THE LAST WEST

THE LAST WEST

A History of the Great Plains of North America

BY RUSSELL McKEE

THOMAS Y. CROWELL COMPANY
New York   Established 1834

For
SHIRLEY

Designed by Ingrid Beckman

Manufactured in the United States of America

Library of Congress Cataloging in Publication Data

McKee, Russell.
   The last West; a history of the Great Plains of North America.
   Bibliography: p.
   1. Great Plains—History. I. Title.
F591.M15   917.8'03   73-22242
ISBN 0-690-00508-3

1 2 3 4 5 6 7 8 9 10

Looking Back,
with Kindest Regards . . .

The Great Plains are not a comfortable land, and their history has often been violent, or desperate, or foolish. That's one of the fascinations of the place. The original idea was to write a descriptive book for those who would rather read about the region than have to travel through it. As the project progressed, it changed. This was unexpected, and not clearly understood by anyone connected with the matter, although histories frequently have a way of doing that. All those people who are believed to be really dead and gone begin to rise up and move about, becoming at times extremely independent, even fractious.

The whole thing probably took a decisive turn about the time it arrived at consideration of the Great Medicine Lodge Creek Kansas Peace Conference and Pipe Smoke of 1867. That gathering has passed here without chronicle, though not unnoticed. A peace treaty was signed there on the plains of Kansas—so of course that meant war had to follow, which it did. These events are quite in keeping with numerous other confusions that arose during the length of the book project. The peace conference was in fact the end of the beginning of white occupation and the beginning of the end of red occupation of the Great Plains. It was not a large moment in plains history, and coming as it did during the Moon of the Changing Season, such departure from reason might have seemed natural. It did not, however, until later reflection, at which time it simply joined the great corps of other Great Plains anomalies. The milling clusters of early peoples; the uncertainty and brutality—and fragility—of the Spanish; the push-pull-and-shove of Indian tribes; the near success and constant failure of the French; the raucous but vaporous presence of the cowboy set off against the quiet and slow—yet permanent—spread of the sodbuster: all are threads in the seamless coat of this land's history. And far from remaining a descriptive text, it comes out as it should: a book of stories about people and their response to an unusual landscape.

A few helped along the way—though for some reason this has been a more lonely venture than usual, in various respects like the plains themselves. Where does one start? Why not with Willena C. "Buck" Adams and her friendly pocket mouse, Nathan, both at the Texas Memorial Museum in Austin. Nathan no doubt has long since gone to his reward and didn't help much anyway, except as a somewhat indifferent companion during a long picture-culling session. Susan Nieminen of the State Historical Society of Colorado in Denver was also most helpful with photos, as were Harriett C. Meloy and Berniece Boone of the Montana Historical Society—Mrs. Meloy as librarian, while Berniece, her photo chief, provided a pleasant afternoon recalling her frontier roots as the great-great-great-great-granddaughter of Dan'l's brother, Squire Boone. Mrs. Meloy and Bill Schneider, editor of that excellent publication *Montana Outdoors*, helped mightily with some late-hour research efforts. Dayton W. Canaday and Mrs. Bonnie Gardner of the South Dakota State Historical Society in Pierre provided other research help, as did Hallett Hammatt at the Museum of the Great Plains in Lawton, Oklahoma. Jim Davis of the Denver Public Library made valuable suggestions and led me to most useful sources and photos. Ed Morgan at the Provincial Archives in Regina, Saskatchewan, was particularly helpful with documents and photos late one Sunday afternoon—when he could as well have taken his ease in a nearby park. Liess Vantine of the State Historical Society of North Dakota gave me several good leads, and Pat Cathcart in Norman, Oklahoma, and Sally Wagner in Santa Fe did their best to set me straight. Cynthia Vartan at Crowell has been an excellent editor. In fairness, readers should know the important heavy role an editor plays in creating any book they'll ever hold. So don't knife these lines, Cynthia, or I'll complain. Lastly, one particular friend over the entire term of this project has been the Michigan State University library computer. It has faithfully reminded me, month after month, of books overdue but has always been gentle even about books long overdue.

CONTENTS

In regard to this extensive section of country, I do not hesitate in giving the opinion, that it is almost wholly unfit for cultivation, and of course uninhabitable by a people depending upon agriculture for their subsistence.

From Major Stephen H. Long's
Journal of his expedition
across the Great Plains in 1820

The prairie and the pampa now emerge as the only major food potentials remaining on the globe. The North American prairie, especially the United States portion is, as discussed in *The Hungry Planet,* a pivot for the future world.

From Dr. Georg Borgstrom,
*FOCAL POINTS—A Global
Food Strategy,* 1973

CHAPTER 1

The Last West

The Great Plains of North America hold this continent together. To the east lie the broadleaf forests, frequent waters, and broken old mountains; to the west lie the rugged new mountains, the Great Basin, the high pine country. Between these two halves stretch the Great Plains province, dead center on the continental landmass.

Nothing about the North American continent has been done in pinched measure, and the Great Plains offer no exception. For two thousand miles north and south, the plains sprawl to an average width of four hundred miles. To outside observers they are a flatland beyond belief. People from east and west proclaim the plains a dreaded hurry-across place, dull, unbelievably monotonous, spooky, unspeakably boring, crossable only at night by fastest jet. That's when they talk to other easterners or westerners about this great landmass separating one coast from the other. But the wheat farmer from Manyberries, Alberta, and the west Texas jeep buster and all the long viewers of far horizons who live between have other thoughts about this land they call home. In their view any piece of land so studiously avoided by small dogs and most people can't be all bad. This loyalty was perhaps expressed simply and best by a plainswoman out of place. She was in a state park in Michigan some years ago, looking at a woodland waterfall locally proclaimed as beautiful. "It's nice," she said without enthusiasm, "but I'll be glad to get out

1

from under all these trees. I can't breathe." Out on her Dakota plains she could stretch out, breathe deep, move about.

Easterners and westerners do not readily understand this truth. It's a failing seen by plainsmen as human enough, possibly an aberration raised by residence in tree-lined eastern landscapes, by living with muddy feet in miasmic southern swamps, or by stumbling over western stone piles. The plainsman thus views foreigners with a generous sympathy. Most outsiders, he knows, can never meet the high standards necessary to become a plainsman. He cites our national history to prove his point. Very few people have made the grade in years past, and there is no indication this trend will improve in the future.

The simple fact is, however, that training and a measure of understanding can produce in outsiders a more temperate, even rational view of the Great Plains. It is rather like sailing. To pass out of sight of land on a broad unknown sea is suicidal without training and a certainty of direction. Similarly, on the Great Plains, men on horseback or afoot have been lost for days in a shallow ocean of waving grasses. They came to such a situation without understanding the plains, and it left many as raving lunatics. They were people of the eastern woodlands. They knew trees and meadows, and rivers that ran someplace. But they did not understand the sea of grasses on which they launched themselves, like buoyant rowboats, at any season in the last four centuries. Such immodesty proved the undoing of more pioneers and wanderers and home-seekers than history counts, most not surviving to appear on the record. Those who did survive inserted one strong chromosome for plains avoidance into the national gene pool. It still has not been bred out of us, and remains today as important a part of our psychological life as in the time of prairie schooners. We remain, in subtle psychological ways, two nations—the East, and the West Coast —divided by the immensity and monotony of the Great Plains.

But the flaw here, say the plainsmen, lies in the sailors, not in the ocean. Adept plainsmanship is learned, not acquired. While others hurry across in straight-line fright, the veteran plainsman moves about freely and without fear, possessed of Great Plains learning gained not out of books but firsthand, out there, by doing.

In his stretching out and moving about, during his steady erosion of new automobiles and pickups into rattly range runners, the plainsman sees what the frightened, hurrying outlander does not; namely, that this homeland, this flatland beyond belief, is not all that simple a patch of geography. The plains are big and open and to some they do look all the same. So does an ocean. But the sailor knows the reefs and shoals and currents that dominate his world, and the practiced plainsman likewise sees many distinctions in his. Both also know an essential truth about far horizons. Sameness of scene all around casts panic in a man who dares look always and only at that distant straight line where earth meets sky. It's a line that can never be walked up, sailed to, or chased away. To survive is to concentrate on close surroundings. Think about your feet, a plainsman suggests, look at the grass a blade at a time. The horizon will take care of itself.

Unfortunately, however, we keep alive in the name itself—Great Plains—an implication of total sameness throughout. That raises in today's traveler a continuation of the long-standing urge for plains avoidance. In the nineteenth century, the region was avoided with even greater determination, being known through most of that century as "The Great American Desert." Before that, the Spaniards also had their doubts about the region—though probably with more good reason. Having large areas of flat country in their homeland, the Spaniards thought the plains worthy of their energies, and so sought to occupy them. Francisco Vásquez de Coronado's magnificent six-hundred-mile passage straight across the panhandles of Texas and Oklahoma and deep into central Kansas was a truly bold effort in search of his lost golden cities. Llano Estacado, he named the region—"Staked Plains"—probably because everywhere across it he saw the stakelike yucca stems. Another explanation is that the only landmarks he saw were some distant cliffs which gave the appearance of stone fortifications, hence the Stockaded Plains, or Llano Estacado. In any case, Coronado came in 1541, and after that the Comanches and Apaches, real owners of the plains, gave later Spaniards an advanced course in flatland appreciation. One lesson the Spanish learned, at some expense, was not to approach the plains in anything less than battalion strength, nor without numerous canteens, all full. Despite this training, and despite 250 years of attempted occupation, the Spaniards never did settle more than the fringes of the plains, at Santa Fe, San Antonio, and a few other outposts in Texas, New Mexico, and Colorado.

The French, arriving a bit later, used better sense. They intermarried with the resident Indians, and in the eighteenth century, crossed from St. Louis to Santa Fe on trading missions. Theirs was the first complete crossing of the Great Plains by white men, though Coronado had come very close. But the French were few in number and their trade merely a slender thread on land moody with the madness of lost men, bone-aching thirst, dust storms, and hostile Indians.

Regular plains crossings began with the American mountain men in the first four decades of the nineteenth century. They came in far greater numbers than the French, borrowing, however, some French survival methods and being driven by strange motives whose wellsprings emerge but dimly in their writings. What was it the mountain men sought? Was it fame or adventure? Money? The power of leadership? None of those really explain why men like Jim Bridger, Jim Beckwourth, the Sublette brothers, Tom "Broken Hand" Fitzpatrick, and two or three hundred of their kind entered the mountain service. Supposedly they were there to collect beaver pelts, worth money. But few made any money from their years of plains crossings and mountain rambling. None ever knew much personal comfort. Fame had little part in their lives as most remained unknown, or little known, until long after they were gone. Adventure? Well, the turnover was high and there must have been easier roads to excitement than losing one's hair to a Blackfoot war party.

In any case, these men came and prevailed, and those who survived became superb plainsmen. They could fight, hide behind buffalo grass, walk, endure days of thirst, eat raw meat,

These plains walkers and mountain men, a pair of citizens with the bark still on, represented their clan about the year 1830. On first meeting, they avoided leaden discourse, but only by the narrowest of margins. "I took ye for an Injin," said one, noting the other's ornate coat and hat. (FREDERIC REMINGTON, *Century Magazine*)

drink blood, make such clothing as they needed, wrestle bears, survive snake bites, extract arrows from their own flesh, escape Indian ambushes. Charles Gardner, "Cannibal Phil," survived a plains blizzard by killing and eating his Indian companion. This became known when he was unpacking his mule after returning to camp. Out of a sack tumbled a shriveled human leg. Gardner grumbled about the poor fare—but a bit later, when marooned in another snowstorm, he killed and roasted his squaw. Another mountain man, fighting starvation, recalled how he held his hands in anthills until covered with the little insects, then hungrily licked them off. The same man crisped the soles of his moccasins in a fire and ate them. He boiled water, caught crickets, and dumped them in, eating them "as soon as they stopped kicking." A favored fare called for two mountain men to start gobbling at either end of a length of raw buffalo intestine and eat toward the center. Neither was allowed to use hands, and if one slurped without chewing, cries of "feed fair, damn ye!" rose from the other end. When hunting was good, eating eight to ten pounds of meat at a sitting was common. The liver, a delicacy, was normally eaten raw, flavored with the contents of the gallbladder. A favorite soup was buffalo blood containing lumps of bone marrow. They were called mountain men, but their favorite fare was buffalo meat, mainly a plains animal, and they were clearly as much plainsmen as mountaineers. They dared the West more than any other group, and they came to know the plains as thoroughly as the geography of their own hands.

When the fashion of hats changed from beaver to silk, the mountain men were left to search for work, soon finding it as escorts and guides for American settlers crossing to the West Coast. Members of these wagon trains steeled themselves for the plains crossing on their way to Oregon or California, and despite assurances from their knowledgeable guides, a genuine dread of the plains became imprinted on our early literature, history, and economic outlook. Those who stuck to the trails, guided or not, found the plains the easiest part of their western journey—far easier than the Rockies, the Great Basin, or the Sierras, all of which claimed far more pioneer lives. The plains being flat offered easy wagon travel, grass for livestock, and water for the careful. Hot and monotonous, yes. But the nineteenth-century traveler had more urgent concerns to fret his thoughts, and the plains gave kind solutions to his major needs.

Still, one misconception is as damning as another. If it has taken us a century to realize that the Great American Desert really has grass and should be called a Great Plain, then it may take equally long to recognize that the Great Plains are in fact composed of a diversity of land types and scenery, and if you must cross them going to or from the Rocky Mountains, then at least certain detours and variations can make the way enjoyable.

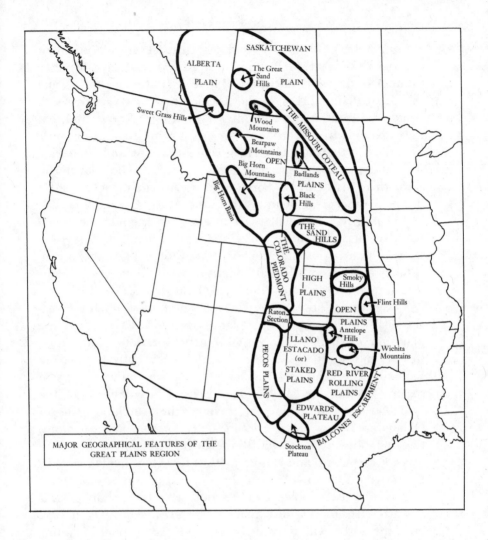

MAJOR GEOGRAPHICAL FEATURES OF THE
GREAT PLAINS REGION

Geographers, historians, and agricultural economists have
defined the Great Plains province in various ways, using a
number of different yardsticks. There's general agreement that
the Great Plains lie east of the Rockies, that they vary in width
from two hundred to six hundred miles east and west, and that
they extend from southern Texas northward to, or into,
Canada, but there's not much agreement on precise boundaries.
For those that include Canada, opinions vary on how far northward the plains extend. Some writers carry them only a short
distance, others roll them north to the Arctic Ocean. Most call
them "prairies" north of the border. Some include the woodlands around and north of Edmonton, others add the well-
watered prairie pothole country of Manitoba. This lack of consistency arises from the many views of what climate, soil, plant
life, and landforms constitute our "Great Plains."

The same variation arises when using levelness of land or vegetation as a measure of the plains province. To say that the
plains are a flatland is a useful generalization—diminishing
steadily in usefulness as one counts the Black Hills, the Dakota
Badlands, the Cypress Hills, several small mountain ranges in
eastern Montana and Wyoming, dozens of hilly landscapes, the
Wichita Mountains, river-cut ravines, the Antelope Hills of
Oklahoma, deep valley gorges in the Raton and Pecos sections,
the one-thousand-foot-high Pine Ridge Escarpment, the Balcones Escarpment, and rolling foothill terrain at many places in
the province. Or to say that the plains is a region of short grass
may also be useful, except in the south where the short grass is
so scattered as to provide actual desert and only a broken forage,
or in the north, where cooler air and reduced evaporation allow
survival of heavier grasses.

Still, the name "Great Plains" is helpful, and can certainly be
a common denominator if used with caution. No single set of
conditions need be used to mark off the region, and the normal
desire to reduce a definition to its simplest terms need not pre-
vail here. A more useful understanding is to see the Great
Plains simply as a central collective geographical region of our
continent, much as we now speak of "The South," or "The East
Coast," or "The West Coast." The definition of the region, in

fact, is the story this book has to tell. It is a story about a piece of land and about the people, plants, and animals that have lived there and created a history for themselves. They, and it, are very durable members of our American community, and in this age of steadily changing values, that is a subject worthy of study. The geological background, the landforms, the use by earliest inhabitants and wildlife, plus the recorded history of the last four centuries all become part of this grand tale. Insofar as these elements develop for us a plains culture, or a chunk of our national history, or an agricultural complex, or a set of land and weather values, then the tale itself may offer new and purposeful meanings. But to understand calls for acceptance of this overlooked land, the last west on our continent.

Early settlers, it should be noted, were on occasion misled by secondhand knowledge about the plains. For them, things got confused. Men who came to the region with preconceived notions often accepted academic, sometimes undigested understandings about the plains. They were told the Great Plains were dry, and later watched as countless small bridges built too low went marching off on boiling streams. Thinking the land level, they watched brakeless wagons bouncing to matchwood down sharp slopes. But thinking it a farmer's paradise, they suffered most of all, being lashed more than men should be by droughts, dust storms, northers, tornadoes, flash floods, and other climatic ilk.

Some, thinking to solve the problems, have produced rash suggestions about ways to stop Great Plains weather from happening. One man proposed to control blizzards—that scourge of the grasslands—by arranging a line of coal stoves along the Canadian border. These would be fired up when the need arose. The heat waves would climb to the upper atmosphere, melt the snow, and divert the cold winds. The Patent Office deserves our everlasting gratitude for disabusing him of that idea before it went too far.

A grander scheme for killing Great Plains tornadoes did get off the ground, however, in a manner of speaking. Mr. J. B. Atwater of Chicago got himself caught in a Kansas twister back about 1885, and vowed to do something about it. He went home

These European immigrants who headed west in a railroad coach in the 1880s, would go to the end of the line, buy a cart or wagon, then head off across the plains to meet their destinies. (*Harpers Weekly*, NOVEMBER 3, 1886)

to Chicago and invented the Atwater Tornado Killer, which received U.S. Patent No. 370,845 in 1887. This mechanism was a box full of dynamite fixed with an outside flap that slapped against the box when the wind rose to tornado proportions. When the box flap slapped the box, percussion caps went off, thereby setting off the dynamite and blowing the tornado apart.

Atwater's invention produced crews of drummers who sold these tornado shooters to the anxious for quite a time. Atwater Tornado Killers were invariably set up along the southwestern edges of towns, in rows, to await any unsuspecting tornado that might happen along. The idea lost its gloss when a passing crow landed on one box just outside a southwestern Kansas village. Somehow, the crow slapped the flap against the box, accidentally set off the dynamite, and the first explosion set off all the other boxes stationed nearby. The townsfolk, who hadn't reckoned on such a problem, had set their Atwaters too close to the village. The explosion flattened their railroad depot, knocked out all the windows in town, and killed two cows and a mule standing nearby—to say nothing of the crow. After that, the people of the region elected to take their chances on nature.

You couldn't exactly blame them, however, for trying to cope with, or against, the winds of the plains. Such blows were a new experience for Americans raised in the protection of the eastern forests. The barren plains and the unceasing wind drove many to madness, while the more durable gradually learned laconic acceptance. Suffering through three days of a howling windstorm some years back, a Great Plains greenhorn struggled to open the front door of a general store which turned out, fortunately, to be a waterhole as well.

"Good grief, is it always like this out here?" he asked, choking down a dust quencher.

The barkeeper, chewing a toothpick, wiped the counter and drawled, "Naw, it'll only be like this four, maybe five days at a time. Then it'll take a turn and get a mite windy."

Great Plains rainmaking, however, remains the durable center of all weather-control activities on the continent, and is the one single subject that always heats up the genes of a confirmed plainsman. So many ways have been found to make rain that it's hard to reckon with them intelligently. Great Plains clouds, the most reluctant on earth, have been shot at, shaken, yelled at, cursed, beckoned, and seeded. One crew of otherwise moderate men even got a flatcar and an old Civil War cannon and went about Kansas selling their cloud-shooting services. Nothing like a good cloud shoot to turn people on.

Jim Bridger, most famous mountain man of them all, once claimed to have heard "A peetrified bird sitting in a peetrified tree, singing peetrified songs." He also claimed to know the location of a valley so large it had an eight-hour, alarm-clock echo. "When you go to bed aside that valley," he said, "You jest yell 'Time to Get Up!', and eight hours later the echo wakes you up." (WESTERN HISTORY COLLECTIONS, UNIVERSITY OF OKLAHOMA LIBRARY, NORMAN)

The lack of rain on the plains has created other interesting problems. Our eastern habit of squaring off land into townships, sections, half sections, and smaller patches of acreage was at the heart of the Homestead Act. That law, passed in 1862, "bet a man 160 acres against five years of his life that he couldn't raise enough to stay alive." At least that's what the law demanded. He could have the 160 acres, it said, but he had to live on it and improve it for five years. In the eastern woodlands, with plenty of water, that law made sense. But that wasn't where the homesteading took place. Homesteading was a Great Plains game most of all, and the first homesteaders into a region staked their 160-acre claims around available waterholes. Others then realized the folly of trying to settle a quarter square mile of dry land, and soon drifted west, leaving the man with the waterhole all the surrounding land as well. A township with one waterhole could expect thin population; those endowed with three could form a society and gather hands for poker. Congress had a hard time adjusting the Homestead Act to fit this waterhole pattern, so most land sooner or later passed to speculators and railroads. Both tried to peddle it for high profits, using uproarious advertising claims, mainly on wide-eyed immigrants from northern and eastern Europe. Scattered communities of Russian, Ukrainian, German, Polish, Scandinavian, and other ethnic farmers and ranchers persist on the plains to this day, completely ignorant of the fact that they were supposed to starve out and blow away long ago. These groups, in fact, became the spine of Great Plains settlement, and like the grasses that surrounded them, they became deep-rooted and wind resistant.

But most North Americans know the Great Plains only from their reading, from photos, and from infrequent beeline transit across this land while going somewhere else. Such land avoidance serves to perpetuate the general image of flatness and prevents growth of any new understandings about the region. Most Americans are as ignorant of the Great Plains today as were their pioneer forebears in the nineteenth century. In fact, those pioneers who crossed the plains in wagons gained far greater knowledge of the region than we ever could in high-flying jets or fast-moving cars, buses, and trains.

For all these reasons, we still know little of this vast landscape, yet it constitutes roughly one-fifth of the land area of our continent and provides the most important single piece of agricultural terrain in the world. It's time now for all of us to take stock of this massive piece of our continent.

CHAPTER 2

Rock Bottom

The Great Plains of North America are bounded in the west by the high spine of the Rocky Mountains, in the south by a string of green Texas hills, in the north by the trees of Canada, and in the east by weather. The northern, western, and southern boundaries have stayed in place a long time. The eastern boundary moves back and forth from year to year along a line midway between the Mississippi and the Rockies. For centuries, this line has been a battleground where from season to season short grasses struggle against long grasses for dominance. In a wet year the long grasses march west. In a dry year their strength fails and the tough little short grasses reclaim the territory. The no-man's-land in this unceasing warfare is a strip of open country fifty or more miles wide lying between the true prairies and the true plains, its width depending on the severity of the season. A weather-softened farmer in eastern Kansas has learned to live with it. "Every year this is a new land," he says. "I don't plan crops too far ahead. When the snows come heavy in late winter and it looks a wet season, I'll try corn. But usually it's dry and usually it's wheat."

All along that borderland, variations on this theme can be heard. People who have stuck to this land have learned that the way to survive is to keep an eye on the western sky. Some claim themselves to be plainsmen, others determine their roots to be of the prairie. Drop the question at a coffee shop anywhere through that country and the answers will likely start a discussion that continues long after coffee is gone and the questioner is twenty miles down the road. That's because people of the plains and the plains edge spend a great deal of time thinking about and talking over the land on which they live. Outsiders who don't know the arguments find this old plains versus prairie discussion merely bewildering.

Those who live there aren't the only ones who can't tie the plains to a definition. Walter Prescott Webb, an old Texas cowpoke turned history professor, claimed the Great Plains were that chunk of mid-America lacking hills, trees, and rain. He proclaimed that view in his great book, *The Great Plains*, published in 1931. Webb had a tough-minded sense of the land where he'd lived and roamed, and his book bears the flavor of arid simplicity one finds in life on the plains. But his definition of plains geography fails. It's too simple and too inclusive.

Nevin M. Fenneman took the other tack. A careful, classical geographer, he also set out to define the Great Plains in his extensive work, *Physiography of Western United States*. Fenneman's work likewise appeared in 1931—a year when the only Great Plains bumper crop seemed to be books about that drought-ridden land. He defined the plains very precisely, divided them into ten subunits, and left readers who didn't know better with a clear and concise understanding of all those boundaries. Unfortunately, to anyone but a classical geographer, many of his boundaries between zones either can't be found, are shrouded, or are so subtle as to be essentially nonexistent. Where Webb was too simple, Fenneman was too detailed.

A much more useful approach is to view the plains not as a fixed piece of geography with specific boundaries and subsections, nor all flat and dry and treeless, but rather as a living assemblage of constantly changing natural units—landforms, plant types, and human and animal habitats—all lying on a strip of ground 400 to 600 miles wide and 2,000 miles long just east of the Rocky Mountains. Some of these land units are

unique, others are seen again and again. All, however, lend
themselves warily to that uneasy totality we have decided to call
"Great Plains."

The force of this definition runs deeper than casual observa-
tion might indicate. In fact, the force of the Great Plains lies
not in its singleness of topography nor its arid quality, but in its
variety, movement, and surprising differences. Perhaps that's
why the plains have for so long resisted verbal arrest. They
change from boring flatland to sudden extrusions of mountains
or deep-cut river gorges. They contain lush green oases armed
with fierce bands of marauding mosquitoes. Hard by these will
be virtual desert conditions with cactus, sand blows, and lake
mirages glimmering in the sun. An hour or half a day farther on
and you are suddenly aware that something else has happened.
Trees have appeared or rolling hills all grassy green and covered
with cattle, or sheer cliffs, or Wisconsin-style farm countryside.
How and where these changes begin or leave off is not always
clear. It is in fact an old landscape that shifts about gentle and
sly, like an old man who has mellowed and slowed and is easing
through. Such subtle changes make it a surprising landscape.
Not in the sense of picture-postcard scenery but in unexpected
turns of color demanding total attention, or fascinating evening
vistas that draw you from your car, or violent changes of
weather that hammer you into the earth—or an oppressive and
sudden awareness, panic fringed, at the land's monolithic brutality and strength. The plains were not necessarily designed for
scenic attractiveness—quote, unquote. And yet their scenery is
extremely forceful in an almost mystical way.

The formation of the plains into their present aspect goes
back a long way. In fact the entire central tableland of North
America did not begin to emerge as a continent until a billion
years ago. The continental shelf is of course much older, but a
billion years ago the main upland of North America was taking
shape as a shore and shallows sometimes above water, more
often submerged. Nearly the entire continent was then a battleground between oceans and isolated patches of mountains. For
now, in our time, the mountains have won. Water that could
flood most land areas of the world is fortunately locked away at

the Polar caps. But it wasn't always so. Many times in the last six hundred million years oceans have rolled across nearly the entire continent, their attack being halted only by the durable Canadian Shield in the north and sometimes by low mountains scattered here and there. Water then was supreme. The oceans advanced because the earth was warm, a warmth that melted Polar ice and brought unbelievable depths of water spilling over the world's landscape. These oceans flooded North America and softened the surface into silts and sands. Rivers stormed down off the few mountain uplands, carrying boulders, stones, sand, and silt, and adding these to the salty depths. Many times this happened, and many times it appeared the oceans might flatten the entire continent and roll their tides westward across the whole North American upland. But the Shield of the north held out and was never completely overrun. And with a slow, determined pace the land continued to build, to push up, to replace surface materials carried away to the ocean.

Somewhere in that distant past the tide finally turned and the land began to emerge. When that happened is unknown. Certainly it began with cooler weather. The earth's water was then being locked into the Polar ice regions, the oceans beginning a long retreat homeward to their present basins. They would not be allowed to continue their assaults on the land, at least for now. As they withdrew they left behind the debris of the battleground, heavy sheets of sediment lying wherever the oceans had flowed. Exposed to the sun and the pressures of their own weight, these sediments baked and hardened into layers of bedrock.

Again and again, this process took place. Each time the earth would warm, oceans rolled forth. Then cooler weather would draw the oceans home and the land would emerge. Each time new sheets of debris would cover those of the past, hardening as they dried. Today these stacked platters of rock dominate the entire substructure of most of central North America, and this is especially true throughout the Great Plains province. It's the basic reason for their general quality of flatness. However, as the process progressed, other things were also happening.

Each time, as water drew back, rivers on the land lengthened

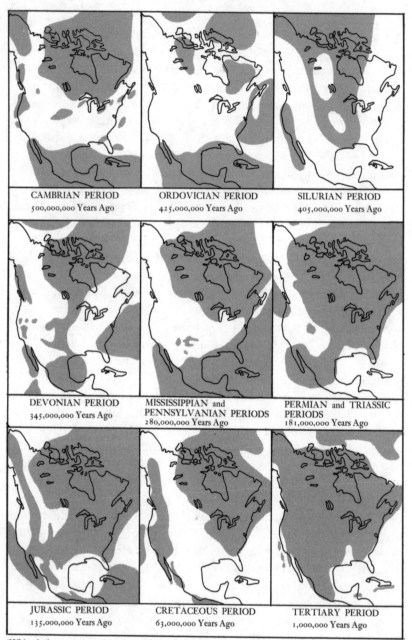

CAMBRIAN PERIOD
500,000,000 Years Ago

ORDOVICIAN PERIOD
425,000,000 Years Ago

SILURIAN PERIOD
405,000,000 Years Ago

DEVONIAN PERIOD
345,000,000 Years Ago

MISSISSIPPIAN and
PENNSYLVANIAN PERIODS
280,000,000 Years Ago

PERMIAN and TRIASSIC
PERIODS
181,000,000 Years Ago

JURASSIC PERIOD
135,000,000 Years Ago

CRETACEOUS PERIOD
63,000,000 Years Ago

TERTIARY PERIOD
1,000,000 Years Ago

(White depicts area covered by water; dark area is land)

their ties to the oceans. That sharpened their cutting edge. Being farther above sea level with each advance of the land, such rivers had to work harder to reach home waters. They gouged channels and canyons, at places hundreds of feet deep, into the still soft levels of Great Plains bedrock. Everywhere the upland was veined now by smaller streams clearing away to the sea. So as the centuries passed, victory lay with the land, and cooling temperatures steadily locked more and more water into Polar ice lodes. Gradually, the river canyons of the Great Plains grew quiet and dry and stony white under the pale winter sun, like bleached skeletons at battle's end. The war had taken a long time.

Much much later, in fact 70 to 90 million years ago, the Rocky Mountains began to rise from a crusty trench left behind by the oceans. The Rockies began as cracks in the surface where small hills thrust upward and they grew gradually, forcing those overlying slabs of rock into gnarled and twisted masses. As they rose, volcanic heat from the earth's interior transformed most into granites. Steadily these granites spread along the continental spine, gradually becoming the basic strength of the Rocky Mountain chain.

The scene then must have been harsh, the landscape grotesquely carved. On the west loomed these new growing mountains. At their base lay the river-clawed badlands sloping in ruptured tangles eastward for hundreds of miles to the Mississippi. There were then no Great Plains, no broad expanse of flatland. All seemed chewed and eroded and chaotic. And yet the rivers had cut only the surface, the skin of the land. Down deep the foundation of the Great Plains remained flat and untouched. The stacked rock layers from the time of oceans were still intact. They had not been corrupted by volcanoes or severe earthquakes or upthrusting mountains. The deposits of limestone, sandstone, shale, and other sediments remained in platelike levels and still formed the basement structure of the plains. Now only that river-ripped surface needed filling and flattening.

Remembering old wounds, the mountains and plains soon conspired to further humble the forces of water. In fact the mountains and plains soon began to use water for their own

designs. They would work together to create a flatland across
which water could not pass. They would tie the land down
tightly and build upon it. And so the alliance was struck and
the Great Plains as we know them today began to grow.

   The rains were now falling with lessening force, bringing
earth materials down out of the Rockies and onto the plains
somewhat more slowly. The rivers that formed in the mountains could carry everything up to the size of boulders and what
they couldn't carry they were forced like road gangs to carve
down to needs. At the base of the mountains, where these rivers
poured out onto the plains, the flatland slowed them enough to
claim their largest cargo. Out a bit farther the flowing streams
were slowed even more and the plains pulled other rocks from
their grip. Farther on the small stones, the sands, and the silts
were claimed. Gradually the meandering stream beds were filled
with these wastes. As this happened, the rivers were lifted out of
their troughs and forced to spill across the nearby countryside.
Soon this spilling became a habit, occurring over and over, for
centuries, until that canyon-marred landscape was completely
filled. Dozens of fan-shaped deltas had formed at the base of the
mountains with scores more building on the originals and thousands of smaller ones flattening every tiny slope that appeared.

   As the centuries passed, the rivers of the Rockies gave their
strength to the plains in this way, smoothing the land into a
dead-level tabletop. Today most water is simply unable to
escape the awesome flatness that grew there. Rivers meander
this way and that looking for the lowest path to the sea. The
more stones and silts the rivers drop, the more their progress
slows until they are split into crippled fingers probing weakly
for that final lowest route home. The remains of old water-
courses lie everywhere beneath the grasses of the plains, a deep
herringbone weave of ancient riverbeds, buried strings of stone
and silt left behind when the rivers drained away. Any stream
that passes here today faces this same bleak future. To see a
High Plains stream in August or September of most any year is
to see dry riverbed, evidence that a stream flows here when the
land and the season allow it. Most plains streams are never
given a normal life of continuous flow like a Columbia or a Mis-

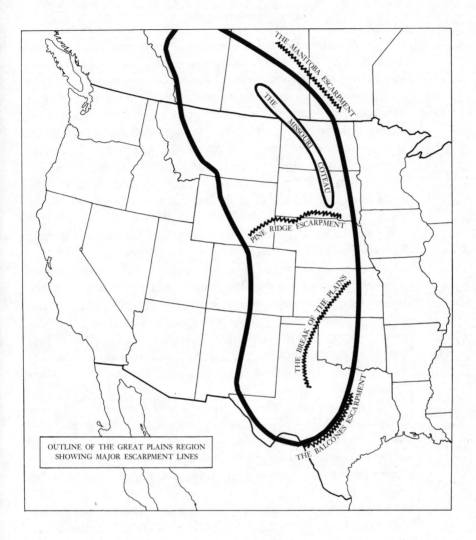

THE MANITOBA ESCARPMENT

THE MISSOURI COTEAU

PINE RIDGE ESCARPMENT

THE BREAK OF THE PLAINS

THE BALCONES ESCARPMENT

OUTLINE OF THE GREAT PLAINS REGION
SHOWING MAJOR ESCARPMENT LINES

sissippi or any of the great eastern or western rivers. Plains streams, the Missouri excepted, either roar in flood stage and move earth materials wherever needed, or they whisper softly as underground trickles, unseen, with no life evident. Zebulon Montgomery Pike, one of our first plainsmen, noted this habit on the Arkansas River in 1807. He suggested boats that might try to navigate the whole length of the Arkansas ". . . should embark at its entrance on the 1st of February when they would have the fresh flow quite to the mountains and meet with no detention. But if they should start later, they would find the river 1,500 miles up nearly dry . . . for the extent of 400 or 500 miles before you arrive near the mountains, the bed of the river is extensive, and a perfect sand bar, which at certain seasons is dry; at least the water is standing in ponds, not affording sufficient to procure a running course. When you come near the mountains, you find the river contracted, a gravelly bottom, and a deep navigable stream. From these circumstances it is evident that the sandy soil imbibes all the waters which the sources project from the mountains." And so the land wins again, allowing each river only enough strength to maintain the plains in their chosen conformity.

About a million years ago this work of plains building was completed. Today it is difficult to realize how effectively, how completely this effort transformed the land. The mountains had never stopped building and the soils and stones they gave to the Great Plains transformed that entire vast region into an unbelievable flatland.

Fortunately, earth forces never rest and in the last 600,000 years this vast flatness has been radically changed by two major events. In the north, four extended periods of flowing glaciers have corrupted the flatlands and left them a network of potholes, moraines, and outwash river valleys. In the south, slow and subtle erosion has replaced the delta-building process and now nibbles at the eastern edges of the plains incessantly, marking them with a cover of gorges, badlands, and canyons.

The four glacial periods left us some interesting geological history. They were divided from one another by strings of warmer weather during which the great ice masses melted back.

Each time these big melts occurred the glaciers left piles of
stone and soil tumbled where they fell, earth materials gathered
up or pushed ahead by the glaciers. These moraines and hill
regions are scattered everywhere through the northern plains.
The Missouri River, which once flowed to Hudson Bay, was
shunted southward to the Gulf of Mexico by a ridge of this glacial debris. Today we call that ridge the Missouri Coteau. The
Turtle Mountains on the North Dakota-Manitoba border and
many rolling moraines in Alberta, Saskatchewan, and Manitoba
were created. The Black Hills and Badlands of the Dakotas,
formed millions of years earlier, were sculptured into the forms
we know today. Countless saucer-shaped lake beds were gouged
into the plains surface, and today are filled with annual runoff
waters. The courses of all rivers in the region were altered one
way or another.

In the south the glaciers also left their effects, though indi-
rectly. When cold weather encased North America in an icebox
climate, rain, snow, and sleet lashed the land. During times
between glaciers the climate was warm and dry. On the southern plains where the glaciers never reached, this translated into
raging rivers and heavy erosion in cold times, followed by
drought and dust blows in warm periods. The rivers cut gorges
and chewed away the eastern and southern flanks of the plains.
Dust blows turned them almost to deserts and left a scrubby
brush-covered arid land similar to marginal areas seen there
today. The four glacial periods, in the order of their occurrence,
were the Nebraskan, Kansan, Illinoian, and Wisconsin. Each
lasted more than 60,000 years, with the Kansan continuing
160,000 years. Each of the three warm interglacial periods—we
are now in the fourth—also lasted 60,000 years or more. The
extended carving process carried out by these actions of land
and weather whittled at the plains topography and added their
own dimensions of change to the already sculptured surface.

But changing the stone face of the Great Plains was only one
event brought about by the glaciers. The Ice Ages also contributed to three other important changes on the plains. First, the
plant growth changed radically with each washing and drying
over the last 600,000 years. Second, the spread of wildlife from

MAJOR RIVERS OF THE GREAT PLAINS REGION

Asia to North America was trafficked over the land bridge at Bering Strait. And third and most important, man arrived on the continent.

Changes in plant and animal forms have been under way for as long as life has existed, of course. However, our North American wildlife faced an unexpected challenge when Asian birds and animals began their march here 600,000 years ago. With these animals and birds came diseases and parasites, and many new plants as well, transported as seeds on the feet of birds, on the fur of animals, or in the stomachs of both. East here began meeting west in a migration that brought our hemisphere a rich new tapestry of life forms. How many plants and animals came to our continent in this way is impossible to reckon, though the number of both is known to be extensive.

But the Great Plains of North America were changed most of all by the coming of prehistoric man in the last few moments of this continent's geological history. All that had gone before was merely a prelude to the rapid changes this upright, two-footed mammal soon burned into the land.

The significance of man's role on the Great Plains has been steadily underplayed. Perhaps the overbearing strength and size of the land hide man's very durable, persistent, and demanding efforts at control. Whatever the reason, man's struggle for control of the Great Plains remains an absorbing drama, one that began 30,000 to 20,000 years ago. Somewhere in that range of time man crossed from Asia in the same way, and on the same narrows, as the migrating wildlife. That sweep of land used by all travelers linked Siberia to Alaska along a broad front extending far southward into the present Pacific Ocean. The date of man's crossing here is the subject of a long-standing and highly absorbing debate. Western Alaska was never covered by glacial ice and so at first provided a narrow continental toehold for man. He could go no farther until glacial ice began to melt.

How long man was locked behind that cold wall is uncertain. The glaciers were rivers of ice thousands of feet thick, in continual though unseen movement. Like glaciers today, but far larger, pressures of their own weight and movement tore them into treacherous crevasses, or pinched them into icy pinnacles

Great Plains rivers do not have a "normal" rate of flow. They range from flood stage to bone dry while traveling from March to October. This stream, seen in early summer, moved an island of stones during the winter, carrying it from near the camera down toward the bridge in the background. (PHOTO BY THE AUTHOR)

past which there was no advance. At times they howled and roared under these immense pressures. Nothing grew there. No animal life existed on the glaciers to give man sustenance. Most of all the glaciers were enormous, covering at one time nearly the entire northern half of North America. The Cordilleran Ice Field, one large lobe of this great ice mass, first grew in the Rockies of western Alberta, spread westward to the Pacific, northward into Alaska, and eastward across the present Great Plains, there to meet the Keewatin Ice Field. The Keewatin formed in east central Canada and spread south and west to lock into the Cordilleran. Man therefore was kept at bay in western Alaska until the heat of the earth slowed and then reversed the spread of these two ice fields. Hundreds of centuries passed as this melting pushed the glaciers back toward their centers. As the glaciers melted away, they eventually split apart at a seam line along the east face of the Rockies, just where the mountains join the plains. And here, between towering walls of ice, along a narrow wind-swept pathway, began one of the momentous human movements of all history—the peopling of the New World.

It was a very ragtag movement. The people were short in stature, few in number, and constantly afraid of their surroundings. They moved only when forced to. It took them centuries to trickle out of Alaska and move southward into the plains of Alberta, Montana, and Wyoming. Generations lingered in single river valleys, or along the outwash of some mountain stream. When wildlife moved away, these fragile people followed. When streams dried up, they traveled in search of new water. When blizzards came, they hid in mountain redoubts or found shelter in valleys—or froze. But slowly, slowly, by these bits of movement, for century after century, these tentative, fearful people kept edging southward into the continent.

At times, the earliest people were pushed hard by scattered bands of new peoples who came behind—and who were themselves often pushed by others stronger or more numerous. All of their lives were short and desperately lived. They were armed only with stone-tipped spears, flint knives, perhaps a few simple bone tools. They wore skins and spent their nights in caves or rocky niches.

And yet they thrived as they moved south because of the uncommon generosity of the Great Plains. The western margin of the plains, hard by the Rockies, was then one of the lushest, most inviting environments on earth. The new people of the New World held themselves flush against the base of the Rockies and ventured onto the plains only when necessary. Yet along that plains margin they found ample natural shelter. Water from nearby mountain streams was plentiful and pure. Fuel for camp fires was everywhere as wood or dried animal droppings. But most important of all, game animals by the millions crowded the grasslands and wooded coverts of the nearby plains.

And so here on the Great Plains were the New World peoples first able to gather their strength and grow in numbers and steadily colonize new territory. Some also slipped through mountain passes and filtered down our West Coast. Others crossed into the Great Basin, then a lush land, or moved even farther to find a life in the Southwest, also a rich postglacial environment. The movement kept on and on, and within 4,000 years after the glaciers parted, the entire length and breadth of

the Western Hemisphere had been visited by man, all the way
to the southern tip of South America.

Yet for all this scattering the Great Plains remained the
favored homeland and most important growing ground for new
peoples. And while staying here and prospering, they gradually
developed the practice of land burning, an activity of profound
importance in the history of the plains. While all the facts
aren't yet known, we can draw some broad suggestions of what
happened in this fascinating period. The time of most interest
begins about 12,000 years ago and extends to about 6,000 years
ago, during which an uncommonly large amount of human and
animal activity seemed to occur. Let's reconstruct the scene on
the plains at the opening of the period:

Twelve thousand years ago, the Great Plains had far more
trees than at present. While basically a grassland even then,
trees are known to have existed on the plains in substantial
numbers from southern Texas northward into Alberta and Saskatchewan. Spruces, pines, oaks, maples, and many other tree
types were found from the Rockies eastward to the Mississippi.
Remnant islands of these trees are still found at many locations
on the Great Plains, at places where water supply or elevation
or a combination of climatic factors have allowed them to persist.
Fossil evidence of trees have been located under today's grasslands at locations often hundreds of miles removed from the
nearest surviving relatives. While a few major species predomi-
nate, a variety of many trees and shrubs is included, indicating
that an unusually rich mixture of plant life existed at that time.

To call it a forest would be misleading, however, and the evidence does not tell how densely these trees covered the region.
The cover could have been quite sparse, or fairly heavy. Doubtless, from the growth habits of some species, at least some areas
of substantial forest probably did exist. In most places, an open
park land or savanna land probably prevailed, with grassy cover
beneath, similar to some big-game lands found today in East
Africa.

The comparison with East Africa goes farther. Consider the
present difference between the wildlife of Kenya, Uganda, and
Tanzania and that of our North American Great Plains. The

Devil's Tower National Monument in northeastern Wyoming is a natural rock tower, 865 feet high, of volcanic origin. It was the first national monument in the United States, dedicated in 1906. That's the Belle Fourche River in the foreground. (PHOTO BY THE AUTHOR)

East African wildlife complex is delicately balanced but extremely rich. It includes at least forty different large animals surviving on a mixture of forests and grasslands about as elevated, and about as dry as our Great Plains. But 12,000 years ago, our plains had a similar richness and variety comprising a mixture of grass and savanna and park land—and about as many large animals as are found in East Africa today. Lewis and

Clark in 1805 encountered about a dozen types of large animals —only a dozen—while today our plains house only the antelope, two kinds of deer, remnant herds of bison, and several small species such as hares, prairie dogs, and coyotes.

How did we lose twenty to thirty species of large animals between 12,000 and 6,000 years ago? And how were our tree-peppered plains converted to an uninterrupted grassland? These were plants and animals that developed on our Great Plains over millions of years of evolution. Many had survived a centuries-long journey from Asia. All had survived three previous ice ages. Yet they were wiped from the face of the earth in the brief span of 6,000 years. What happened? The answer to this puzzle still has many pieces missing, yet it also has some interesting borders and a slowly emerging form. Consider the following possibility:

When man filtered down into North America 20,000 to 30,000 years ago, he found an unbelievable variety of wildlife. There on the plains before him stood millions of large wild creatures. The list included horses, camels, elk, sloths, a four-horned antelope, and a one-horned creature similar to a rhinoceros. There were at least three types of deer, plus black, brown, and grizzly bears. There were elephants, llamas, pigs, and a six-foot creature that seemed a cross between an armadillo and a tortoise. There was the wolf, the coyote, the fox, and the saber-toothed tiger. There were anteaters, grass eaters, tree eaters, and meat eaters. There were giant beavers and giant buffalo. The list is long and our knowledge of it still not complete.

For man, these were the ingredients for survival and steady growth. He had shelter, ample opportunities for food, and skins for clothing in the brutal North American winter. He lived in small bands and hunted in groups. His major problem was weapons, and while this man was a superb craftsman, creating some of the finest stone projectiie points the world has ever seen, he did not have any long-range hunting equipment. The bow and arrow were unknown until much later. His main manufactured weapon was the stone-tipped spear, which he used for jabbing and throwing. He had good stone knives to dispatch wounded animals and for skinning. He may also have had the atlatl, or spear thrower, a short length of wood or bone held in such a way that it lengthened a man's arm and gave a greater arc to his swing, hence more speed to his hurled weapon. However, the atlatl was probably used mainly for throwing lightweight darts at small agile targets such as birds. Heavy spears needed for killing large game were probably too ponderous for the spear thrower.

Man's solution to this need for long-range weapons was fire. On arrival in North America, man had long experience with fire and was adept in using it for hunting, defense against enemies, and attack. Fire was tamed in Asia long before it was carried to North America. In fact, evidence of fire in human use goes back at least 250,000 years. It was used in Asia, Africa, and Europe long before man arrived here. When the earliest peoples came to the Great Plains, they had a wide understanding of fire's uses, and could not have survived the harsh northern climate without it. Literally hundreds of references to uses of fire are found in archeological writings and studies about primitive peoples. A graphic example of one sophisticated use appears in the journal of the Spanish wanderer, Alvar Núñez Cabeza de Vaca, who was a prisoner of a tribe he called Ignaces Indians (probably Apaches) and was the first educated white man to enter southeastern Texas in 1528:

" . . . they go about with a firebrand," he wrote, "setting fire to the plains and timber so as to drive off the mosquitoes, and also to get the lizards and similar things which they eat, to come out of the soil. In the same manner, they kill deer, encircling them with fires, and they do it also to deprive the animals of pasture, compelling them to go for food where the Indians want."

For the Ignaces Indians, fire as a weapon was supplementary to their bows and arrows. But on the Great Plains, primitive man depended on fire much more heavily, and for many reasons. First, he had no other long-range weapons—no bows and arrows, for example. Second, the land was level and a fire once started could race along without serious interruption. The generally arid nature of the Great Plains aided this spread of fire, the fuel being mostly grass, which started easily and burned rap-

The dead-level High Plains, one region of the Great Plains, were created over millions of years by water action that washed surface materials back and forth until they were completely flattened. The depression is believed to be an old buffalo wallow, where the big woolies dusted themselves. (WESTERN HISTORY COLLECTIONS, UNIVERSITY OF OKLAHOMA LIBRARY, NORMAN)

idly. Third, the plains are almost continually swept by prevailing westerly winds which fanned these fires and drove them forward. Finally, the lands being burned were a mixture of grassy openings and scattered trees, a habitat that supported all the many kinds of wild animals of North America. The grazing animals could graze, the browsing animals could browse, and the predators could keep their eyes, claws, and teeth on both.

Hunting methods no doubt depended on the terrain, but primitive man investigated all uses of fire. The simplest and most direct was the fire drive. Fires were set along a front that grew wider as it moved forward, and animals driven before it would mire in a river or swamp, fall over a cliff, or be caught in ravines. Also, open areas of plains might be burned to deprive animals of hard-to-hunt pasturage. Then rocky areas or narrow strips of grass along a shore or below a ledge would remain for easier hunting. Sometimes large herds were stampeded by fire, the animals trampling over one another, with hunters following to pick up the dead and injured. Fires were useful against all

these animals throughout the warm months, and the chances of
bagging at least something with fire were always good.

The net result of this fire hunting—and of changing climate
and Great Plains ecology—was that primitive man, in the brief
span of about six thousand years, systematically destroyed one
major species after another until a score or more had been
wiped from the Western Hemisphere. Those not totally
destroyed by fire hunting were scattered and driven to such low
numbers that extinction was inevitable. Along with destruction
of the wildlife, trees that had been scattered across the plains
were burned away, leaving the land to the stubborn grasses.
Both the Great Plains and neighboring long-grass prairies farther east were routinely burned year after year. By the time the
first white men arrived, they found unending seas of open grasslands from Illinois westward to the Rockies. Only the coverts
and coulees through that country, with their greater supplies of
water and more broken terrain, kept some hardy trees alive,
while rugged oaks in the grassy openings of Illinois and Indiana
probably represented, at that time, the front line between western fires and eastern forests.

Extinction must always be viewed as a natural process of evolution, and if man can see himself as part of this natural thread,
then it may be said that here on the plains he served as a preda-
tor to help the evolution of species. But in so doing he deprived
us of a momentary richness of wildlife, more varied and colorful
even than that seen today in East Africa. We are far poorer for
the loss, and the fewer wild species on today's Great Plains
mock our thoughts. What might have been is no more.

CHAPTER 3

The First Plainsmen

When Coronado clanked his column of conquistadores across western Kansas in 1541, he met Indians who were sharply different from those we have come to know in pioneer journals, early western literature, and old movies. For in the three hundred years between Coronado and the nineteenth century westward migration of new Americans, the Indians of the Great Plains were transformed by wars and the horse from part-time farmers and rabbit eaters into colorful nomadic hunters of big game. They were men who ran at the sight of the first Spanish warriors, while with horses they became the toughest light cavalry the world had ever seen. Some farmers who earlier had been hunters returned to the hunt when the horse arrived, providing an interesting local reversal of the more common path man has trod in his rise above hunger. The spiritual life of these plains people was also radically changed by the horse; it lifted the Indian off his feet, gave him mobility, and great stores of food. It freed him for social and spiritual change and growth. In Coronado's time, an Indian's days were filled with scratching to survive. In the nineteenth century, Indians were food rich. They turned their days to ceremonies, fraternal activities, games, warfare. Because of the horse, their material culture broadened steadily. They became virtually a different people.

The first society—the people Coronado met—have their own

story to tell. They remain a shadowy family despite heroic efforts by many to uncover their beginnings, their life style, and their cultural heritage. The central dimness concerns their link with the past. Despite years of study and intensive work by specialists in many fields, the picture of man's North American past still remains unclear.

Our ignorance today, however, is as nothing compared to that of the past. Early explorers had virtually no knowledge of the people they met, though their theories were highly enthusiastic. Columbus called them "Indians," believing he had landed on the outer edges of India. Later, in Europe, his Indians were sometimes seen as exiled children of Babel; or they were the lost tribes of Israel, original descendants of Adam and Eve, Red Devils. They were cast outs, or castoffs, or cast ups from Mediterranean, Scandinavian, African, or Asian peoples. They were sailing people blown off course to America. They evolved from animals, they came from God, they came from Hell. They came from any place other than the homeland of those holding the opinions.

With enough such thoughts floating freely in the western mind, it wasn't necessary to invite forth factual influences. And except for a small band of doubters who finally appeared late in the nineteenth century, we might have remained serenely on course with such notions indefinitely. Fortunately, a growing cadre of tough-minded types has now scratched up sufficient evidence to successfully throw all those old beliefs in the trash bin. The searchers are a precinct of academic detectives, shrewdly extracting hordes of information from bits of stone and bone left by early man. About twenty-five authenticated very early human skulls or skull fragments have been located and several dozen important habitation sites have been excavated. Some methods of dating this material are truly ingenious. One uses fossil tree rings; another the rate of language change among Indians; a third the declining amount of radioactive carbon found in ancient organic materials; a fourth the depth and arrangement of old materials uncovered at each site. As time passes, all these dating techniques are being improved and now serve as checks against each other. However, many uncertainties from this period still exist.

The argument now centers on who came here, and when. Did several waves of *different* peoples settle North America, thereby accounting for the many different tribes and life styles? Or did only a single distinctive people come here, though in bunches, with all differences arising from circumstances on this continent?

Until recently, the wave theory held sway. Under this belief, at least five waves of peoples came to North America, each bringing its own load of cultural equipment and physical traits. Supposedly, they started coming as long as 30,000 years ago and the most recent group did not invade North America until about 3,000 years ago. All came from Asia across the land bridge between Siberia and Alaska.

This wave theory provides easy answers to a lot of nagging questions. For example, if the Indians did not come here in waves, how could certain tools or weapons or styles of pottery appear at roughly the same time in both Asia and North America? How could so many diverse Indian languages take root here? How could there be such enormous life style differences between, for example, the impoverished Paiute Indians of the Great Basin and the highly civilized Aztec or Mayan empires? Just a few hundred years ago, explorers found the Paiutes—Shoshones—digging roots, eating grasshoppers, sleeping under bushes, and keeping a life style extremely barren of cultural baggage. The Aztec by comparison built cities, divided labor for maximum efficiency, created a written language, and produced all the basic religious, social, and military institutions we know today in "modern" society.

How easy it is, therefore, to imagine that these different cultures came from different beginnings. Yet for all the logic it presents, the wave theory is doubted by many specialists who favor the theory of cultural evolution. While tougher to accept, evolution as a source for tribal differences is far more fascinating and complex than the simplistic wave theory.

Basically, theorists of cultural evolution say that early peoples drifted or were pushed across the Asian land bridge into Alaska probably not earlier than 20,000 to 30,000 years ago. There is thin evidence that man arrived here 50,000 or 60,000 years ago, but if so, he exerted no important influence on his surroundings. That question aside, early North American people apparently filtered down into the continent as soon as glaciers allowed them to pass, probably 20,000 to 18,000 years ago. As we have seen, they followed the Great Plains route taken by migrating wildlife. No humans were here during the 2,000,000 years of man's evolution in the Old World, and the men who finally arrived here across the land bridge were nearly the same in physical appearance as modern man. If similarly clothed and groomed, they might pass unnoticed today on any city street.

Evolutionists believe that with two later exceptions—the Eskimos and Athabascans—all early men arrived here before 10,000 years ago. That's the end point of migrations because the glaciers were melting and soon flooded the land bridge under rising seas. These early peoples, split and fractured into tiny bands when they came, were nonetheless kinsmen at their Asian source. Yet by the time of white contact late in the fifteenth century, enough cultural changes had occurred so that the Western Hemisphere was a veritable patchwork of polyglot peoples. Columbus complained that he couldn't understand the language of the people he met. Yet to converse with all the people of this hemisphere, he would have needed to understand more than five hundred separate languages and dialects. North American Indian cultures in his time ranged from complex city states to insect-eating bands. Some men were over six feet tall while others stood five feet or less. Hair color ranged from jet black to light brown. Skin colors included a similar wide range and extremes placed side by side would appear as almost different races.

Yet it's fascinating to realize that all the early peoples of the Americas are linked by inescapable bonds of blood, and this is where the wave theory, with its many spillings of diverse peoples into our land, must come tumbling down. The plain fact is that the Indians of the Western Hemisphere are all of a single cluster of blood types. For all the cultural differences that developed, a basic physical kinship of one to the other was never erased. In fact, the Indians of the Americas have been classified medically as one of the most homogeneous groups of humans ever to spread over a large area of the earth. As though pulling

Mesohippus, about the size of a collie dog, was an early ancestor of the modern horse. He grew from eohippus, an animal about the size of a large house cat. Both were native to North America 30,000,000 to 50,000,000 years ago. (MUSEUM OF THE GREAT PLAINS, LAWTON, OKLAHOMA)

a plug from a bottle, they spilled down through our continent from Alaska and spattered into tiny groups throughout the hemisphere. Then during a hundred intervening centuries they established the social, political, and linguistic differences noted during the last hundred years. Many were long thought independently different peoples. Yet they all came from a common ancestry and their blood type has not varied from that brought here by those early Asian peoples. There are, of course, other physical similarities. For example, skull shapes show certain similarities, as do fingerprints with their high proportion of arches rather than whorls. There is a general tendency among all American Indians not to turn bald or grow whiskers, and they reveal certain color-vision acuity patterns. But the similarity of blood types and the consistency of blood patterns from group to group provides the basic key to the evolutionist's position.

And yet there are those obvious physical and cultural differences that need explanation. What caused the variations in skin tone and physical height, the color differences of hair and eyes, the language and social differences? Great Plains tribes show extensive differences in these areas. Also, during our westward expansion in the eighteenth and nineteenth centuries, American pioneers found striking cultural varieties among the more than thirty tribes then resident in the plains region. Some Indians grew crops while others only hunted big game. Some split their time between hunting and farming. Some lived in earth lodge houses, some in buffalo robe tipis. There were six basic Plains Indian languages and so many dialects that some members of the same language family could not understand each other. The only language known to all was the one that didn't depend on sound—that esperanto of the western plains, sign language.

These differences merely reinforce the evolutionist theory. Language, the evolutionists say, provides a good example. Some linguists believe that a language will change about one-fifth of its words in a thousand years. According to this theory, if a group of people all speaking the same language divide in two and set themselves up as independent nations, then five thousand years later the two groups should be speaking totally different languages. If this is true, it could account for the striking variety of verbal sounds that developed on the Great Plains during the time early peoples lived there.

The wide variety of life styles might also be explained in another evolutionary way, these theorists say. People who live as a group constantly bombard themselves with new ideas about ways to live, things to do, decisions to make. Out of this welter of random possibilities they select those choices right for the moment and right for them as a people. If they grow accustomed to change and their physical surroundings allow or require such changes, then tradition and fixed values will hold less meaning. The culture of such a group will change quite rapidly. Conversely, a traditional society will by definition change more slowly. Thus one group might evolve into an Incan or Mayan empire while another continues to dig roots and eat insects.

The observed physical differences between groups of Plains

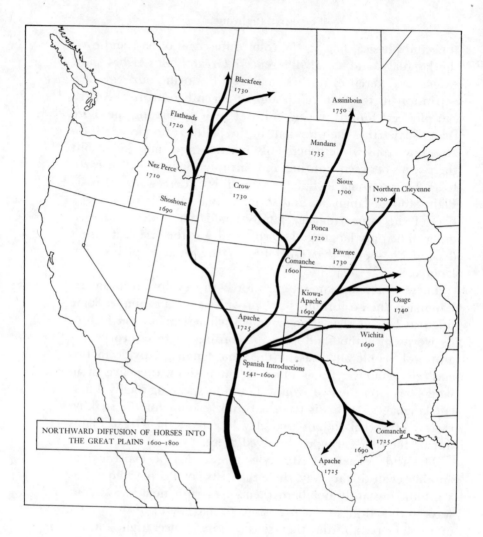

NORTHWARD DIFFUSION OF HORSES INTO
THE GREAT PLAINS 1600–1800

Blackfeet
1730

Assiniboin
1750

Flatheads
1720

Mandans
1735

Nez Perce
1710

Crow
1730

Sioux
1700

Northern Cheyenne
1700

Shoshone
1690

Ponca
1720

Pawnee
1730

Comanche
1600

Kiowa-
Apache
1690

Osage
1740

Apache
1725

Wichita
1690

Spanish Introductions
1541–1600

Comanche
1725

Apache
1725

1690

Indians are a related subject. Such differences can arise from
random genetic drift, Mendelian law, and natural selection. In
a primitive situation, when one family splits from another, certain physical traits will soon begin to dominate in each. One
band may have a few taller people. If tallness begins to dominate in the group's gene pool, then shortness very soon is mathe-
matically removed from the group. Soon only tall people are
produced as members of the band. Because of the vastness of the
North American continent and the cohesive nature of early
tribal bands, such physical differences could develop rapidly.
From such beginnings the people of the Great Plains were able
to present many different faces to the homogeneous white world.
By the same token, and unfortunately for them, they stood as
groups divided from one another and thus easy to conquer.

Populations of all these plains groups were fairly small before
the horse arrived. Until recently, in fact, it was believed that the
Great Plains were mostly barren of human life before horses
arrived. That idea has steadily eroded as dozens of primitive
Great Plains campsites have been found. All were small, however, and used by only a few people, but their antiquity and
location cannot be disputed. At first, the theory grew that these
pre-horse people were either seasonal travelers passing through,
or nomadic hunters moving within their chosen territory.
Today even that idea is losing ground. More likely they were all
semipermanent residents who learned to glean a life from plants
and animals of the plains. Their movements from place to place
were clearly quite limited, with survival based on hunting. Fire
drives, stalks, surrounds, and stampedes over cliffs or into creeks
provided the main techniques. These people probably supple-
mented their diet by digging edible roots while living as small
bands along streams. In dry seasons and winter time, they must
have migrated to nearby coverts and sheltering foothills, or eastward to the prairie borders. Others simply stuck it out along
creek beds or under rock ledges. Inevitably those who moved
with the seasons flowed back onto the plains with the coming of
better weather and the annual wildlife migrations.

Prior to 2,500 years ago, none of the plains peoples raised
crops. Each small family group invariably greeted the new day

hungry, and began the search for food along river banks and surrounding grasslands. At day's end if enough snails, fish, snakes, turtles, rabbits, and birds' eggs were collected, then they lived a while longer. If they could toll an antelope within spearing distance, if they could pounce on a young deer, if they could fire bison over a cliff, they became food rich for many days. In the winter they were seldom so fortunate; in other seasons life was not fuller, only less tenuous.

Slowly as the centuries passed these family clusters began to increase and then to merge into bands, so when the Middle Ages were gripping Europe, many plainsmen were living in communities of one hundred to two hundred people. They were, that is, until something happened to end their existence on the plains. For some reason, in the period from the twelfth to fifteenth centuries, these early people disappeared from the plains. What caused this loss is unknown, but they simply evaporated, leaving little trace of their former existence. A study of ancient tree rings showed that a severe and lasting drought hit the plains from 1276 to 1299. That might have cleared them away. Also, larger bands of roving hunters from eastern prairies or western mountains might have gradually wiped out these smaller, more precarious groups. Whatever the cause, the plains were almost barren of humans for several centuries before gradually refilling with tribes from east and west. Mainly these immigrants were farmers and hunters who settled on the plains in colonies even larger than before.

These were the people Coronado met. Only fragmentary accounts of them survive in the Coronado documents, and in other journals of the period. The earliest, and one of the best, came from the pen of a common soldier who served under Coronado. This is the memoir of Pedro de Castañeda de Naçera and it stands as one of the most important documents in early Great Plains history. Simply written, it describes the country and its people in a brief, solid style. Castañeda was with Coronado when he crossed the Staked Plains in Texas, Oklahoma, and western Kansas, and wrote from memory this account of that experience:

"Now we will speak of the plains. This country is spacious and level, and is more than four hundred leagues wide [1,000 miles] in the part between the two mountain ranges—one, that which Francisco Vásquez de Coronado crossed, and the other that which the force under Don Fernando de Soto crossed, near the North Sea, entering the country from Florida. No settlements were seen anywhere on these plains.

"In traversing two hundred fifty leagues [600–700 miles], the other mountain range was not seen, nor a hill nor a hillock. Several lakes were found at intervals; they were round as plates, a stone's throw or more across, some fresh and some salt. The grass grows tall near these lakes; away from them it is very short, a span or less. The country is like a bowl so that when a man sits down, the horizon surrounds him all around at the distance of a musket shot. There are no groves of trees except at the rivers, which flow at the bottom of some ravines where the trees grow so thick that they were not noticed until one was right on the edge of them. There are paths down into these, made by the cows [buffalo] when they go to water, which is essential throughout these plains.

"As I have related in the first part, people follow the cows, hunting them and tanning the skins to take to the settlements in the winter to sell. These people are called Querechos and Teyas. They have better figures, are better warriors, and are more feared. They travel like the Arabs, with their tents and troops of dogs loaded with poles and having Moorish pack saddles with girths. These people eat raw meat and drink blood. They do not eat human flesh. They are a kind people and are faithful friends. They are able to make themselves very well understood by means of signs. They dry the flesh of the cows, cutting it thin like a leaf, and when dry they grind it like meal to keep it and make a sort of sea soup of it to eat. A handful thrown into a pot swells up so as to increase very much. They season pemmican with fat from the cow. They empty a large gut and fill it with blood, and carry this around the neck to drink when they are thirsty. When they open the belly of a cow, they squeeze out the chewed grass and drink the juice that remains behind, because they say that this contains the essence of the stomach. They cut the hide open at the back and pull it off at the joints, using a flint as large as a finger, tied in a little stick, with as much ease as if working with a good iron tool. They give it an edge with their own teeth. The quickness with which they do this is something worth seeing and noting. There are very great numbers of wolves on these plains, which go around with the cows. They have white skins."

Coronado was arriving on the Great Plains in 1541 at a time when the native peoples had reestablished their hold on that land. Castañeda's account does not deal with farming activities of the people he found, but recent study has shown that they produced crops of corn, beans, squash, sunflowers, and probably other vegetables as well. Most of this agriculture was east of the 99th Meridian, in west central Kansas, lying toward the bitter end of the long road Coronado traveled. Here a more abundant rainfall and richer humus in the river valleys made such primitive farming possible. Here the native peoples built their earthlodge villages beside the rivers, and tilled their garden plots nearby.

The villages were a keen disappointment to Coronado. Rather than the golden cities his government had expected, they were merely collections of mud huts, and as the hopes held by his officers drained into bickering and intrigue, he must have realized the collapse of his career was near. Yet the greater wonder was that he found even these native peoples. Had he known the history of the natives he found, and been less preoccupied with his own affairs, he might have wondered at the marvel of his discovery. These people he met were the descendants of truly great travelers and explorers, peoples who had come far greater distances over the earth than he, peoples who had braved the glacial lands, the mountains, endless forests, endless plains.

Quite in keeping with this tradition, it was the native peoples who now became the discoverers. Where Coronado was disappointed, they were awe struck and terrified, overwhelmed at the sight of horses, unbelieving of the armor and guns. Seeing man riding the backs of large animals must have shattered their prior

Native stocks of horses disappeared from North America sometime before white men arrived. But Cortez reintroduced them to Mexico in the sixteenth century and they soon spread throughout the hemisphere. Coronado and his conquistadores brought them to the Great Plains in 1541. (FREDERIC REMINGTON, *Century Magazine*, JANUARY 1889)

images of wildlife. None could have dreamed how completely horses would soon change their own way of life, and yet Coronado must have seeded that thought among them as he paced his columns along their dusty streets.

West of the 99th Meridian, on the high open plains, Coronado also met small clusters of nomads roaming the grassy coverts in search of bison, antelope, and deer. These people lived as simply as Bedouins, following the herds and sleeping in the open. They were few in number and skittish as the noisy column of Spaniards approached. Sometime before these white invaders arrived, such nomads had learned to trade dry buffalo meat to the river dwellers for corn and other vegetables. Both groups lived by the thinnest threads of survival at each end of a tough little economy where all people made best use of their skills on a hard, unyielding land.

Along the rivers, as the sixteenth century drew to a close, the villages slowly grew larger. Garden plots were more extensive, more productive, and more numerous. Out on the plains the nomads also increased in numbers, as they did on the eastern and western plains margins. But it was still the rivers that veined the plains into a whole. Lands between the open plains were broad, dangerous places to wander. River valleys were the mainstays to provide a day's food, places where fish, turtles, frogs, snakes, and crayfish were usually available, where the soil could be tilled and edible plants might grow. Trees grew here and shaded big game. On the open plains, the heavily matted sod was impossible to work, and so those who braved its dangers were the hunters. They had no horses, but in their travels they used dog travois. They had fire and bows and arrows, and they were the forebears of the Great Plains Indian tribes of a later day. They could hold their own against weather, thirst, and hunger.

However, when the horse arrived, deep and rapid changes occurred. Indian populations now increased almost to the explosion point. By the end of the seventeenth century, Pawnee towns on the Upper Republican River in eastern Nebraska and northern Kansas often had three thousand inhabitants and two hundred large earthen lodges. To support such communities,

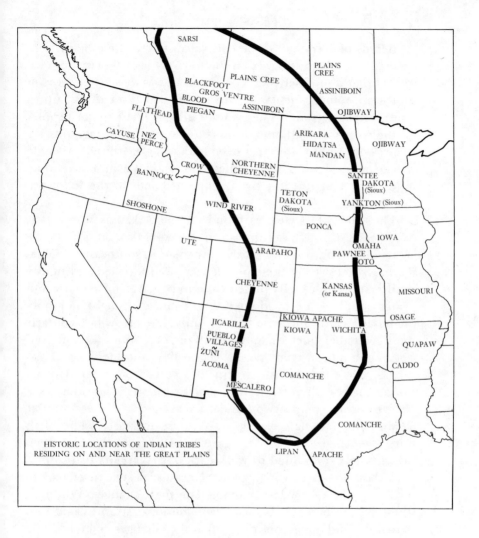

SARSI

PLAINS CREE

PLAINS CREE

ASSINIBOIN

BLACKFOOT
GROS VENTRE
BLOOD
FLATHEAD   PIEGAN   ASSINIBOIN   OJIBWAY

CAYUSE NEZ
        PERCE   OJIBWAY

                                ARIKARA
                                HIDATSA
                CROW   MANDAN
BANNOCK   NORTHERN
                CHEYENNE   SANTEE
                                       DAKOTA
                         TETON   (Sioux)
SHOSHONE   WIND RIVER DAKOTA   YANKTON (Sioux)
                            (Sioux)

                UTE   PONCA
                                               IOWA
                         ARAPAHO   OMAHA
                                        PAWNEE
                         CHEYENNE   OTO
                                                    MISSOURI
                                KANSAS
                                (or Kansa)
                JICARILLA   OSAGE
                         KIOWA APACHE
                PUEBLO   KIOWA   WICHITA
                VILLAGES
                ZUÑI   QUAPAW
                ACOMA   CADDO
                MESCALERO COMANCHE

                                        COMANCHE

HISTORIC LOCATIONS OF INDIAN TRIBES
RESIDING ON AND NEAR THE GREAT PLAINS
                         LIPAN   APACHE

hundreds of acres had to be cultivated. Often these fields were located five to ten miles from the town. One authority has estimated that a productive third of an acre was needed per person to sustain some tribes, while for others that hunted less, up to one acre per person was kept under tillage. These plains peoples of the river valleys dug enormous underground storage pits for their food, eight to ten feet deep and as large around. A single village might have dozens of these pits, and all would have to be filled each year to carry townspeople through to the following harvest.

The same life style was found on the Arkansas where that river eases through southwestern Kansas; also on the Platte system in Nebraska, and on the Canadian in southeastern Oklahoma. The towns of these people were well fortified and tightly built, and were usually placed close to the river for defense and water supply. They had to be. The horse brought not only material wealth and ease in the hunt, but arrow-fast contacts between tribes. Such a rapid growth in populations soon put old social customs on trial. We have seen how automobile and airplane have changed America in fifty years from a rural to an urban society, all very often in social turmoil. When the horse arrived on the plains two hundred years ago, it brewed similar changes for our native peoples. Warfare increased. The birth rate steepened. With many garden plots located miles from town, tillers commuted to work each day. Warriors had to protect those exposed work parties. New social structures had to evolve in the villages to accommodate these changes. While all these people had full bellies, new emotional strains came into tribal life and dangerous new physical challenges emerged. The horse cut the anchor line holding these people to the land, and set many tribes adrift on fruitful but untried waters.

The history of the horse on this continent is intriguing. The earliest recognizable granddaddy of all horses, a fox-sized creature called eohippus, first appeared in North America about fifty million years ago. He also appeared about the same time in Europe, and a theory now current suggests that these early horses probably evolved on our Great Plains, then migrated to the Old World across an early north Pacific land bridge. Eohippus was an animal with three toes on hind feet and four on front feet. He existed in large numbers throughout the American West and particularly on the plains. Gradually this animal evolved into mesohippus, the size of a small donkey, and finally a million years ago into an animal about the size and shape of our present horse. Over this long span of time, horses kept losing toes until only one remained, the nail of that last toe hardening on each foot to become the hoof. These early horses also continued to disperse across the globe and to grow in size, speed, and variety so that several kinds of horses such as zebras, wild asses, donkeys, Mongolian ponies, and others roamed the plains and grasslands of the entire world during the last million years.

Sometime in the past 10,000 years, however, all horses disappeared from the Americas. They were part of the general disappearance discussed earlier. Why this happened or how is another of those prehistoric mysteries for which no total solution has yet been found—though hunting by man no doubt played a role. The early human migrations into North America included people who had traditionally hunted horses for meat and hides, and they may have driven the horse to extinction here, as they did other species. Or a killing disease may have come across the land bridge to claim American horses. They may have been steadily reduced by fires, or predators, or blizzards before reaching extinction. However it happened, they disappeared here but continued to flourish in the Old World. As civilization spread, man domesticated the horse and made it his chief beast of burden in parts of Asia, in Europe, and in the Middle East. By the time the Spanish began their conquest of the Americas in the sixteenth century, the horse was a common military figure in Europe. He was also the principal companion of Christian liberators during the Crusades. After an absence of nearly 10,000 years, the horse returned to North America as a conqueror on March 13, 1519 when Hernando Cortez landed near Vera Cruz with a tiny army and sixteen of the animals.

At first the Indians were terrified of the horse, a fear that provided the Spaniards with one of their best weapons in the New World. Rapidly, as the Spanish conquered Mexico, they

increased their supplies of horses. Coronado, for example, left
Mexico City on his northern expedition in 1540 with 336 men,
about a thousand Indians, and "an equal number of horses." He
returned to that city in 1542 with less than a hundred men and
an unknown but far smaller number of horses. Most of the
horses had either been killed or had gone astray. How many
escaped to the Great Plains is unknown, but the number was
probably not very great. The Indians meanwhile had no experience with horses and their early contacts—not inclined to
endear them to the animals—came when they were run down
by Spanish cavalry. "We dressed the wounds of the horses with
grease from dead Indians," wrote one of Cortez's captains. As
time passed, however, the Indian's fear wore away. As settlement proceeded, the Spaniards began to use Indians as stable-
hands and handlers. In sixteenth-century mission villages of the
southwest, that meant a kinetic relationship between Indian
and horse was beginning to develop. The Spaniards, sensing
danger, set up prohibitions against Indians riding horses. The
law changed natural curiosity into natural desire, and before
long horses and their Indian handlers began to disappear over
the horizon.

But the change came slowly. A century and a half after
Coronado's expedition, the Caddo Indians of Texas, living next
door to the Spanish settlements, had gathered only about thirty
animals. These were seen in their villages along the Red River
in 1690. Thirty years later, a trader reported seeing about three
hundred horses in a pair of small Pawnee villages on the Arkansas River, much farther north. But that was still less than one
horse per man. As late as 1724, a group of Kansa Indians in
northeastern Kansas did not have horses, and as late as 1735,
there were no horses north and east of the Missouri River. By
that time the horse had been on American soil 216 years. It was
1750 before horses began to replace canoes in Minnesota and
the eastern Dakotas.

Along the slopes of the Rockies, however, the horse traveled
northward somewhat faster. The Blackfoot Indians of Wyoming
and Montana had horses soon after 1730, while the Shoshone,
Nez Perce, and Flatheads farther west probably had them even

This first known drawing of the American buffalo appeared in Europe in 1552, shortly after the Spanish conquerers reached the Great Plains. (GO-MARA's *Historia de los Indio Saragossa*)

sooner. The Crows got horses about the same time as the Black-feet, but that was still nearly two hundred years after Coronado entered the plains.

As their capabilities in hunting and warfare were realized, tribes began to seek horses through trade and barter. There was also that change of ownership we call theft that Plains Indians knew as a cultural form of honor seeking and coup counting. Whatever the term used, Spanish horses were steadily becoming Indian horses. Strays also began to multiply on the open range, providing another source of supply.

In addition, there was the Indians' almost legendary handling of the horse. The Great Plains in fact provided an excellent training ground for horsemanship, and an entire life style soon began to develop around it. The redmen designed and built their own saddles, bridles, and other tack, usually based on Spanish models. Learning to ride was another challenge for the ground-bound Indian. By jeers and cheers from his peers, a native enthusiasm for firm-ground safety was steadily overcome. Through all of this, the horse quickly became the basic unit of value in trade and barter. An Indian's most valuable possessions were his horses and he expended great energy obtaining and keeping them. Without a fine horse, the Plains Indian of the eighteenth century was something less than half the man he had been before horses arrived. But give such a man a horse, a good horse, and together they became a powerful food-getting, horse-racing, heavy gambling, brave and vain chunk of plains society. Captain R. B. Marcy on a trip to Texas in 1849 wrote:

"It is when mounted that the Comanche exhibits himself to the best advantage. Here he is at home, and his skill in various manoeuvres . . . is truly astonishing. . . . Every warrior has his war-like horse, which is the fleetest that can be obtained, and he prizes him more highly than anything else in his possession, and it is seldom that he can be induced to part with him at any price. He never mounts him except when going into battle, the buffalo chase, or upon state occasions. On his return he is met at the door of his lodge by one of his wives, who takes his horse and attends to its wants with the utmost care. . . . I once made an effort to purchase a favorite horse from a chief of one of the bands of the southern Comanche, and offered him a large price, but he could not be persuaded to part with him. He said the animal was one of the fleetest in his possession, and if he were to sell him, it would prove a calamity to his whole band, as it often required all the speed of this animal to insure success in the buffalo chase; that his loss would be felt by all his people, and he would be regarded as very foolish; moreover, he said, patting his favorite on the neck, 'I love him very much.' "

For a considerable time, then, the Indians kept the Great Plains locked in their grip primarily through their horseman-ship. In fact, some have said that the entire Spanish hope of col-onizing the southern plains failed because of horse-mounted Indians. Cortez unleashed an equestrian tide that ultimately swept his Spanish descendants back to Madrid. It took nearly three centuries for this to happen, but when it did, the collapse of an empire resulted. And the first crack in that empire's armor was seen first of all on our American Great Plains.

CHAPTER 4
Arrivals from Europe

Spanish exploration of the southern Great Plains in the sixteenth century was extensive, brutal, and courageous. Led across
those plains by visions of God, glory, and gold, the Spanish conquistadores took their Indian battles in stride, wrote superb
reports of their adventures, and never found the yellow metal
that led them forth. The reports they left were their greatest
treasure and the failure to find gold their greatest defeat. From
Cabeza de Vaca's incredible journey in 1528 to Juan de Oñate's
military campaign at the end of the century, five major expeditions ventured onto the southern Great Plains. Cabeza de Vaca,
first white man on the scene, skirted the southern edge of the
plains, saw much, and laid the groundwork for all later beliefs
that gold lay to the north. Two later expeditions reached as far
north as central and eastern Kansas. One other, led by the rene-
gade Antonio Gutierrez de Humaña, reached at least to the
Republican River in central Kansas and perhaps to the Platte in
Nebraska. A fifth led by Gaspar Castaño de Sosa explored the
length of the Pecos River from the Rio Grande to Taos, New
Mexico.

Conversion of the "heathens" was cited as one reason for
these explorations, and Franciscan monks were usually mixed in
the columns of armored Spanish gentlemen, foot soldiers, and

53

subjugated Indians. Service to the King was another reason for
the push northward. But gold was the real quarry. They all
sought gold. "We came there to serve God and get rich," wrote
one of Coronado's captains. On horseback, on foot, pushing
dusty carriages and pulling heavy cannons, the tiny bands of soldiers, settlers, and Christianizers threaded north and east from
their Mexican and New Mexican strongholds, gradually coming
to understand the Llano Estacado, its borders, and its resident
owners, the Apaches and Comanches. In each case, they learned
one important fact: Gold could not be found north of the Rio
Grande. True, the Spanish wanted Indians converted and settlers settled. But that was frosting. The real stuff these brave,
brutal men sought was the bright yellow metal. None found it
and none received the royal plaudits. Consequently, none died
as Spanish heroes.

Still, the Spaniards did make a stab at colonizing the region
and by the eighteenth century were holding to it rather stubbornly. For this they suffered steady losses through all the years
of their endeavors. When small clusters of friars and settlers
went eastward or northward from the major settlements, they
often failed to return. When sizable columns of mounted soldiers accompanied these explorations, they often passed through
untouched. The Indians meantime kept up their disjointed
guerrilla warfare, a military approach the Spaniards seemed to
understand only very dimly. Through this give-and-take, the
Spaniards continued to maintain varying degrees of control over
the entire region for nearly three centuries, and their influences
of language, church, place-names, and culture will long remain
woven into the fabric of that land. The bloods of the Spaniard
and Indian were mixed both in battle and in bed, and though
their land policy failed, colonization did succeed, if uneasily, as
a lasting social ferment.

For all of that—taking the view of the Spanish Crown—the
colonies were a failure. They did not establish more than a
handful of lasting settlements north of the Rio Grande. Santa
Fe was their biggest success, and even that outpost was not thoroughly Spanish; it proved a cultural crossroads dominated in
numbers by Indians and mixed bloods. During the Pueblo

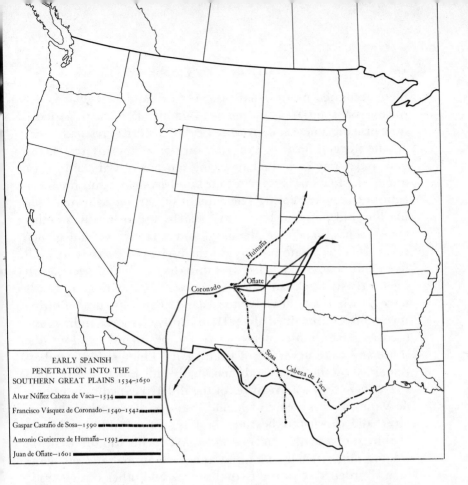

Revolt of 1680, Santa Fe fell with all the rest of the northern settlements, and the Spanish were driven back to El Paso. Most missions established in the southern plains region during those bloody decades were smeared away as quickly as they were settled. Of the many Indians met, almost none accepted Christianity from the friars. The brilliant cities sought by commanders of the military columns and the provincial governors—*adelantados* they were called—were never found. Pueblos, tipi villages, clusters of earth or grass lodges, and a few scattered silver mines; these were all, and they had to suffice.

During the entire period, the written reports have left us an extraordinary history. They tell us more about early life on the Great Plains than any other documents. They are uniformly clear and descriptive and provide graphic and often very com-

plete accounts. As time has passed, more and more have been
uncovered, translated, and made available. The entire period is
now proving a new and growing field of historical research.

The story of Spanish explorers on the southern Great Plains
gets under way with the fascinating journey of Cabeza de Vaca,
one of the few survivors of a four-hundred-man Spanish expedition to the New World. The expedition set out to search Florida for gold in 1528. It was wrecked by ocean storms, swamps,
fevers, starvation, poor planning, and a failure to find golden
cities. In a desperate bid to save themselves, the survivors built
five small boats and headed west into the Gulf. They were adrift
for nearly six weeks and most were lost, but about eighty finally
were blown ashore at Galveston Island, Texas. By the following
spring fifteen remained alive. Held captive by local Indians and
used as slaves, most attempted to escape inland or along the
shore and were never heard from again. Three sickly members
remained on the island and then finally only one was alive. This
was Cabeza de Vaca, treasurer of the ill-fated expedition. Cabeza
de Vaca was educated, tough, and resourceful. Somehow he survived the capricious beatings of his captors and the diet of
grubby roots, snails, and raw meat. When his captors went on
trading missions they used him as a pack animal and medicine
man. Burdened with their coral, shells, and other coastal trade
goods, they marched him inland for long distances. On these
brutal journeys Cabeza de Vaca became the first European to
see the southern margin of the Great Plains. How far north he
traveled is unknown, but in his *Narrative* he reports having
seen buffalo and having eaten their meat with his captors.

After nearly six years of captivity, he finally escaped, fleeing
inland in 1534 and traveling from tribe to tribe as a medicine
man. To assure his safety he stayed at each tiny village long
enough to minister to the sick. One day he came to Indians who
told of seeing other white-skinned people. They led him to a
nearby village and there held prisoner were three of Cabeza de
Vaca's companions from the Florida expedition. One was a
black slave named Esteban, the others were Spaniards named
Andrés Dorantes de Carranza, and **Alonso de Castillo de
Maldonado**. Together they conspired to escape and one dark

night in 1534 fled as a group across the hardpan of southern
Texas, the eastern star at their backs and visions of Spanish
Mexico ahead.

As the four men wandered westward, the tribes they met
became convinced that Esteban and his white companions were
gods sent to earth. For the Spaniards this became their survival
equipment. Slowly the four were passed from tribe to tribe
across western Texas and into southern New Mexico, then
south and west into Mexico performing "miracles" for the Indians as they went. Somewhere in their wandering, Cabeza de
Vaca was given a "hawk bell of copper, thick and large, and
figured with a face." That bell would later play an important
role in Spanish expeditions, inflaming the thoughts of men who
wished for more important metals there to the north.

One day they came upon an Indian carrying a nail and a
European belt buckle. They were stunned with hope, and a few
days later, wonder of wonders, met a pack of Spanish slavers
hard at work in the hills of Sinaloa. It was April 1536, nearly
eight incredible years after they had landed at Galveston Island.
The slavers were as stunned as the naked thorn-torn wanderers.
The dead had returned to life, and their stories electrified
Mexico City.

Gradually, however, the privations they endured were transformed into unusual adventures across fabled lands, then into
exploration of richly ornamented places. Soon the remembered
Indian huts became the Seven Lost Cities of Cíbola. They had
long been a legend in Europe and now were finally located in
the New World, north of the Rio Grande. Gradually these
stories grew and changed and then were heard in the Spanish
court. More time passed but finally the royal favors were sorted
out so an expedition could explore the mysterious north. In the
winter of 1539 the King agreed that a military column could
move north, with the fabled golden cities the main object of
conquest.

The front runner to lead this expedition was General Francisco Vásquez de Coronado, a dashing young conquistador,
handsome, of noble birth, and ripe for adventure. Soon after
arriving in the New World, he married Doña Beatriz de

Francisco Vásquez de Coronado (1510–54) was born in Salamanca, Spain and went to Mexico in 1535. No drawings or paintings of Coronado are known to exist. This portrait was drawn from a written description of the great explorer. (ROSWELL, NEW MEXICO, MUSEUM AND ART CENTER)

Estrada, a favored if illegitimate daughter of King Ferdinand, and a woman of marked beauty, wealth, and position. Coronado and his wife took up residence on an immense estate at Tlalpan, Mexico, and in 1538 he was named governor of Neuva Galicia, a northern province of the growing colonial empire. In 1539 Coronado was thirty years old and his charm and wealth and position were enough to carry the day. Though besieged by glory-hunting hopefuls, Viceroy Antonio de Mendoza acted on the King's wishes and chose Coronado to lead the Spaniards north.

Coronado's army left Compostela, the Mexican provincial capital, in the spring of 1540. He had 336 soldiers, several hundred Indian helpers, a sizable number of Indian women and children, 1,500 horses, and a mixed herd of cattle, sheep, and hogs. They clanked along through the dusty Mexican country-side for weeks, always moving northwest, to finally arrive in southern Arizona in early summer. There the army turned eastward into central New Mexico to the land of the Zuñis. Expecting the best, they found the worst. Their Cíbola, that supposed cluster of golden cities, proved to be only pueblo villages in west central New Mexico. The Spaniards captured the first pueblo, Hawikuh, on July 7, 1540 near present Gallup, then pressed on and captured others before settling down to winter at Tiguex southwest of present Santa Fe.

Being Spaniards, they were accustomed to the region's cold, dry winter approximating that of their homeland, and they dwelled well enough in Indian pueblos, eating Indian food. The dispossessed Indians survived not nearly as well, however, and the steel-hard hatred that developed later toward the white man began to build right here in New Mexico.

While Coronado rested through the winter, he learned of an unusual Indian held captive by the nearby Zuñis, and on investigation found "The Turk," probably a Pawnee. The Turk—called that by the Spaniards "because he looked like one"—was one of those unfortunate pawns who cast their lot unwarily into the web of history. He told tales, and the more he told, the more the Spanish listened. Pedro de Castañeda, chronicler of the Coronado expedition, recounted the meeting of the Turk and the Spanish leaders in his *Journal*:

"The Turk told them such great things about the wealth of gold and silver in his country that they did not care about looking for cows [buffalo], but returned after they had seen a few to report the rich news to the general. . . . The Turk said that in his country there was a river in the level plain which was two leagues wide, with fishes large as horses, and numbers of very big canoes, with more than twenty rowers on a side. These canoes carried sails, and their lords sat on the poop under awnings, and on the prow they had great golden eagles. He said also that the lord of the country took his afternoon nap under a great tree on which were hung many little golden bells. These put him to sleep as they swung in the air. He said also that everyone had their ordinary dishes made of wrought plate, and the jugs and bowls were of gold. He called gold *Acochis*. They showed him metal ornaments and he said they were not gold; he knew gold and silver very well and did not care anything about other metals. For this reason, and because of the ease with which he told it, he was believed."

So there the die was cast. Coronado would go east into the plains to find his el dorado. Never mind that other Indians doubted the Turk. His words were soothing to the general's ears. The Spaniards waited impatiently for the spring, and on April 23, 1541 started east. For weeks, the army marched across the grassland with the Turk in the lead. Gradually, however, with only grasslands to view day after day, patience thinned to a growing anger. Finally one morning, when pressed for directions, the Turk admitted he had lied. He did not know where he was. He insisted, however, that the golden city of Quivira really did exist. He urged the general to continue. With desire still forcing belief, Coronado placed the Turk in irons, sent most of his force back to New Mexico, and pushed on with thirty men and the best horses. Castañeda then tells what happened:

"The general followed his guides until he reached the village of Quivira, which took forty-eight days marching, on account of the great detour they had made toward Florida. They asked the Turk why he had lied and had guided them so far out of their way. He said that his country was in that direction and that, besides this, the people at Cicuye had asked him to lead them off onto the plains and lose them, so that the horses would die when their provisions gave out . . . The Turk said all this like one who had given up hope . . . They garrotted him. Neither gold nor silver nor any trace of either was found among these people. The lord of Quivira wore a copper plate on his neck and prized it highly."

Only a copper plate and highly prized at that. The inhabitants of Quivira lived in Indian huts beside a Kansas creek. Only that and nothing more. And so the deception was complete. Coronado's great venture into history became nothing more than a grand mistake. For this the Spaniards wrapped a cord around the Turk's neck and strangled him. After resting twenty-five days and pondering what to do, Coronado returned to New Mexico by a shorter route and arrived back at Tiguex on October 20, 1541.

During the journey north, the entire force had been preoccupied with the gold they felt must certainly lie ahead. On the march home, disillusion clouded every step and Castañeda recalled the spooky ability of the Great Plains to swallow up whole columns of travelers:

"Who would believe that one thousand horses and five hundred of our cows and more than five thousand rams and

ewes and more than one thousand five hundred Indians and
servants, in traveling over those plains, would leave no more
trace where they had passed than if nothing had been there—
nothing—so that it was necessary to make piles of bones and
cow dung now and then so that the rear guard could follow the
army. The grass never failed to become erect after it had been
trodden down, and although it was short, it was as fresh and
straight as before." Later settlers were to be swallowed up by
the emptiness of the plains in the same way, and those who
straggled behind or wandered from any main column might be
found days later, insane or dazed or dead. Many never were
found.

One subject fascinated all Spaniards who traversed the Great
Plains, and that was buffalo. They called them cows and bulls

The Spanish were fascinated by buffalo, which they called "the cows." This
early drawing by George Catlin shows a small herd dusting themselves
in the circular plains "wallows." (GEORGE CATLIN, IN *North American
Indians*)

and all chroniclers described them in their own way. Here's
Castañeda's version:

"All the horses took flight when they first saw the bulls. They
have a narrow, short face, the eyes sticking out at the side so
that when they are running they can see who is following them.
They have very long beards, like goats, and when they are running they throw their heads back with the beard dragging on
the ground. There is a sort of girdle round the middle of the
body. The hair is very woolly, like a sheep's, very fine, and in
front of the girdle the hair is very long and rough like a lion's.
They have a great hump, larger than a camel's. The horns are
short and thick, so that they are not seen much above the hair.
In May, they change the hair in the middle of the body for a
down, which makes perfect lions of them. They rub against the
small trees in the little ravines to shed their hair, and they continue this until only the down is left, as a snake changes his
skin. They have a short tail, with a bunch of hair at the end.
When they run, they carry it erect like a scorpion. It is worth
noticing that the little calves are red and just like ours, but they
change their appearance and color with time and age."

The buffalo must have numbered in the millions. Castañeda
tells of one amazing sight observed during Coronado's expedition to Kansas:

"Another thing was a heap of cow bones, a crossbow shot
long, almost twice a man's height in places, and some eighteen
feet or more wide, which was found on the edge of a salt lake in
the southern part, and this in a region where there are no
people who could have made it. The only explanation of this
which could be suggested was that the waves which the north
winds must make in the lake had piled up the bones of the
cattle which had died in the lake, when the old and weak ones
who went into the water were unable to get out. The noticeable
thing is the number of cattle that would be necessary to make
such a pile of bones."

Coronado had planned another journey into the Great Plains
the following spring, but in December 1541, he fell from a
horse during a race and received a severe head injury from
which he never fully recovered. The next summer his bedrag-

gled column returned to Mexico City, he on a stretcher and his men in disgrace. Coronado was tried for wasting royal funds in his unsuccessful northern campaign. Because of ill health and a lingering royal favor, he was acquitted of all charges, but was relieved of his post as provincial governor and died a broken man in 1554.

His second in command was not so lucky. Don García López de Cárdenas also was tried, found guilty, fined, banned from the New World for ten years, and exiled. The charge was misuse of government funds and property. Cárdenas had been an exemplary soldier and leader, and had taken over after Coronado was injured. However, he did not have illness as an excuse and Spanish wrath at the lack of gold had to settle on someone.

With Coronado's trial, northern exploration ended for nearly half a century. That was enough time for tough memories to fade to reflection, then rejection, then correction, and finally speculation. With innocence restored and a new century in sight, more probes of the north began. Walking across the eastern desert, in the summer of 1582, several Franciscan friars took up residence among the Indians of New Mexico. The padres were promptly murdered—the Indians perhaps failing to understand that crosses were more powerful than crossbows. In revenge, Antonio de Espejo, a wealthy landholder, mounted a punitive expedition to the north. Espejo moved up the Rio Grande to central New Mexico, and after "disciplining the Indians," turned westward into Arizona. He had heard local rumors of a lake of gold somewhere to the west, and now determined to find it. After traveling several hundred miles he found signs of minerals, and in western Arizona soon located several silver deposits. Silver! At last a precious metal had been found. The year was old, however, and not having resources or authority to work such mines, he returned to Mexico to obtain both. His story captured the city once again—as Cabeza de Vaca's had half a century earlier.

But the remoteness of the region and the mining effort needed forced the Spaniards to pause and reflect—an act which only served to heighten interest. During the time that the Viceroy temporized, Luis de Carabajal, governor of the northern

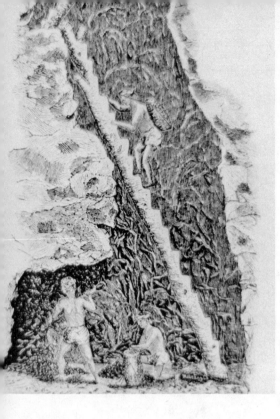

Rumors of silver mines in Spanish-held portions of the Great Plains contributed heavily to French attempts to reach Santa Fe. This early engraving depicts Indian slaves, as they might have looked working in such a mine. (*Official Report of the Territory of New Mexico*, BY WILLIAM RITCH, SANTA FE, 1882–83)

province of Nuevo León, was arrested by the Inquisition and taken to Mexico City for trial. That left Gaspar Castaño de Sosa, the lieutenant governor, in charge. The date was 1590, and Sosa had heard as many rumors about silver mines as anyone else. As soon as Carabajal was safely packed off to the city, Sosa called together the settlers then living at Monclova, his provincial capital, formed them into a mining company, and headed north. His only authority for such a move was simple greed. The column included everyone—men, women, and children, as well as goats, sheep, and cows.

After reaching the Rio Grande, they pushed upstream to the junction of the Pecos, then followed that river along its deep and magnificent gorge northward to the Taos pueblo. This was the first time any Spaniard had ascended the Pecos, which crosses the northern end of the Coahuila desert and enters the southern margin of the Great Plains. But Sosa's venture was not viewed with official approval. In fact, the Viceroy was livid with anger. Almost as soon as Sosa reached Taos, a military detachment, out of breath, arrived from the capital. Sosa was arrested and he and his followers were marched back to Mexico City, all in a dismal row.

Three years later, a much more secretive expedition ventured onto the plains. Without authority from the Viceroy, two renegades named Francisco Leyva de Bonilla and Antonio Gutierrez de Humaña led a column out of New Mexico and northward into the Great Plains. It wasn't a large column, but a number of Indian helpers had joined the force, including one named Jusephe, plus an unnamed black slave girl and at least one other Spaniard named Alonzo Sanchez. The group poked about over the plains of Oklahoma and western Kansas for several weeks, apparently enjoying themselves thoroughly. They came to great herds of buffalo and hunted steadily. For a time, all went well. Then dissension grew between Bonilla and Humaña, possibly over the course of the expedition. After some time, the group passed through a large village of Wichita Indians on the Arkansas River. Jusephe recalled that the Indians lived in grass lodges and farmed great garden plots nearby. The travelers continued northward, split now by growing discord between the leaders. A few days after leaving the grass lodge village, the two men started an open quarrel that lasted all one day and into the night. Finally, in a rage, Humaña murdered Bonilla.

The next day the group continued northward under a gloom of distrust, the Indian followers nervous and uncertain. On and on they went, doggedly, hunting buffalo, until they reached a "second large river." Almost certainly this was the Platte in southcentral Nebraska. And here they stopped, having come farther into central North America than any other white men. They had reached the geographical heartland of the continent fifteen years before Samuel de Champlain, first white settler in eastern North America, would land on the St. Lawrence River. By overland passage, Humaña's hunting party had penetrated from Mexico City a straight-line distance of nearly fifteen hundred miles to the north, and though these men did not display the Spanish flag, they represented their nation at the farthest extent of its North American expansion.

By now, however, morale in Humaña's group had fallen

apart. Among other troubles, the buffalo herds thinned out, there were no more Indian villages, and a broad river blocked their path. It must have seemed useless to continue. One night after all were asleep, six of the Indian followers slipped away from camp and headed back toward New Mexico. Without protection from the Spanish guns, they were openly exposed to surrounding tribesmen, and in a short time four disappeared into the plains, and a fifth was dead. The sixth, however, was Jusephe. After being separated from the others, he was captured by Apaches and held as a slave somewhere on the central plains. After a year, he escaped and made his way back to the Spanish settlements in New Mexico.

His story stirred Santa Fe, but for a time nothing more was known of the Humaña expedition. Then some years later, in a northern Indian village, a monk stumbled onto Alonzo Sanchez, the other Spaniard who traveled with Humaña. Sanchez had elected to live out his life among the Indians, either by choice or from fear of prosecution for his part in the expedition. Sanchez now added further details to what was known. He said that after Jusephe and the Indians deserted, the remainder of the party turned homeward. One night they were forced to camp on an open plain where the grass was dried to tinder by the late summer sun. Just before dawn, Indians crept up, surrounded the camp, and set fire to the grass. At the height of the confusion, they burst through the smoke and killed everyone except Sanchez and the black girl. These two were taken by the Indians and forced to join their tribe, the black girl becoming an Indian's wife and Sanchez gradually becoming a leader in the group. Though troops were sent to find him, he was never seen again.

The next important northward mission was that of Juan de Oñate. His story began as the century was drawing to a close. Time had healed earlier wounds, and the Spanish government decided to try once again to colonize the north, to develop the silver mines found by Espejo, and to search further for gold. Not since 1541 had any authorized expedition been sent to search the Great Plains. The right to make this venturesome journey finally fell to Oñate, a wealthy, haughty Spanish nobleman. After a lengthy period of organization, he led a colonizing force into New Mexico in the spring of 1598.

For three years, he "pacified" Indians, settled land, and searched for gold and silver mines. During all this time, he stayed in the mountains of New Mexico and the deserts of Arizona. Finally, on June 23, 1601, he started east and north into the Great Plains. He had talked with Jusephe, lately returned from the Humaña expedition, and he had the benefit of Coronado's experience during that grassland adventure. But though Oñate searched diligently and traveled extensively on the southern plains he did not find gold, and his journals are chiefly important for their descriptions of the land and its peoples. The path he followed to Quivira was roughly similar to Coronado's and the Indian community there was still intact. The numbers of Indians encountered by Oñate, however, had increased substantially from those reported by Coronado sixty years earlier. Oñate wrote of discovering " ... a large rancheria, with more than five thousand souls." This was en route, while still in Oklahoma. His map shows the village to have six hundred houses, and some sources reckon the community numbered up to six thousand inhabitants. Yet this was merely a temporary camp, as these Indians " ... were not a people who sowed and reaped, but lived solely on the cattle."

Farther on, Oñate recalls: " ... we came to a settlement containing more than 1,200 houses, all established along the bank of another good-sized river which flowed into the large one. The houses were all round, built of forked poles and bound with rods, and on the outside covered to the ground with dry grass. Within, on the sides, they had frameworks or platforms which served them as beds. Most of the houses were large enough to hold eight or ten persons. They were two lance lengths high. ... " These were the Wichita Indians and Oñate fortunately found them peaceful and friendly, for his force was heavily outnumbered.

A few days later and farther north, he traveled in one day about nine miles " ... all the way through a populated district, and seeing that the houses continued beyond, and having positive knowledge of the large assemblage of people which awaited us, it was necessary to take counsel as to what should be done."

During this journey through Kansas, the Spanish enjoyed quantities of new and interesting foods: "Each day the land through which we were traveling became better, and the luxury of an abundance of fish from the river greatly alleviated the hardships of the journey. And the fruits gave no less pleasure, particularly the plums, of a hundred thousand different kinds, as mellow and good as those which grow in the choicest orchards of our land. They are so good that although eaten by thousands they never injured anybody. The trees were small, but their fruit was more plentiful than their leaves, and they were so abundant that in more than one hundred and fifty leagues, hardly a day passed without seeing groves of them and also of grapevines such that although they hid the view in many places they produced sweet and delicious grapes." Farther on they found " . . . many walnut trees loaded with nuts which were nearly as good as those of our country, the trees being taller and having more abundant foliage, and the land being so grown with pasture it could scarcely be seen . . . the cattle [buffalo] were innumerable, and of all kinds of game there was a great abundance—Castilian partridges, turkeys, deer, and hares. . . . "

The Indians, too, grew numerous vegetables, and their success with the land comes home in this comment: "We remained here for one day in this pleasant spot surrounded on all sides by fields of maize and crops of the Indians. The stalks of the maize were as high as that of New Spain and in many places even higher. The land was so rich that, having harvested the maize, a new growth of a span in height had sprung up over a large portion of the same ground, without any cultivation or labor other than the removal of the weeds and the making of holes where they planted the maize. There were many beans, some gourds, and between the fields some plum trees. . . . It was thought certain that it had a warm climate, for the people we saw went about naked, although they carried skins on their shoulders. Like the other settled Indians they utilize cattle in large numbers. It is incredible how many there are in that land."

Finally, the way of life of these nomadic Plains Indians fascinated Oñate. "The Indians are numerous in all that land. They live in rancherias in the hide tents hereinbefore mentioned. They always follow the cattle, and in their pursuit they are as well sheltered in their tents as they could be in any house. They eat meat almost raw, and with much tallow and suet, which serves them as bread, and with a chunk of meat in one hand and a piece of tallow in the other, they bite first on one and then on the other and grow up magnificently strong and courageous. Their weapons consist of flint and very large bows, after the manner of the Turks. They have some spears with long thick points, although few, for the flint is better than spears to kill cattle. They kill them at the first shot with the greatest skill, while ambushed in brush blinds made at the watering places."

Oñate completed his journey to Quivira, found no gold, and returned to New Mexico. His failure, like those of the men who went before, would cost him dearly. He was later discredited, then tried for mistreating colonists, fined, banished forever from the north, and not allowed in Mexico City for four years. He later returned to Spain where he died in 1624 or 1625.

Thus ended a colorful but uncertain century of Spanish discovery in North America, a time that included the first white penetration of the southern and central Great Plains. Of the five men most involved, only one came through unscathed. Coronado suffered severe head injuries, was tried, and lost his position as governor of Nueva Galicia. Sosa and Oñate were tried and convicted. Humaña killed Bonilla and was himself killed by Indians. Only Cabeza de Vaca, that remarkable wanderer, returned to Spain to live in peace and royal regard.

But if the Spanish crown was disappointed at the lack of gold in the new lands, it would now be jolted by other problems. Invaders from north and east were coming to the plains. The French were on the move, and the Spanish would have to face a serious new challenge. Soon, French, Spanish, and Indians would come together in locked contest over control of the New Mexican silver mines and the rich Santa Fe mercantile trade. The central and southern Great Plains would prove the battleground over which this struggle would now work its designs.

CHAPTER 5

Three Flags from Four Directions

In the seventeenth and eighteenth centuries, explorers from three nations were at work exposing the Great Plains to European view. English, French, and Spanish had hopes of finding more than the plains could provide, and all who came sought the magic keys to instant wealth, glorious adventure, and royal favor. Curiosity, as a fever, could be quelled by sizable doses of exploration. Wealth and royal favor proved tougher to secure. Many who trekked to the plains died violently. Most were broken and left impoverished by the struggle. The land itself seemed to drain away their resources, giving in return only a few fragile bits of knowledge.

These were men who came to the plains from west, south, east, and north. Most history books leave the impression that exploration across our continent proceeded like a wave from east to west. The Daniel Boone genre presents its explorers drawn across the land by the magnet of the unsettled West. Boone himself first crossed the Cumberland Gap in 1767 and was followed by thousands of frontiersmen who steadily increased in number, leap frogging their settlements across the nation in the late eighteenth and early nineteenth centuries. Following Boone came Lewis and Clark, the two best-known outriders of American history, then Zebulon Montgomery Pike, Jedediah Strong Smith, Joseph Reddeford Walker, John

Charles Frémont, Kit Carson, Jim Bridger; and also the Astorians, the Mormon migration, the Overland Stage, the Pony Express. All left east to west trails across our land and plenty of print in our history books.

The fact is, however, most exploration of our heartland had been completed long before that chain of events began. Much of the early exploration was made on south to north routes and even, for the Spanish, along west to east routes. Coronado explored the Llano Estacado more than two centuries before Boone was born, and he approached that flatland from the south and the west. The state of Colorado—Spanish for "red" —was then a region owned by Indians, but invaded from the south by the conquistadores before 1600. Many unknown Frenchmen, likewise, had moved into and across the plains in the 1600s, generally traveling from the Great Lakes region south and west.

While these early probes were critically important to the nations involved, they were not very numerous. It was really the 1700s that proved the grand age of Great Plains exploration. More than a dozen important, recorded expeditions sliced back and forth across the region during that century. Many of the journals and diaries left by French and Spanish wanderers in the south and central plains have been translated and are now available to the general public. Some have only recently been reprinted. In the north, the English provided well-documented expeditions, but a bit later. The main play guiding all exploration was a durable state of rivalry between the three contending nations. Their contest spins out over the 1700s and is webbed with intrigue, ambush, and sudden slaughter.

As might be expected, the most significant activities of the 1700s really have their roots in the previous century. In 1680, for example, Spain was in firm control of Mexico, but had grown lax along the New Mexico-Texas borderlands. That year the Pueblos revolted. Without mercy, they gave their oppressors some bloody lessons in frontier warfare and quickly drove all Spaniards back to El Paso and south of the Rio Grande. In 1684, the Spaniards suffered a second setback. That summer, René Robert Cavelier, Sieur de La Salle, famed Great Lakes explorer, suddenly and without notice landed four hundred French settlers, traders, and soldiers at Matagordo Bay, Texas. They had sailed from France, intent on placing a colony a short distance up the Mississippi. But they missed the mouth of the river and landed instead on the eastern flank of the Spanish provinces. La Salle's move, coupled with the Pueblo Revolt, shocked the Spanish to action. They soon launched a series of moves aimed at cementing a wall of Great Plains tribes between French and Spanish frontiers. To do this, they had to push north and east into the Great Plains, eastern Texas, and Louisiana—although knowing from past losses the heavy cost of such distant military ventures. The age of the free-booting Spanish conquistador had passed, and the new wave of presidial soldiers now demanded regular pay, barracks, and three daily rations. Nevertheless, the Spanish had to hold on. The New Mexican silver mines still promised enough returns to make the northern venture profitable. Trade with the Indians also might pan out—if they could ever be converted to industrious Christian farmers! Meantime, the French pressed in from the East, and had to be contained.

The game soon proved tricky. The Indians found they could sell their support to the side with the most tobacco, axes, guns, and kettles. They also realized that white soldiers and cavalry could be most helpful in destroying rival tribesmen. In the shifting sands of these loyalty patterns there were few certainties, and what was true in one season might be reversed in the next.

Another uncertainty arose because France and Spain were nominally allied at home, but virtually at war on the Great Plains. This was especially true in the last years of the 1600s. Further, the problem of having to smile at each other while shooting for the gut was suddenly heightened in 1700. That year King Charles II of Spain died, leaving no heirs. Europe was immediately steamed in a royal kettle over who should succeed him, with all reigning monarchs offering their children as replacements. The turmoil soon engulfed Europe in the War of the Spanish Succession, a period of trouble that lasted thirteen years, from 1701 to 1714. All contenders vied for Spanish favor, forcing the Spaniards to play a cautious political game. France finally won, and Prince Philip of Anjou took the Spanish throne in 1713. He was the great-grandson of Louis XIV, king of France.

Imagine, however, the difficulty these years of political intrigue presented to a Spanish commander on the New Mexican frontier. On one hand, he was expected to protect the region against all invaders—particularly any who might try to drain away commerce or invade the silver mines. On the other hand, he was expected to prevent war, particularly with the French who might be, and finally did become, allied to the Spanish court by ties of blood.

For their side, the French acted as though New Spain was a plum to be picked, and they moved confidently onto the Great Plains battleground. As early as 1678, French traders had probably reached the Pawnee villages in central Nebraska. By 1694 they were regularly among the Osage in Missouri. By 1706 and probably much earlier, they were threading out along the river valleys of the central plains, trading steadily with the Indians. All this activity led to open clashes with the Spanish military and, by 1719, matters were so strained that war broke out on the continent as well as on the plains. However, it soon proved only a spat between brothers. Hostilities lasted a little over a year, drained away the angers, and left the territorial and trade situation about as it had been. Still, the Spaniards realized the French traders were too aggressive to take lightly, and they kept their guard up.

All these French invaders were basically traders and trappers. Most were illiterate and left no record of their travels. Mainly their footprints may be seen in other ways—through the record of Indian wars, for example. Their work with the Pawnees is a good example. The Pawnees hated the Navajos, resident Indians among the Spanish settlements in New Mexico. Each summer, as the Spaniards recorded it, the Navajos were accustomed to making long journeys to central Kansas. There they traded with tribes Coronado had discovered in 1541. However, by the 1690s these expeditions were being harassed in transit by French and Pawnees. The Spanish knew the French were there because the Navajos kept bringing back bullet wounds and captured guns. The Spanish enforced strict laws against selling firearms to Indians, but the Pawnees had guns aplenty, so their traders almost certainly were French. Further, the French effort was widespread and persistent—as witness their war against the Navajos:

It all started with sniping between the Pawnees and French on one side and Navajos on the other, a friction that continued in a minor way for some years. Then in 1694 the Navajos captured some Pawnee children during their annual trek to the plains and brought them back to New Mexico. They hoped to sell them to the Spanish as slaves. But no one wanted to buy children so outside Santa Fe one fine morning the Navajos simply beheaded them. Three years later the Pawnees and French collected vengeance by slaughtering a reported four thousand Navajos. A year after that, the Navajos returned to this bloodletting, and after fierce fighting, wiped out three Pawnee settlements and a French-Pawnee fort.

The Spanish did not participate, but the noise of all this warfare was clearly heard in Santa Fe. They realized the danger was growing. Finally, on July 13, 1706 Juan de Ulibarri was dispatched with a small military force northward from Santa Fe into southeastern Colorado. Ulibarri was a thoughtful, observant man, and levelheaded. He moved north and then east over a tough ridge of mountains to the Great Plains. Soon he met a band of friendly Apaches who warned of trouble ahead—warring Indians. Ulibarri turned north and for four days marched along the base of the great Rocky Mountain spine. The Spaniards, the French—and later the Americans—knew the Rockies by various names, such as the Shining Mountains, Spanish Mountains, Mexican Mountains, and Anahuac Mountains. Whatever the name, they were magnificent peaks along what we now call the Front Range. And here, Ulibarri must have mused on his homeland. It was late July and the snow-capped Rockies and nearby Great Plains resembled the cold, high Sierra Nevadas and barren plains of Spain. His journal reveals a stern but gentle man, who allowed his troops no mischief against the scattered poor Indians met along the way. To each impoverished native he gave some small present, so that the column passed

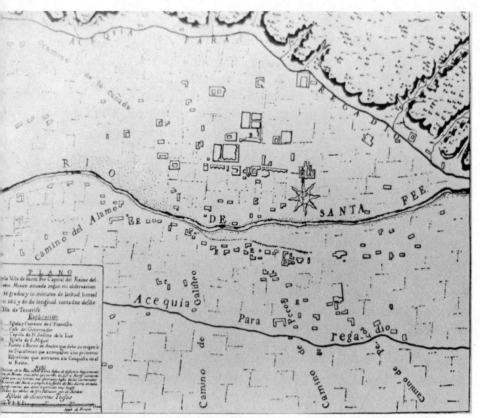

This is the earliest known map of Santa Fe, drawn in 1766 by José de Urrutia. By that date, the Spanish had occupied the city for more than two centuries, but they never constructed heavy fortifications, and the settlement remained a scattering of adobe buildings straddling the Santa Fe River. (ELEANOR ADAMS, *The Missions of New Mexico, 1776*, ALBUQUERQUE, 1956)

through the countryside in peace. South of present Pueblo, Colorado, Ulibarri came to the Arkansas River, which he named Rio Napestle, after a local Indian community. The Arkansas is a strong river at that point, just issuing from the Rockies, and was wide enough to worry Ulibarri while crossing it: "I was particularly surprised to observe that the time taken to cross it was about the equivalent of thirty-three Credos recited very slowly." One wonders if he was measuring or praying for deliverance.

Turning east, Ulibarri and his band now experienced for the first time that common danger facing anyone who dared cross the plains. As the commander recorded it: "We set out from

this spot and marched to the east guided by the Indian. He took
his direction from hummocks of grass placed a short distance
apart on the trail by the Apaches, who lose even themselves
here. In this way they had marked out the course. All of this was
of no use to us, for, although the Indians took especial care, we
became lost entirely. The Indians, according to their shallow
natures, were overcome with fear to such extreme despondency
that they almost wept. I, the sergeant major, used all possible
measures and placed myself under the patronage of Our Lady
the Virgin Mary. ... It was the good fortune that two scouts
who searched the land found water very far above where we
were. The news of this filled the whole camp with joy. ... " The
next day they were lost again, and Ulibarri sent scouts in all
directions before finding another spring.

By August 4, they had arrived at El Quartelejo, an Apache
village near present Crowley, Colorado, well out onto the Great
Plains. The Apaches reported being harassed by Pawnees and
French to the north and east, and they welcomed the Spaniards
warmly. At a council, Ulibarri told the village chiefs he had
come to free sixty Picuris (Pueblos) they were holding as slaves.
His journal at this point is instructive of the sort of political
dealing under way between whites and Indians, even then. Ulibarri wrote:

"I advised them that they should not make the slightest objec-
tion in handing over the Picuris, for otherwise they would experience the severity of our arms. To that they all answered they
were ready to obey and carry out that which our captain had
ordered. They said they would give up all the Picuris, not only
those who were there but also those who were scattered about in
the rest of the rancherias, and that in order that they would
understand that our words were true and our friendship honest,
while the Picuris were being gathered, we were to go with them
to attack their enemies, the Pawnee Indians, since it was only a
seven days' journey across level land with sufficient water. To
this I responded that another occasion would not be lacking in
which to aid them; at that time I was determined only to bring
back the Picuris. Further, I might lose the largest part of my
horses, as their feet had become very sore. Also, in order not to

frighten and drive them away, I had not brought with me a bugle and a drum. Finally, it was very necessary for me to return shortly because of the winter which was coming; and that I would come another year in May or June and we would succeed in helping them against their enemies. They assented to this explanation and others that I gave them. It is supposed that the Pawnees and French are united. They told me that I could leave with them one of our useless guns, as the other white men who live farther in also gave them to the Pawnees their enemies."

Ulibarri left an unworkable gun with the Apaches, and after a ten-day stay, returned to Santa Fe with his troops and the Indians he had freed. His arrangement with the Apaches thus included a military assistance pact, delivery of arms to maintain balance of power, and agreements by the Apaches not to war on the Picuris, allies of the Spanish. The French, on their side, were doing the same thing among the Pawnees. Already, the Indians were being divided into blocs to serve as buffers between French and Spanish. Such moves were turning the Great Plains into one large permanent battleground. It had perhaps long been such an Indian battleground on a more fragmented scale. Now, however, efforts of the two nations were polarizing the many small tribes into either pro-French or pro-Spanish units.

Ulibarri's expedition in 1706 proved one other important truth. While visiting the Apaches, the Spanish were shown a gun taken from a white man. The Apaches had killed him during an encounter with the Pawnees the month before. Juan de Archeveque, an interpreter in the Spanish troop, identified the weapon as French, thereby providing dramatic proof that both nations had arrived at the foot of the Rocky Mountains by that date, and probably earlier. They were there seventy to eighty years before Boone crossed the Cumberland Gap, and a century before Lewis and Clark would start their transcontinental journey up the Missouri River.

A number of other Spanish expeditions invaded the plains during this period. Juan Hurtado led a military column into the plains to discipline some troublesome Apaches in 1715. He left

This lithograph of Santa Fe was made in 1846, and depicts the simple adobe architecture of the city. During the Spanish period there were fewer buildings, but the city served as the nerve center for all their northern colonial activities. (STATE HISTORICAL SOCIETY OF COLORADO LIBRARY, DENVER)

Santa Fe on August 28 leading a column of 36 soldiers, 52 Spanish settlers, and 149 Indians, plus 36 mules and 239 horses. His journey is principally important in showing the strongly disciplined way in which the Spanish handled these frontier expeditions. Very little was left to chance. Hurtado received written orders that spelled out in detail all he was expected to do. He was instructed by Provincial Governor Juan Mogollon to "take every precaution so that the heathen Indian allies who may be met on the route shall not be maltreated in any respect by the soldiers, the settlers, and the Indians of the pueblos. The purpose is only to punish the Apaches, Chipaines, or Limitas who are causing damages and robberies that have been experienced and as appear in the affidavits. On these war will be made, taking care that the women and children of the Chipaines are not killed by the natives and are apprehended and brought to my presence. . . . The commander shall not allow the soldiers to gamble, nor barter arms or horses, with warning that I shall judge his tolerance."

Hurtado signed an affidavit proving he had received these

orders, and then proceeded out onto the plains with his command. He traveled east along the Canadian River, then turned north about to present Stinnett, Texas, high up in the Panhandle. All he found was empty Apache rancherias, and after exploring the region carefully, he returned to Santa Fe without incident.

Antonio Valverde, governor of the New Mexican provinces, personally led another military expedition out of Santa Fe in 1719. The plan was to discipline Comanches and Utes, then ravaging all local Indian tribes. They were especially tough on the Apaches and Navajos, who had lately become allies of the Spanish. Valverde left Santa Fe on September 15 with an army of more than 600 and at least 850 horses and mules. He first moved northward into Colorado, then turned east on much the same route followed by Ulibarri thirteen years earlier. Now, however, France and Spain were at war, and the column was large enough for a full-scale battle with the enemy. It never came, but the general's journal tells us much about the Spanish, the Indians, and life on the plains.

Soon after departing Santa Fe, as the army neared the Colorado border, Valverde found seven terraced houses where some friendly Apaches lived. "It was seen that they had already gathered their crops of corn because they had placed it in the shape of a wall about half a yard high. Many rows of the same were seen in abundance, from which it was evident that the land is very fertile. On it they have many ditches and canals in order to irrigate their fields."

Canals and irrigated fields. Fertile lands. An abundance of corn. The year 1719 and the place southeastern Colorado. The scene there today has many similarities to this pleasant pastoral view, with much of the cropland still under irrigation and corn an important mainstay in the economy.

On October 2, the weather was warm, and after a short morning march, Valverde called a halt at midday. He clearly was not a driving military leader and preferred instead to ease his way north in gentlemanly fashion. Camp was made at the junction of two branches of the Huerfano River, south of present Pueblo. The country, he wrote, ". . . has many plums, which though wild are of fine flavor and taste. .... It was leafy here and the command took a nap, enjoying the coolness and shade of the many poplars and deep woods."

Hunting was good throughout the journey, and Valverde's journal, which he wrote in the impersonal third person, is larded with notes on their successes afield: "October third— Here they hunted and caught many deer and a lot of good fat prairie hens with which they made very delicious tamales."

"October fourth—On this road today many deer and prairie chickens which moved about in flocks were caught to such an extent that nowhere else were more caught because of their abundance in this region. . . . The governor hunted deer and chicken. . . . On this day a mountain lion and a wildcat were killed. At about sunset some Indians came in, running from a bear which plunged into the middle of the camp, throwing the people into confusion. With great shouting and uproar, they killed him with many spear thrusts and arrows. His strength and size were so formidable that the governor was impelled to go with the chaplain to view it."

As the column pushed farther east into the plains, buffalo were killed and buffalo chips were used to cook them. On the fifteenth, even the governor himself took part in the hunting: "Having seen a great herd of buffalo, the señor governor mounted his horse and with his adjutant and other soldiers went among them. He isolated a cow and ran it a good distance until he killed it with a spear. He told the soldiers to avail themselves of the meat and to bring him the tongue only. On this day all the command killed many buffalo."

A campaign afield was not going to subdue Valverde's instincts for the noble life. One night one of the chaplains visited the governor in his tent, and later that evening he wrote, again in the third person: "They celebrated together with the military chiefs the eve of the glorious patriarch San Francisco, having ordered out a small keg of rich spirituous brandy made at the Pass of the Rio del Norte of the governor's own vintage. It was of such good flavor, taste, and quality that the wine of Castile does not surpass it." The next day the governor's aide brought out the "best rich bread and melon preserves he carried for such an occasion . . .," all this taking place in a ". . . very cheerful spot, with a beautiful view and excellent springs and many thick poplar groves. On the left hand, about three leagues away, there is a range of mountains, and on the right, a very extensive plain. . . ."

The only martial note to intrude on this country idyll appeared on October 22, near present Las Animas, Colorado. There on the banks of the Arkansas River, the local friendly Apaches brought the governor one of their braves who was recovering from a gunshot wound. The man told Valverde that he and his people had been planting corn far out on the plains to the east when they were attacked from ambush by French, Pawnees, and Jumanos. The Apaches fought off the attack, then escaped from their camp when night fell. The Indians also told Valverde of other French activities, so that the governor wrote:

"The French have built two large pueblos, each of which is as large as that of Taos. In them they live together with the said Pawnee and Jumanos Indians, to whom they have given long guns which they have taught them to shoot. With one of these they had wounded this man. They also carry some small guns suspended from their belts . . . likewise, they added that the French have three other settlements on the other side of the large river, and that to these they take arms.

"The governor told the Apache chief and all the rest who were there that they were admitted to the protection of our king and lord. . . . As his minister and servant, he offered them his aid against the French and the nations with which they were confederated. . . . He would expel the French from it as the lands belong only to the majesty of our king and lord, Don Philip V. . . . They would see that the Spaniards were coming with their power and strength to attack and drive the French out of the land and destroy their pueblos and villages. With this discourse the Apaches were consoled and pleased."

Brave words, but when the Indians asked him to stay and secure the land against the hated French Valverde backed off, saying he had to return to Santa Fe. It was turning cold, the rich bread and melon preserves were gone, "the spirituous brandy as good as that of Castile" was running low, and he had no news of the kingdom in his charge. In short, he would not back his words with deeds. The field would be left to the French. Besides, Valverde could return to New Mexico knowing that the Colorado Apaches were numerous and could serve as a buffer at least for awhile longer. As for the Apaches, they were left with their thoughts—and no guns to oppose the rampaging enemy.

Meantime, the French doubtless knew all about Valverde's campaign to the frontier of their territory. Who could rattle a column of that size through the plains without being seen? The Spanish reported finding numerous deserted enemy encampments, all small, many recent. Pawnee bands, it seems, were melting away from Valverde's column and carrying news of his arrival north and east. Clearly the Spanish enjoyed this outing, but forgot they were out there to fight guerrillas. *Guerrilla*— that word came into our language from the Spanish, and was one the governor must have understood. Yet he failed to engage the enemy, a failure probably sealing the fate of the next expedition to the Great Plains, that of Pedro de Villasur, which left Santa Fe the following spring.

The Villasur expedition was important to Spanish designs in several ways. After Valverde returned to Santa Fe in the fall of 1719, numerous councils of war were held. The Spanish were uncertain how they might best blunt the growing French intrusion. That winter, the various proposals and counterproposals were studied. The Spanish military was uncommonly democratic and sensible in these affairs, and often called on all participants to take part in decisions, including experienced presidial soldiers, settlers, and Indian leaders. Usually all were asked to present signed opinions regarding proposed campaigns or placement of military strongpoints. The opinions were then summarized, and the strongest arguments used in forming a decision. Such was the case in the winter of 1719–20, when the Spaniards mulled placement of a new military stronghold on the Great Plains. Two locations were discussed, but indecision continued through the winter, occupying the government both at Mexico City and Santa Fe.

Perhaps in this framework the selection of Colonel Don

With the Spanish came the horse, and soon the Plains Indians were mounted and on their way to becoming a food-rich society—as well as a dangerous threat to the Spanish. Here a group of hunters begin to butcher a downed buffalo. (PAINTING BY CHARLES BODMER, FROM *Travels in the United States*)

Pedro de Villasur as leader of the next expedition north may best be understood. Villasur was not experienced in frontier warfare, but he was young and trusted and held high military rank in Governor Valverde's New Mexican government. Valverde, then deeply engaged in the question of the Great Plains fortress, perhaps expected Villasur's northern journey to be as untroubled as his own the year before. In any case, the young colonel was chosen to lead a mixed column of 105 presidial troops, settlers, and friendly Indians north out of Santa Fe in late June or early July 1720. His route followed that of earlier expeditions and took him first to the large Indian settlement at El Quartelejo, visited by Ulibarri in 1706. From there he turned north until he reached the Platte River, fifty miles northeast of Denver, and well out onto the High Plains. The troop followed the river east to the junction of its other branch, near present North Platte, Nebraska, arriving there on August 6. The remainder of the story came from testimony of the few Spaniards who survived.

As they told it, Villasur here called a council of war. He was frustrated that the column had come farther north than any other Spanish expedition and still had not encountered any French. They decided after some debate to push ahead and collect what information they could from any resident Indians they might find. The next day, Naranjo, the scout, reported Pawnees ahead, engaged in war dances. A Pawnee had accompanied the Spanish troop, and Villasur sent him ahead to arrange a meeting, but he soon returned. He told Villasur that when he got opposite the Indians' village they had brandished tomahawks at him from across the river.

The next day, Villasur moved his column opposite the village and sent his Pawnee over to investigate. The messenger swam across, was helped out, and accompanied into a tipi. After a time he reappeared and called across the river that they would not let him return. He also said he didn't learn anything about the French. The next day, some of the Pawnees came over to the Spanish camp to visit. While there, Archeveque, the French interpreter, wrote a note for them to carry back to their camp. The following day, they returned to the Spanish camp, carrying a paper bearing some illegible writing.

For Villasur, all this heightened the frustration, and he began to talk of crossing the river to see for himself what lay in the Pawnee camp. His officers, most of whom were old frontier hands, urged caution, and the troop decided instead to withdraw. They broke camp, moved back to the west, crossed a small river and at four in the afternoon of August 13 made camp. That night, Villasur posted Indian sentinels to guard both camp and horses. Soon after dark, the troop heard noises that sounded like someone crossing the river. They also heard a dog bark. Villasur sent scouts to check, but all seemed safe enough, and everyone went to bed.

Just at daybreak, the camp was jolted awake by a turmoil of howls and shrieks as a band of Pawnees came out of a thicket, encircled the camp, and poured flintlock, pistol, and archery fire into it with deadly effect. The Spaniards were caught in their beds and Villasur was killed in the first volley. As the fighting continued, down went Archeveque and the veteran scout Naranjo plus about twenty-five other Spanish soldiers, a dozen Indians, the chaplain, and several others. All told, forty-four were killed in the brief, bloody encounter. Despite the surprise, however, the Spanish rallied and began to inflict casualties on the attackers. Within a short time, the engagement broke off, and the Pawnees failed to pursue the battered remnant of the Spanish force. Sixty-one escaped, including forty-eight Indians and a dozen Spaniards.

Inquiry into the Villasur disaster continued for six years, and Governor Valverde was finally found guilty of poor judgment. The court told him he should not have chosen so inexperienced a leader for so important an assignment. But Valverde's only punishment was to pay 50 pesos for charity masses and 150 pesos for purchase of church hardware. His long service and his friends in Mexico City probably spared him a tougher fate.

Villasur's expedition was the single bloodiest loss the Spanish had experienced in two centuries of bloody northern conquest. It was also their northernmost exploration, and would prove to be their last major military expedition into the Great Plains. Nearly a third of the best soldiers in the New Mexican province were killed in that fight. Ironically, the battle occurred after the war between Spain and France had ended. No one on the frontier knew it at the time, however, and some months would pass before fear of an invasion could drain out of Santa Fe.

But though French military columns never came, they would send their individual traders, in growing numbers, as the middle years of the eighteenth century were soon to show.

CHAPTER 6
The Forgotten Plainsmen

His name was Etienne Veniard de Bourgmond, better known as de Bourgmond, or more commonly as simply Bourgmond, and he was one of a small number of extraordinary men who have the distinction of being the most overlooked figures in North American history. Bourgmond, Louis Juchereau de St. Denis, Jean-Baptiste Bernard de la Harpe, Pedro Vial, Pierre and Paul Mallet, Claude Charles du Tisne, and a few others unknown; these were the white men who most effectively explored the southern and central Great Plains in the first two-thirds of the eighteenth century. All were French. They were traders, trappers, woods runners, and plains walkers. They covered vast amounts of ground, lived by their wits, and left almost no records of the lives they lived. Each worked his own way into the plains, separated from the others by time and distance. For most, the rewards were merely a brief time of survival in a tough, hostile land.

From earliest contact in North America to the final collapse at Quebec in 1759, French explorers were the men who opened the eastern gateways into the continent. After fanning out through the Great Lakes region in the seventeenth century, they picked their way along waterways into the Great Plains, moving westward from Lake Superior and up and down the Mississippi. They threaded up the Missouri, the Republican, the Canadian, the Red. The Canadian, in fact, became the Canadian because French Canadians traveled that river in its naming time. Yet it lies in New Mexico, north Texas, and Oklahoma.

These French explorers—part-time merchants and full-time adventurers—lived in a web of shifting, uncertain Indian alliances. Friends of one season might be mortal enemies the next. Yet somehow, the French penetrated the vast emptiness of the Great Plains when no one else dared pass, not even Indians. While British colonists were still walled up along the eastern seaboard, these travelers had reached the Rockies, unknown and unheralded. Bourgmond saw western Nebraska fifty years before our Revolution started. The Mallet brothers traveled from St. Louis to Santa Fe eighty years before William Becknell founded the Santa Fe Trail that traveled the same route. The Mallets then emphasized their plainsmanship by crossing the following year from Santa Fe to New Orleans. Yet their journey remains almost unknown to Americans. Our histories of the plains bear frequent witness to the travels of Zebulon Pike, John Wesley Powell, John Charles Frémont, and Stephen F. Austin, but references to St. Denis, Du Tisne, La Harpe, and others are rare. St. Denis, known as St. Denis the Elder, was the first to travel from Nacogdoches in eastern Texas to San Antonio, then on to San Juan Bautista on the Rio Grande. He made the five-hundred-mile journey on foot in 1714 through Comanche country and survived to tell of it. La Harpe edged into the southeastern plains during 1719–20, canoeing and walking from Natchitoches in Louisiana up the Red River, then overland to the Canadian and downriver to the Arkansas before returning. Du Tisne made an extensive riverine and overland exploration of the central plains in 1719. He traveled from Kaskaskia in lower Illinois up the Osage River to western Missouri before striking out overland to reach the Kansas River west of present Topeka. From there he followed the north shore of the Republican, then continued northwest until he reached the Platte, where he visited a group of Pawnee villages west of present Kearney, Nebraska. All this travel was on foot or by canoe, and all of it was done alone or in the company of resident Indians.

Such travels perhaps occurred too early to be remembered,

taking place before American history was being written. These men did not know or recognize a frontier as such, and as a habit, Americans tend to look for frontiers, new or old, and ignore or pass over confusions outside that framework. The French, traveling as individuals, took Indian ways and wives and lived seminomadic existences, far from white settlements. And so they've been forgotten. But the knowledge they gained of the plains was passed by word of mouth to those who followed—and wrote—and whose names are now more familiar in our versions of this fascinating period.

Bourgmond provides a fair example of the breed. His history expresses the vigorous joy of life and precious regard for freedom that seemed to grip these men of the open west. They moved about freely, as easy masters of the land despite the danger of their surroundings. Though only sketchy accounts of Bourgmond remain, and almost no accounts of some of the others, he at least led a full life. Born of an old Norman family, son of a renowned physician, young Bourgmond entered French military service, was soon shipped to America, and in the spring of 1706 found himself an ensign commanding the tiny garrison at Fort Detroit, now Detroit, Michigan. One night soon after he arrived, a large and determined force of Fox Indians attacked the post. After an all-night battle, Bourgmond and his fifteen-man army succeeded in driving off the attackers. The residents of the village were pleased by the courage the little garrison had shown, and generous in their praise. The settlement's most luscious member, Madame Tichenet, was especially generous to the gallant young commander. The pair eloped from her bedchamber to join a colony of deserters tenting through the summer on the shore of Lake Erie. Monsieur Tichenet, understandably annoyed, raised a posse of fifty men and marched off to capture the fugitives. The battle was brief and all the renegades were hauled back to Detroit. Despite the obvious evidence of desertion and wife theft, Bourgmond was acquitted by the court at Fort Detroit. His judges also saw fit to reinstate him in the army and soon after rewarded him with a promotion. As French officers, they recognized merit when they saw it.

No drawings of Bourgmond are known to exist, but his garb for the plains may have looked similar to this, here worn by a French trader of the eighteenth century. (FREDERIC REMINGTON, *Harper's New Monthly Magazine*)

His next amorous encounter was with an Indian girl named La Chenette, and she led him to still another Indian charmer who has remained nameless, but who proved so fascinating that Bourgmond again deserted, this time for the land of the Missouri River, where he set up housekeeping and lived with his new mate from 1712 to 1719.

It was during this period that he began to change from a simple frontier rogue to a political power among the Indians of the eastern plains border. As his prestige increased, his sway with the Missouri Indians soon built a bastion of French influence against the Spanish farther west. There seemed to grow from Bourgmond an element of trust that the Indians found easy to accept. One story that has survived tells of Bourgmond going alone and unarmed to an Indian village where a French trapper had been murdered. Bourgmond called for a public trial of the killer. It was held on the spot, and the murderer was sentenced by his people to die. Before Bourgmond left the village, the condemned man had been executed by his own brother.

Bourgmond's influence also became widespread. During all his years along the Missouri, he traveled extensively, reaching deep into Nebraska and Kansas and coming in frequent contact with many different Indian groups. Maps of the Missouri from that period are based on his observations, and as a political force, he clearly dominated the region during the crucial opening period of French exploration. Through such valuable service, the French forgot about his earlier desertion from Detroit. In fact, they soon sought his help for a special mission against the Spanish.

The Spanish at that time controlled Texas and New Mexico, plus much of Oklahoma and Colorado, either with garrisons or through the allegiance of friendly Indian tribes. Now, however, the French proposed to bring this "Red Wall" under both commercial and military siege, and Bourgmond was asked to play a key role. The question was how to approach the matter.

Ever since the Treaty of Cateau-Cambrensis in 1559, France and Spain had carried on a curious relationship in the New World, and conditions Bourgmond now faced on the Great Plains exemplified this. The treaty itself meant little in Europe, but certain unwritten agreements caused interesting repercussions in American history for the next two centuries. These verbal agreements placed Spain and France at peace in Europe, but allowed each to pursue its own course in North America. Sometimes this proved extremely bloody. At other times, both nations acted with a curious restraint, as if too much American provocation might rupture European peace.

On the Great Plains, the game was played with Indian tribes as the pawns. Here the situation called for ingenuity. The authority of the French Crown had been invested in the Company of the Indies, generally known as "The Company," a trading firm using New Orleans as its American base. Louisiana at that time was a vast undefined inland empire, stretching north to Illinois and west to the Spanish lands. The Company imported large quantities of frontier needs to this New World port, including cloth, kettles, guns, powder, rum, and other commodities. Mostly these goods were consumed by settlers in the lower Mississippi Valley. But the main goal of The Company was a profitable trade with the people of Santa Fe. The French knew the Spanish operated silver mines in New Mexico, and rumors about production from those mines floated back and forth across the plains for more than two hundred years. Many individual Spaniards also wanted to develop this French trade. It obviously offered a shorter, faster, cheaper source of European goods than the long haul from Spain to Mexico City to New Mexico and Texas.

Official Spanish policy, however, prevented northern colonists from direct contact with the traders. The French, seeking to overcome that policy with kettles and calico, pressed westward along several routes, laden with tempting burdens, during much of the eighteenth century. What they met time after time was that wall of Indian tribes kept loyal to the Spanish by gifts, by passions inflamed against tribal enemies, and by Spanish promises of military assistance. The Company, meanwhile, kept up its trade with French colonists in the lower Mississippi Valley and with local fur-trapping Indians. But they saw this merely as bread-and-butter trade, not a cake frosted with Spanish silver. That vision kept The Company's appetite keen for nearly a century.

For all the maneuvering, however, commerce across the plains to New Mexico kept eluding the French. And when the Villasur expedition was massacred in 1720, another damper fell between the two nations. The Spanish were furious over the Villasur loss, and claimed the French aided the Indians with arms and leadership. Perhaps they had. Bourgmond was a well-known figure in lower Nebraska at that time, and guns used against Villasur almost certainly passed through his hands on their way west. His life along the Missouri since 1712 had included a variety of trading ventures. Also, gun sales to Indians were not forbidden by the French. Clearly, Bourgmond was in a position to blunt any Spanish military moves toward Missouri, having the wholehearted support of all surrounding Indian tribes. His mate, a "young savage," had produced a son soon after he settled on the Missouri, and such a blood tie to the tribe was invariably viewed by the Indians as a sign of allegiance and trust. The Indian, being a strong family man, preferred visible signs of outward white grace to easy promises of friendship. Bourgmond further advanced his good reputation by displays of personal vigor and fair-minded cooperation with the people of his adoption. They responded in kind. He became, in short, one with them yet a man who could deal for France as well.

The Villasur massacre, while in his territory, was not however his personal affair. Late in 1719, a year before the bloody ambush, Bourgmond took his young son and left on a long journey to France. He had not visited his homeland since coming to North America nearly twenty years earlier, and as he paddled his canoe down the Mississippi that spring, a series of new ambitions began arranging themselves in his brain. He was well aware of his position on the blade edge of French imperial and commercial desires. He knew The Company needed him for its work and that need would feed his plans.

In France, he gave officers of The Company all the solid information they ever received about the upper Missouri country. He told them the Missouri River was at least eight hundred leagues long—two thousand miles—and on that guess he wasn't far wrong. He mapped the region crudely and located Indian tribes by name and strength. He knew the beaver marshes along the riverbeds, and the hardpan of the plains, and could list the material needs of his Indian neighbors.

So officers of The Company soon offered Bourgmond a special mission. He would return to the New World and carry forward their designs, they said. Ah, he said, not so hasty. There were other matters to handle, namely a certain wealthy widow. And with that, he turned to enjoy some local amours.

The officers again approached. Time, they said, was passing. What about all those Spanish silver mines across the plains? Did he know of them? Yes, they lay to the west. What of the people there, were they friendly? He did not know for sure, but to find out, he would have to cross the plains, at least six hundred leagues west of his Missouri country. That would be costly.

And so the officers were baited, and the more they talked the more convinced they were that true wealth lay out there beyond the American plains. Bourgmond simply waited them out. Besides, he was busy courting his rich widow, daily made more beautiful as the extent of her properties unfolded. Which he loved more, the land or the lady, the record does not say, but they were soon married, in a church, with his bastard son in attendance—and a boat ticket to New Orleans in his hip pocket.

Shortly after, his indifference swaying their reason, officers of The Company came to terms. He sailed for Louisiana in the spring of 1722 with all his demands reluctantly met. His son was with him and his frontier mate lay ahead while his new wife remained in France to care for his newly owned property, formerly hers alone. At New Orleans, jealous subordinates of The Company gave him meager aid, but he soon had his small troop of Frenchmen assembled, and as new commander in charge of all the Missouri country, his expedition began to ascend the Mississippi. It was a long, slow summer trip, and he did not arrive in his old haunts until mid-autumn. The greeting he received from his chosen people was overwhelming, and the feasting went on for days before he could get to the core of his project.

The site he chose for "Fort Orleans," the promised French stronghold, was on the north shore of the Missouri, about fifty miles east of present Kansas City. He was not able to start construction until mid-November, however, and it took his crew all winter to complete the palisade, living quarters, chapel, and storage buildings. This was a difficult and trying winter for the little band, most of whom were new to frontier life. Also, throughout his career, Bourgmond somehow had problems with French compatriots. With Indians, he seemed always in strong accord, but his white brothers surrounded him with endless dispute. Here was no different and before long several letters of complaint were on their way downriver from Fort Orleans to

New Orleans. His soldiers wrote of rough treatment and indifference to pay and rations and regulations. To Bourgmond, it hardly mattered. He knew what The Company really wanted, and with a trusted lieutenant named Galliard, he now began to plan his approach to Santa Fe. This second part of his mission —peace with the plainsmen—would be difficult and ticklish. Indian wars were easily stirred, while the trader's peace was tough to keep.

The tribe he faced was called Padoucas by Spanish and French, a group now known to us as Comanches. Plains tribal names were confused at this transitional period, most having come from early Spanish contact and being related more as geographic clusters of peoples than specific language groups. Spelling of Indian tribal names also was inconsistent; as pronounced to the literate Spaniard or Frenchman, so were they written down, some spelling the name one way, some another. The Comanches that Bourgmond faced were a tribe long at war against allies of the French—the Missouris, Pawnees, Otos, Osages, Kansas, and others—but Bourgmond hoped to sway them with trade goods and kindness.

In late June 1724, he set out from his fort with a few Indians and French, angling southwest toward Kansas and Santa Fe. Soon after leaving, he fell critically ill, and was hauled back to Fort Orleans in the bed of a canoe under a raging fever. Galliard was left to carry the project forward. Included in his party were two Comanche women and a boy, captured years earlier and held as "slaves" by the Missouris. That word—slaves— should be viewed with caution, however. Our modern interpretation of slavery contrasts sharply with that of general Indian tradition. Indian warriors taken in battle were normally tortured and killed. But women and children were frequently adopted into the victorious tribe and were generally treated as family members. This had been the case with the Comanches in Galliard's following.

On reaching enemy territory, the three Comanches were sent ahead, and after lengthy and touchy discussion finally convinced their kinsmen that the French and their allies had provided them a secure home and good treatment. Galliard was then allowed to "harangue" a circle of seated but doubtful Comanche leaders. Haranguing—a mix of brag, oratory, and diplomacy—was standard peace talk during which each side measured the other for strength and weakness. Among many promises, Galliard included the offer of a visit from the great French peacemaker—Etienne Veniard de Bourgmond, chief of all the Missouri country. He would come to sit in peace with the mighty Comanche, and he would carry with him the flag of the French king. Galliard also gave out numerous presents—beads, candles, kettles, knives—and to the chiefs, guns and powder. That was big medicine. The Comanches couldn't even buy guns and powder from their Spanish allies, yet the French gave them away. Enemies began softening into silent acceptance. Soon after, Galliard turned homeward, hopeful of peace but accompanied by five Comanches who needed more proof. He arrived at Fort Orleans in early September to find Bourgmond nearly well and ready for travel. Together the two men conspired. Galliard reckoned that a show of French strength would convince the Comanches peace was in their best interests. Bourgmond countered that their little army was far too weak to display much strength. On the other hand, a great show of pomp and excitement, plus the great harangue by Bourgmond as Galliard had promised, plus many presents, might conclude the peace.

And so it happened that on the morning of October 8, 1724, a little band of 14 French soldiers and 19 chiefs from the Missouri, Kansas, Oto, and Iowa nations, with 10 horses and 5 Comanche visitors, all set out in a parade for the land of the doubtful Comanches. In the lead was Bourgmond's half-Indian son, bearing the golden fleur-de-lis, waving in a north Kansas breeze, while following the French leader was a French drummer, beating the rhythm of the march. Ten days on the trail carried them to the great Comanche encampment, where the joy of the greeting—more than expected—told Bourgmond his goal was nearly at hand. Galliard had done his advance work well. The location was dead center in Kansas, near present Ellsworth. The tipis were circled beside a narrow creek, nearly dry in the

French plainsmen, like Bourgmond, were well trained for the peaceful diversion called "haranguing" in the council tipi. Here a trader holds a peace pipe and lectures the assembled chieftains—just as Bourgmond did. (FREDERIC REMINGTON, *Harper's New Monthly Magazine*)

fall heat. Buffalo meat was racked about in strings, drying for the winter, while the inevitable bounce of dogs yelped and raced in confusion.

Next day, the Comanches prepared themselves for the Big French Chief's harangue by assembling in a semicircle where they sat cross legged on the ground. About two hundred gathered while Bourgmond had his soldiers open the pack bags and lay out quantities of kettles, cloth, knives, beads, powder, shot, guns, tobacco, and all those other marvelous trade goods. The desire showing on the faces of Bourgmond's audience that morning urged the Frenchman on, and for two hours, in the grand tradition of the best Indian diplomats, he exhorted them on the strength of the French nation and its Indian allies, on their earnest desire for peace with the great Comanche nation,

on the happy result of such an alliance. As he spoke, Bourgmond gave presents to all the Comanches, with the greatest
reserved for the chiefs and leading warriors.

When he finished, the big chief of the Comanches rose: "You
see here the French," he said, "whom the Big Spirit has sent to
our village to make peace with us. This is done. He has given
his word and a large quantity of merchandise without asking us
anything; therefore, we believe him and we see very well that he
does not want to deceive us. Go, you people, men and women,
and get food for the French, our friends. This is the Big French
Chief, who has established peace between us and our greatest
enemies. Now we can hunt in peace and now we will go and
visit those who made war on us and they will visit us; they will
return to us our women and children whom they took and who
are slaves with them and we will give them horses. . . ."

It was a speech the French had waited decades to hear. Bourgmond gave the chief the French flag, urging him to keep it
"always as white as I give it to you, and without spots," and
with that the entire assemblage gave way to feasting and displays of friendship that lasted for days. The Red Wall was
breached, and Santa Fe lay like a ripe plum only 250 leagues to
the southwest, over peaceful ground all the way. The French
could now press on, with friendly Indian escorts, and complete
the journey to the land of the goods-hungry, silver-clanking
Spaniards. With passports in hand and letters of introduction
they might finally end frontier bickering between the two
nations. Bourgmond's commanding presence could lead such
negotiations, and Indian tribes could prosper all along the mercantile way.

"It's out there, and not far," Bourgmond must have thought.
We can imagine him on those golden October afternoons, looking westward across the Kansas plains, the sun a pale orange
globe drifting down into the buffalo haze. Yet he had arrived
too late for the journey that year. He knew the plains blizzards
would soon roar down off the Rockies. His trade goods were
gone, too, and he had only a few horses, not nearly enough for
his whole column. So he elected not to try for the big prize, and
instead made ready to return to Fort Orleans. Though he had

no way of knowing, this would be his last long look at the Great Plains, and where he then stood was the high watermark of his travels in America.

Before departing the Comanche village, he announced that he would go to France in the next season, taking with him a group of Indian chiefs to meet with the king. This had been a promise made earlier to his Missouri River friends, and now with the triumph of his peace treaty in hand, he could impose on The Company for expenses of the journey. And so, after an uneventful return to Fort Orleans, and a quiet winter among his people, he set off toward New Orleans in the spring of 1725. Fourteen Indian chiefs accompanied him, with one "Princesse de Missouris"—a new mistress drawn from his adopted family of Indians. Company officials in New Orleans were dismayed at the expected cost, however, and demanded that the group be reduced in size to save expenses. After some haggling, five chiefs were permitted to make the trip with Bourgmond, plus of course his new-found girl friend. The parsimonious company allowed the chiefs only the fare of common sailors, forcing Bourgmond to buy them meat and wine from his own pocket.

In Paris the Indians were an immediate sensation. They hunted running stags in the Bois de Boulogne while the Court watched at a discreet distance. They performed war dances at l'Opera and Théâtre des Italiens. They harangued the king in frontier style and complained to the queen that the perfumed ladies of Paris "smelled like alligators." Meantime, in the background, Bourgmond found himself in a tangle betwen his Indian mistress and the propertied French widow he had married the previous year. Finally the mistress was baptized in Notre Dame and Bourgmond returned to his wife. The Indian maid then married a Sergeant Dubois from one of Bourgmond's old frontier commands and in the following season the couple returned to America.

In December, Bourgmond received the letters of nobility he had insisted on as part of his bargain with The Company, and settled down in France as a prosperous landed gentleman, rich with tales of the frontier, and a success at every dinner party. He had quit The Company's employ when he became a nobleman and that organization was now left to muddle along its own path to Santa Fe. French caravans that might have traveled Bourgmond's route never materialized, and the peace he nailed together slowly fell into bickering and broken promises. In September 1726, just two years after Bourgmond set out on his mission of peace from Fort Orleans, that outpost was reduced to a garrison of only eight men, and the year following the fort was abandoned. The cost of maintaining northern strongholds had been too high, and the hoped-for rewards of the Spanish trade never swelled The Company's ledgers. Bourgmond's personal strength and political position among the Indians had misled The Company into believing the shortest route to Santa Fe lay along his Missouri River. With the leader gone, they now saw the weakness of the plan. Soon they were left to trade only in the lower Mississippi Valley. But that didn't quell French interest. They still believed the Spanish were out there, across the plains with ample stocks of silver and a hunger for European goods.

From Bourgmond's peace in September 1724, to the late 1730s, no known attempts were made to cross the southern plains. Then in 1739 one of the incredible journeys of American history took place. The men who made this great trek of two thousand miles, most of it on our Great Plains, have been all but forgotten, and the fact that it was they who finally tied eastern and western America into one great landmass is remembered in only a few ancient and dusty volumes. They were the brothers Pierre and Paul Mallet, French wanderers. Unfortunately, very little is known of them. They kept a journal of their travels but it was lost, and what remains is writings about them found two centuries later in official French documents. Nevertheless what survives is important.

The Mallet brothers seem to have arrived in Illinois from Canada. Their destination was Santa Fe, though they had no sanction from the French government to attempt such a journey. At an unknown date in the spring of 1739—probably early April—they departed from Kaskaskia in southern Illinois accompanied by at least six other Frenchmen and an unknown group of Indians. Passing St. Louis, they continued a slow ascent of several weeks up the Missouri River. They pursued on this route at least one long-standing belief that New Mexico lay at the headwaters of the Missouri River. They may also have pursued a second belief as well; namely, that located at the center of North America was a height of land from which four rivers flowed to the four corners of the continent. This was an old belief, conjured up dreamily by eighteenth-century map makers —who didn't have to canoe and portage and walk across their mistakes. It was supposed that whoever attained that central high ground at the source of the rivers could travel at will, and on choice, by canoe or boat to the Southern Sea, the Western Sea, the Northern Sea, or the Eastern Sea.

Despite the fanciful nature of this belief, there was by the 1730s at least some expectation it might come true. After all, the Missouri and Mississippi did lead, more or less, to an "Eastern Sea," and other major rivers drained the continent to the north, emptying into James and Hudson bays. The Spaniards also knew of the Colorado, which emptied into a semi-Southern Sea, the Gulf of California. It was the Western Sea that eluded all travelers, and yet all believed it *must* be there. The Western Sea was the source of hope for an easy route to Cathay, India, China, and the longed-for riches of those far-off, fabled lands. Perhaps the Mallets, when they departed St. Louis, hoped to bag this bigger game.

Whatever their original purpose, they seem to have changed their minds after reaching the Niobrara River in northeastern Nebraska. What provoked this decision is not known, but on May 29, 1739, they turned abruptly southwest, going out overland, possibly on horses purchased from the Indians. From the Niobrara, they moved to the Platte, then turned west a short distance before crossing that river. From here they headed southwest over the High Plains in an almost straight line toward Santa Fe, crossing the Republican, Solomon, and Smoky Hill river systems until they reached the Arkansas near present Dodge City, Kansas.

Somewhere during this period, they lost nine horses loaded with most of their merchandise. Despite this personal disaster, the Mallets pressed on, apparently determined to reach their

The Comanches obtained horses shortly before Bourgmond arrived in their territory. Though this drawing was made a century later, the hunting method and equipment is that of the early eighteenth century. (*Graham's Magazine*, 1844)

goal, with or without trade goods. After reaching the Arkansas, they followed that great river west to its junction with the Purgatoire, then angled southwest to the foot of the Rockies. They were now near the north border of New Mexico, 150 miles from Santa Fe, in a region sparsely settled with Indians, all loyal to the Spanish. Day by day the Mallets encountered small bands, but were allowed to continue toward the capital, guided by fleeting conversations with the few inhabitants they met. They found stones with Spanish inscriptions along some of these rivers and their line of march, while not the shortest, never swerved from a general southwesterly direction. They were on the trail to Santa Fe, and they seemed to know it.

It was now early July 1739, and though footsore, weary, and nearly starving from the months of travel, promising signs began to appear. An Indian told them he knew the way to the

Spaniards, and volunteered to lead them there. Soon after, they reached the Spanish Mountains, then a small river beyond which a Spanish mission was located. On the fifteenth of July, the Spanish commander at Taos sent them runners with loaves of white bread, and as they approached that village a great crowd of Spanish and Indians came in greeting. Where was the war and the animosity? How could these smiling Spaniards, so long feared and distrusted, move to such ready acceptance of a band of wandering Frenchmen? On July 22, 1739, they entered Santa Fe, thus completing the first known complete crossing of the Great Plains by white men. They were battered, nearly naked, and with almost no provisions or merchandise, but their hosts accepted them fully, then housed and fed them for nine months. The viceroy at Mexico City had to pass judgment on their presence in Santa Fe, but meanwhile they were welcome. As only one caravan plied that long southern route each year, an answer from the Mexican capital was slow in coming. Finally the letter arrived. They were accepted. It was as if a whole nation had suddenly been pardoned for past excesses. They were allowed free movement throughout the colony and as observant travelers they soon began to record their impressions.

On May 1, 1740, seven of the Frenchmen, including both Mallets, left Santa Fe for New Orleans. Their route home was more direct, following the Canadian eastward to the Arkansas, then continuing on to the Mississippi. After reaching the Arkansas, three of the group decided to return to Canada, but the Mallets and two others continued southeast to New Orleans. Their arrival in that French outpost produced a mercantile sensation.

Later, an official of The Company at New Orleans converted the Mallets' information about Santa Fe into an official report: "There are about 800 Spanish and mestizo families, and in the surrounding country there are a number of permanent Indian villages, where in each one a priest does his missionary work. The garrison is composed of but eighty soldiers, a bad band and poorly armed. . . . In the immediate neighborhood there are mines which are not exploited . . . The Canadians [the Mallets] assure that the small quantity of merchandise they distributed

there had a considerable effect and that the Indians would be
entirely ours if we had some post in the country." Also of interest to the French military was the Mallets' comment that Santa
Fe was merely a village "built of wood and without any fortifications."

So ended the first double passage across the Great Plains. It
was accomplished against massive odds, covering a distance of
two thousand miles in a total travel time of only three months.
The crossing occurred exactly two centuries after Coronado first
set foot on the Llano Estacado, centuries marked by warfare and
distrust between Spain and France and laced with uncertainty
about the geography or safety of the plains.

The next year the Mallets tried to retrace their canoe route
up the Canadian toward Santa Fe, but they became lost and had
to give it up. Still, they had cracked the barrier of the southern plains and proved without question that this highly dangerous area could be navigated safely. So far as is known, however,
no one dared follow in their footsteps for half a century. And
then it was another Frenchman—Pedro Vial, who literally made
the southern and central plains his own pathway for several
years.

Vial was born Pierre Vial in Lyon, southern France (date
unknown). He first appeared on the southern plains in 1786,
serving as an explorer—Pedro Vial—in the employ of the Spanish. His task that year was to locate and travel a road between
San Antonio and Santa Fe. It was a tough trip, made with one
companion, during which he fell ill and lived among a settlement of Wichita Indians for several weeks. The route he followed was an erratic course northward from San Antonio to
the Colorado and Brazos rivers, finally reaching the Red River
near the center of the Texas-Oklahoma border. From there,
however, he followed a straighter course west into Santa Fe.

In 1788, after being in New Mexico for about a year, he again
was asked to explore, this time to the southeast. He left Santa
Fe that year and followed a rather direct route to Natchitoches
in northwestern Mississippi. From there he angled southwest
to winter in San Antonio, then returned to Santa Fe in the
spring. On this triangular journey he showed himself to be a

tough, capable frontiersman who seemed absolutely fearless in crossing country notable for its uncertain temper. He traveled about 2,400 miles, taking a little over a year. Several companions accompanied him, though the group kept changing as it passed from place to place.

Then in 1792, Vial again set out at the request of Spanish authorities to chart a route to St. Louis, now the northernmost Spanish colony in their newly owned "Upper Louisiana." There had never been a direct link between Santa Fe and St. Louis, and the journey made by the Mallet brothers had been both long and indirect. They had, in fact, left a general impression with the Spaniards that the distance between the two villages was immense. Vial took two summers to make the 2,300-mile round trip, but he shocked Spanish authorities when he told them he could have made the journey in either direction in twenty-five days. On his route to St. Louis he had been waylaid by Kansas Indians and held prisoner for six weeks, extending the trip over much of the summer. But he had taken a direct route that almost precisely followed what would, in thirty years, become the Santa Fe Trail. Thus he was first to travel that famous track.

Vial made the Spaniards realize how dangerously close they were to invasion by British and Americans. Even, in fact, as he made this first transit of the Santa Fe Trail, American frontiersmen were threading out along the river basins and beginning to invade Spanish territory from the east. But that was to become an issue at the end of the century. First there was more to be learned about the northern plains—this time by one Frenchman and two Englishmen.

CHAPTER 7
A Trio of Canadians

They were tough and unyielding, these first plainsmen, left by the drive of each day's events with little time to brood on their fates. The record of each man so committed corresponds in strength of purpose with that of the others. Yet the caprice of history has selected only some to be remembered. In the sixteenth, seventeenth and eighteenth centuries, those we remember are mainly those who wrote as well as traveled, and they are painfully few in number. It is necessary, therefore, to salt early plains history with the realization that many others, unknown to anyone, were there as well, and traveled and saw and passed on their knowledge by word of mouth.

In short, a gradual infiltration of the plains region took place in those three centuries, and we know from available writings only its outlines. The Spanish, obviously first, threaded into the lower plains from south and west, and were the only sixteenth-century explorers. The French, obviously most persistent, came from the east, ostensibly as merchants, and traveled mostly in the central plains region. But the French also worked the northern flank in the time of, but opposed by, the English. On that northern flank, only three names stand out in the seventeenth and eighteenth centuries—two Englishmen, Henry Kelsey and Anthony Hendry, and a Frenchman, Pierre Gaultier de Varennes, Sieur de La Vérendrye. The journeys of Kelsey and La Vérendrye were separated by half a century—Kelsey went there

in 1690–92, La Vérendrye in 1742–43. Hendry followed La
Vérendrye by eleven years, going out to the western Canadian
plains in 1754 and returning in 1755. Kelsey's journey has been
the most vexing to historians because of his puerile attempts to
write in rhyme and his general indifference to observations on
the land and its peoples. La Vérendrye and his sons suffered
most from their explorations, being continually badgered by
their government and virtually driven onto the plains by
demands of their superiors. Throughout, however, they were
highly courageous and disciplined frontiersmen. Hendry, an
outlawed smuggler who joined the Hudson's Bay Company, was
first to define the northern boundaries of the plains by crossing
to the Rockies on the Saskatchewan River system. These were
all tough men and their niches in North American history,
though little known, are well deserved.

That of Kelsey's, however, was long in dispute. The Hudson's
Bay Company had been chartered by the Crown in 1670 as a
"Company of Adventurers from England Trading into Hudson's Bay." One of its charter requirements was to explore the
western interior regions of Canada. The Company ignored this,
however, and jealous critics soon claimed the charter was being
mismanaged. Either it should be suspended, they said, or broadened to allow other companies to carry out interior exploration. The Hudson's Bay group saw itself as merchants, however, not frontier explorers, and preferred having Indian trappers come to the Bay to trade. The French "Pedlars" meanwhile, being less tidy about their self-images, drilled with great
effectiveness into the fur-laden veins of the interior. The Indians were quite willing to trade with the French who came to
their lands, lived their lives, and brought them brandy and
friendship along with merchandise. The long trip to the Bay,
where the dour Scots and British refused both drink and equal-
ity, was hardly worth the somewhat higher quality English merchandise. So the Company's fortunes were slow in growing, and
various leaders in Parliament, seized with fits of patriotism,
called for others to carry forward this important venture of the
Empire.

A very large brouhaha on this subject developed in the late

1740s, and that's when the Company trotted forth the story of
Kelsey's journey inland. Kelsey's trip of 1690, they said, proved
the Company had in fact been exploring the interior. Oppo-
nents cried fake and foul. They said Kelsey never made the
journey. They called for verification, and for nearly two
hundred years the entire Kelsey journey lay in doubtful shades.
Then in 1926 a man named A. F. Dobbs presented the Public
Record Office of Northern Ireland with a collection of papers
from Dobbs Castle, his long-time family residence. Included was
the original Kelsey journal. It developed that Arthur Dobbs, a
former resident of the castle, had been one of those at quarrel
with the Company in the 1740s and 1750s, and had apparently
obtained and suppressed the manuscript, which has since
proved authentic.

Kelsey, a Company document states, "was a very active lad,
delighting much in Indians' company, being never better
pleased than when he is travelling amongst them." He shipped
out to Hudson Bay aboard one of the Company's ships, and his
youthful years at York Fort were spent learning Indian languages and causing general mayhem to the Company's antifra-
ternization policy. When in 1690 Company officials cordially
invited him to go west, he thought it a splendid notion.
Whether the York Fort governor requested this journey for
exploration or for expulsion is uncertain, but Kelsey did go
west to the Canadian plains in that year.

He left York Fort on June 12, 1690, and probably traveled up
the Nelson River to Moose Lake, then made his way to a mysterious, and still unknown, "Deerings Point" on July 10. From
there he continued westward until "the ground begins for to be
dry with wood Poplo and birch with ash thats very good." Farther on, he notes "leaving the woods behind and finding the
Buffillo great." Probably he was at this point on the high plainy
land between the North and South Saskatchewan rivers, west of
Saskatoon. He had in fact reached the Canadian Great Plains,
first white man to accomplish this feat.

There he remained over the winter, hunting buffalo with the
Indians before returning to his Deerings Point in early July
1691. His stay there was momentary, however, and after collect-

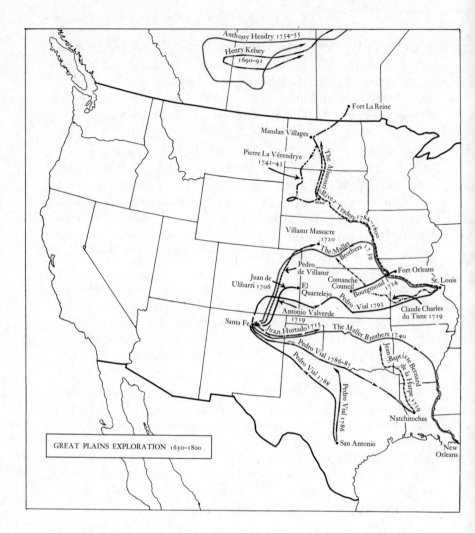

Anthony Hendry 1754-55

Henry Kelsey
1690-92

Fort La Reine

Mandan Villages

Pierre La Vérendrye
1742-43

The Missouri River Traders 1784-1800

Villasur Massacre
1720

The Mallet Brothers 1739

Pedro
de Villasur

Juan de
Ulibarri 1706

El
Quartelejo

Comanche
Council

Fort Orleans

St. Louis

Bourgmond
1724

Pedro Vial 1793

Antonio Valverde
1719

Claude Charles
du Tisne 1719

Santa Fe

Juan Hurtado 1715

The Mallet Brothers 1740

Pedro Vial 1786-87

Jean-Baptiste Bernard
de la Harpe 1719

Pedro Vial 1788

Pedro Vial 1786

Natchitoches

San Antonio

New
Orleans

GREAT PLAINS EXPLORATION 1650-1800

ing supplies he again turned westward. By the end of July 1691, he was once more on the open plains.

Fortunately in this second year he left off his rhyming and recorded many specific details of his surroundings. On August 20, for example, he reported that " . . . this plain affords Nothing but short Round sticky grass and Buffillo & a great sort of a Bear which is Bigger than any white Bear & is Neither White nor Black But silver hair'd like our English Rabbit. The Buffillo Likewise is not like those of the Northward, their Horns growing like an English Ox but Black and short." This was the first description in English of buffalo grass, and the grizzly bear, and for that matter of the plains buffalo, here compared to "those of the northward." Was he confusing the buffalo with the musk ox, common at that time north of York Fort?

He traveled sizable distances on foot, recording each day's travel dutifully, and ranging from 6 to 30 miles per day throughout much of July, all of August, and the first half of September. In all he walked nearly 600 miles across the plains. On one of the days in which he logged 30 miles travel, he had nothing to eat but one wood partridge, and reports his Indian companions having only some grass and berries. On another day, one of the Indians killed a "Buck Muse," and the chief presented Kelsey with "the great gut of the beast." Then for a time there was plenty to eat. But the feast and famine foraging of these people of the plains continued throughout his narrative, and like them he was as often hungry as glutted. The buffalo proved the most consistent food source, and on August 23, 1691, he described one of the Indian hunts: " . . . Now the manner of their hunting these Beast on the Barren ground is when they see a great parcel of them together they surround them with men which done they gather themselves into a smaller Compass keeping the Beasts still in the middle & so shooting them till they break out at some place or other & so get away from them. . . . "

Sometime in 1692 Kelsey returned to the Bay, and in later years became governor of York Fort, dying in England, destitute, in the 1720s. In 1734, his widow petitioned the Company " . . . to give her Something to buy her son John Kelsey Clothes She being wholly incapable to do it herself. . . . " The Company elders ordered that six pounds, six pence be laid out as a gratuity in remembrance of Captain Kelsey's past service.

One curiosity remains. His route west has always been uncertain because the location of what he described as "Deerings Point" is unknown. However, on July 18, 1691, Kelsey was a short distance west of that Point when he wrote in his journal as follows: "I took the Rundlett which the Governor had sent me full of powder and emptied part of it into a leather Bagg so I put one hatchet, 2 fathoms of black Tobacco, 6 knives, 2 Skains of twine, two nettlines, one tin show, and other small moveables into the rundlett and headed it up again so we made a hole in the ground & put that & other things into it & so made of it our storehouse untill we came that way the next spring." From there he continued west to the plains. But in 1692 he went out to the Bay with no further mention of this little cache—and therein lies a question. Did he recover it, or do the six knives and hatchet still lie secretly guarding his unknown route to the West? The uncertainty of that route might quickly be solved if this rusting little treasure trove could be found. Perhaps in this age of the small, portable metal detector someone may yet unravel this mystery of the north.

By 1700, then, the Spaniards had a rough understanding of the southern plains, while Kelsey had outlined the Canadian "prairies" for the English. By 1720 Bourgmond and other French traders had found their way into the eastern margins of the central plains by moving up the Missouri, the Platte, and the Republican. In 1739 the Mallets passed across the southern plains to Santa Fe, and the following year traveled from Santa Fe to New Orleans. But now the La Vérendrye family would pioneer a new route, this time across the north central plains to the Black Hills of western South Dakota. And their journey, coming only two years after the Mallet crossing, would throw more light on this great mass of flatland that was proving so troublesome to western exploration.

The story leading to this event had its beginning in 1685 in the little town of Three Rivers near Montreal on the St. Lawrence. There on November 17 La Vérendrye was born, one of ten children of an industrious French farm family. His father was governor of the Three Rivers district, and at age twelve, the patriotic young Pierre entered the French army. Sent to France, he suffered nine wounds at the Battle of Malplaquet, but somehow survived and returned to Canada in 1711. The next year he married and settled down as a farmer near Three Rivers. Here he prospered and his family grew, but the longer this life continued, the more restless he became. Year after year, he listened to the voyageurs as they came down from the northwest, laden with beaver hides and wilderness tales. Each spring he watched them push off again up the St. Lawrence to those storied western lands he had never seen.

By 1725 his itch had become a rash, and he asked Beauharnois, governor of the colony, to send him out to the frontier. The governor obliged him with command of a fur-trading post on Lake Nipigon, north of Lake Superior, and in the spring of 1726, he went west for the first time, then at age forty-one, tall and powerfully built, a seasoned and disciplined leader with a distinguished war record. For the next eighteen years, La Vérendrye was the mainstay of the entire French effort on the northern frontier. He kept the Indians at peace with one another and drained beaver peltries away from the British on Hudson Bay. He and his four sons built a string of forts and trading posts. French influence under his leadership extended from the west end of Lake Superior northwest to Lake Winnipeg and beyond. The La Vérendryes kept their rendezvous with Indians, traders, and voyageurs, and they kept both furs and trade goods moving on the long supply line from Montreal to the interior.

But Pierre La Vérendrye was nine parts explorer and one part businessman, and his fortunes as a fur trader showed a steady rate of decay during his entire tenure on the frontier. He had borrowed heavily to outfit himself for the frontier, but his fortunes were so bad he couldn't even keep up with interest payments; thus the anger of his creditors was a continuous fire in his life. That, however, was only part of his problem.

Like Bourgmond farther south, La Vérendrye had heard a vexing rumor that a strange people were living beside a great sea far to the west. They wore armor, rode horses, and worked metal. The rumor, and the location of the "Sea of the West,"

were equally vague. In addition, La Vérendrye also was be-
guiled about the four great rivers supposedly draining away to
their four respective seas—North, South, East, and West.

The search for these geographical marvels began for the La
Vérendryes with their first trip to the plains in 1738. To pay the
costs and loss of time, however, the journey was planned as a
trade venture to the Mandan villages near present Bismarck,
North Dakota. Starting out on October 18, La Vérendrye led a
troop of four Frenchmen, plus his two sons, and forty-five Assiniboin natives westward from Fort La Reine. That post was
located near Portage la Prairie, Manitoba, and the little troop
moved from there slowly toward the southwest. As it traveled, it
grew in size until more than six hundred overfriendly Assiniboin men, women, and children had gathered into a lengthy
column. This slowed progress and angered La Vérendrye, but
he finally entered the first Mandan village on December 3 amid
great rejoicing and a crushing mixture of Indians from the two
tribes. His four French soldiers fired off three volleys in salute
to the Mandans, an act that opened the feasting and rejoicing.
The Mandans were in all ways eager to know about La Vérendrye, "their father," and the explorer noted in his journal that
they had carefully preserved "the two collars I had sent them
four or five years before." The festivities were marred immediately, however, when his bag of presents was stolen. That left
him without gifts for the chiefs, and brought a grumble of suspicions between the two tribes over who was guilty.

The next day, a more severe blow hit the expedition. The
one interpreter who understood both Mandan and Assiniboin
conducted a bit of overnight interpretation on his own, and
next morning trooped off across the Dakota plains in pursuit of
an Assiniboin maiden. All hoped-for discussion was now gone,
and despite all their attempts, the French and Mandans could
not converse. After this setback, the observant Frenchman had
to content himself with writings in his journal, producing a
series of careful notations on these unusual people of the plains.

"The Mandan fort," La Vérendrye wrote, "was built on a
height in the open prairie with a ditch upwards of 15 to 18 feet
wide. It could be entered only by steps or posts which were able

The interior of the Mandan Indian village La Vérendrye visited in North Dakota in the 1740s was crowded and busy. He described the domelike dwellings as spacious, comfortable, and neat. Note the fencelike palisade in the background. (GEORGE CATLIN, *North American Indians*)

to be removed when threatened by an enemy." After crossing this moat, the invader would encounter a palisade surrounding a rampart. The palisade "was supported on cross pieces morticed into posts of 15 feet."

One of these moat and palisade systems encompassed an area of nearly fourteen acres, and was probably half a mile in total length. Inside the first village were 130 huts. Each hut was circular and most were up to fifty feet in diameter. The Mandans were, he said, "... of mixed blood, white and black. The women are rather handsome, particularly the light-coloured ones; they have an abundance of fair hair. The whole tribe, men and women, is very industrious. Their dwellings are large and spacious, divided into several apartments by wide planks. Nothing is lying about; all their belongings are placed in large bags and hung on posts; their beds are made in the form of tombs and are surrounded by skins. They all go to bed naked, both men and women. The men go naked all the time, being covered only by a buffalo robe. Many of the women go naked like the men, with this difference, that they wear a small loincloth about a hand wide and a foot long sewed to a girdle in front only. All the women wear this kind of protection even when they wear a petticoat, so that they are not embarrassed when they sit down and do not have to keep the thighs closed like other Indian women. Some wear a kind of jacket of very soft buckskin."

They were great eaters, and every day carried more than twenty dishes to the French leader, including buffalo and antelope, corn, beans, beechnuts, squash, pumpkins, and many other vegetables, always cooked. The meat, however, was eaten nearly raw, and rotting flesh was used as a delicacy. "The men are big and tall, very active and for the most part, good-looking, fine physiognomies, and affable. The women generally have not a savage cast of features."

As he walked about the dry, dusty streets of their village, fifteen hundred miles west of Montreal and close to the geographic center of the continent, he watched them play a "kind of ball" along the open spaces and ramparts, and saw them tattooing each other with willow ink and needles. He observed deep storage pits in which they kept quantities of food for the winter, contrasting this with the feast and famine habits of the Assiniboins. He noticed their fine leather work. And he waited for his son to return from one of the other villages, hoping he might find a Cree-speaking Mandan. But when he returned, it was the same story. No conversation and no more information about the people who were believed to live beyond the plains. No positive evidence in the form of silver or gold, nor any bits of captured armor plate, nor other items of foreign origin.

The Assiniboins left soon after, in a panic when the canny Mandans spread a rumor that a large party of war-toughened Sioux had been seen nearby. The Assiniboins, as guests of the

Mandans, were consuming large quantities of food, and with winter closing down, such provisions grew in importance as they dwindled in quantity. As soon as the Assiniboins dispersed, the Mandan chief gestured to La Vérendrye that the tale of the Sioux was merely a ruse, and not to be alarmed.

The departure of the Assiniboins quieted the camp, but did little to ease La Vérendrye's disappointment or frustration over his failure to learn of the "Western Sea" and its peoples. He remained as the Mandans' honored guest until December 13, then started back to Fort La Reine, leaving two Frenchmen over winter to learn the Mandan language.

La Vérendrye's second journey to the Mandans was also abortive, led in this case by his son Pierre. Pierre set out from Fort La Reine in the late spring of 1741 accompanied by the two Frenchmen who now understood the Mandan language. Their objective was to wait with the Mandans for the arrival of a group of horse-using Indians—unnamed—that lived far to the west. Pierre and his interpreters reached the Mandan villages handily, but the horse users never arrived. When Pierre started upriver to find them, he was chased back by a war party of prairie Sioux.

The venture was not a total loss, however. When they returned to the French base that fall, they took with them two horses, the first seen in that country, acquired in a trade with the Mandans. The young Frenchman also learned that the River of the West known to the Indians was actually only the Missouri. His Indian reporters had been misled where the Big Muddy took some large bends to the west near the Mandan camp. The only real evidence of the Western Sea the young explorer could gather was "a coverlet of embroidered cotton and four mugs of porcelain, articles much used by the people of the sea." The "mugs" were actually tubular beads, items Pierre obtained from the Mandans and carried to his father, to be forwarded to the French court.

But trinkets were not enough. In the face of this latest failure, Comte de Maurepas, the King's minister, moved to replace one of the explorer's sons with another officer, to be paid three thousand livres a year from proceeds of La Vérendrye's fur trad-

This quaint depiction of a buffalo pound came from the Canadian plains region traveled by Henry Kelsey and Anthony Hendry. They may have witnessed such a hunting method. (SIR JOHN FRANKLIN, *Journey to the Polar Sea*, 1819—22)

ing. By now, the frontier commander was more than fifty thousand livres in debt, and adding the burden of another officer's salary was almost humorous. Governor Beauharnois tried to save La Vérendrye this difficulty, but the King's minister was adamant.

Fortunately for history, it would take another year for his order to be paddled into the interior. In the meantime, La Vérendrye, now fifty-eight and in ill health, made plans for a final assault on the Great Plains. Young Louis-Joseph, known in the family as the Chevalier, would lead the third expedition to the West, this year going all the way. He was youngest of the three, but now at age twenty-four, aggressive and sage in his judgments. Brother François, aged twenty-five, would accompany him, along with two other Frenchmen and two Indian guides. Meantime, Pierre, aged twenty-seven, would make a long loop to the northwest and establish a fur-trading post beyond the sphere of local Indian tensions. If battles began near Fort La Reine, his trade there would not be interrupted. Also, he would be at the very frontier of the fur trade, on the main line to intercept pelts headed toward the British at Hudson Bay. He would locate at The Pas, where the Pasquia River joins the great Saskatchewan system, about on the present Manitoba-Saskatchewan border. His mission was to save the family from financial ruin while the western expedition would save it from political destruction. In the meantime, their father would remain at Fort La Reine and do what he could to keep the Indian peace.

And so on April 29, 1742, the Chevalier and his crew cracked shell ice away from shore and launched their canoes up the Assiniboin. They followed the route taken twice before, leaving the river a distance west of Fort La Reine and striking out overland. In twenty days they had reached the Mandan villages. Again they waited for the promised horse-using Indians, meantime mulling the tales they heard, listening to the Mandans night after night, hoping their elusive friends would finally arrive. The two interpreters learned that the horse Indians lived where "people are white, have beards, and pray to the great Master of Life in books," which they described as made of leaves of Indian corn, that they "sing holding their books, in great houses where they assemble for prayer. The women are white and handsome. They play the harpsichord and the bass viol, they use pistols and saddlecloths. The towns are near the great lake the waters of which rise and fall and are not good to drink."

Of course these whites had to be Spanish, and the French explorers must have sensed it, yet they refused the final verdict. There had been so many confusions drummed up in all these tales, always compounded by the language blocks. And that nagging uncertainty about the Western Sea had not been disposed of. The Spanish were at Santa Fe, far from any salt water. But were they also close by, and was the Western Sea also nearby? Or was it possibly a different non-Indian people these horsemen knew? Chinese perhaps? Whatever the case, the Chevalier and his tiny band finally gave up their wait, and on July 23 set out cross-lots, on foot, to see what they could see. Considering that both his brother Jean-Baptiste and a cousin had lately been murdered by Indians, and that the dreaded prairie Sioux might be anywhere nearby, this act in itself showed a courage bordering on the foolhardy.

When they arrived at a mountain, their guides called it the land of the horse Indians. Finding no one, the Chevalier decided to camp and light signal fires from several promontories. Here they sat for nearly a month before an answering plume of smoke rose to the southwest of their camp. One of the guides and one of the Frenchmen were dispatched to investigate, and returned a few days later reporting friendly treatment from "a village of handsome men." The whole group was invited to visit and stay with these people, so the Chevalier hoisted anchor and headed off. His hosts turned out to be a nomadic people of the plains, and the explorers stayed with them for the next three weeks.

In early November, however, this group passed the explorers along to a tribe of Little Foxes, who soon led them to a "Pioya" village, who in turn led them southward to a village of true horse Indians. Unfortunately, as they arrived, the camp was in an uproar. They had just sustained a crippling attack from a band of marauding Shoshones, and their entire tribe had been torn apart. Having no way to help the explorers, the distraught Indians suggested going on to join a group of Bow Indians camped nearby.

All this travel had taken the space of two months, and it was late November when the four Frenchmen arrived in the camp of the Bows. Their two Indian guides had long since returned to the Mandan village, and they were now entirely dependent on the goodwill and food supplies of these nomadic people. As it happened, the Bows were just then mounting an expedition of their own and would soon attack a village of Snake Indians, located at the foot of a western mountain chain. Everyone was mounted now, including the Frenchmen, as the Bow Indians had quantities of horses, mules, and asses. For nearly two weeks the mixed troop of Indians and French continued their advance westward, much of this time in view of the mountains. The enemy supposedly was camped on the lower slopes of the mountain, and as they neared their quarry, the Bows grew nervous.

They set up a base camp as depository for their families and baggage, and there made plans. They would march the warriors ahead, fall on the Snakes, and annihilate them.

On the morning of the attack, the Chevalier left his brother at the base camp and rode forward with the war party. Just as the main body was about to reach the camp, scouts came riding back full tilt to report that the Snakes had scattered up the mountain slopes, leaving their baggage and camp behind. In the confused way frontline warfare sometimes turns, this immediately struck fear in the attackers. Were the Snakes circling around to attack the Bows' base camp? Fearing for their families, the Bows turned and rode pell-mell in a rout for home. "The chief of the Bow people," wrote the Chevalier, "did what he could to get that idea out of their heads, and persuade them to go forward, but no one would listen to him. 'It is very annoying,' he said to me, 'that I have brought you so far and that we cannot go any farther.' I was greatly mortified not to be able to climb the mountains as I had wished."

And there the matter ended. Caught in a wave of mob panic, he was forced to ride away, that mountain range at his back, beyond which he thought lay the vast blue expanse of the Western Sea. But he hadn't seen it, and he couldn't be sure, and now the chance was lost forever. Though he made promises to return and visit these friendly people, he must have known he never would. Leaving the Bows, the Chevalier led his little group, wandering slowly north and east, gradually working his way homeward, arriving there on July 2, 1743. He had been on the trail fourteen months, and his father was greatly relieved to see his two sons alive and safe. But their mission had been a failure and shortly thereafter, as expected, their political fortunes worsened. The old man, under pressure from creditors and his governor, had to resign his post and return with his sons to Montreal.

This was the end of a great era in frontier exploration. It was also the last important attempt Frenchmen would make to penetrate the western darkness of this continent. A few more abortive tries were made to reach the mythical Western Sea, but the driving energy of La Vérendrye and his sons was gone from the

scene, and no one came to replace it. A scant sixteen years after
the Chevalier returned to Fort La Reine, the British sailed up
the St. Lawrence and passed Marquis de Montcalm's flank without a shot. A few nights later, they scaled the heights at Quebec
and defeated the French army on the Plains of Abraham.
French reign on the North American continent had ended.

Two interesting sidelights of the Chevalier's last journey
remain. It is not known to this day what mountain range he
saw. Most authorities agree that it was either the Black Hills of
South Dakota or the Big Horns of Wyoming, those two offshore
islands of the Rocky Mountain chain. No responsible authority
believes they reached as far as the Front Range or the Laramie
Range of the main Rocky Mountain spine. Yet the poignancy of
this near miss must have remained with the Chevalier to the
end of his life. Had the Indian scouts simply not panicked on
that day in January 1743, all might have been well. The Western Sea must have rippled beyond. The King could have been
satisfied, and the La Vérendryes restored to their rightful position in Canada. But the Indians had panicked and the La Vérendryes had lost.

Whatever his thoughts on that subject, the Chevalier noted in
his journal that, while returning to Fort La Reine, he had
buried a leaden plate on a promontory overlooking the Missouri River. "I deposited on an eminence near the fort," he
wrote, "a tablet of lead with the arms and inscription of the
King, and a pyramid of stones for the General. I said to the savages, who did not know about the tablet of lead that I had put
in the ground, that I was erecting these stones in memory of the
fact that we had come upon their land. I should have greatly
wished to take the latitude of that place; but our astrolabe had
not been of any use from the beginning of our journey, the ring
of it being broken."

Nearly two centuries later, a schoolgirl named Hattie Foster
saw a corner of his leaden plate jutting from the ground near
Pierre, South Dakota. It was a Sunday afternoon, February 16,
1913, and young Hattie pried it free and showed it to her
teacher. That plate now rests in the state museum at Pierre,
reading on one side, in Latin: "In the 26th year of the reign of

La Vérendrye and his sons may have witnessed Indians such as this Minnetaree warrior during their travels in the upper Missouri country. Though the Frenchmen did not reach Minnetaree country, the dance, head-dress, rattles, beads, and tough leather-backed bow were common to the northern plains. (CHARLES BODMER, *Travels in the United States*)

Louis XV, Pierre Gaultier de la Vérendrye acting on behalf of the Marquis de Beauharnois deposited this plate in 1741 in the name of our most illustrious sovereign, the King." The date, of course, was wrong. On the reverse side they had scrawled: "Deposited by the Chevalier and de la Vérendrye [his brother], witnesses St. Louy de Londette, A. Miotte, the 30 March 1743."

Unfortunately, the point of discovery of this leaden plate was the only positive geographic location in the entire journal, and speculation about how far they traveled, or where they traveled is fruitless. Yet they were the first white men on the north central plains, and their journal has proved a valuable source of historical interest. They reported the Indians very hospitable, they saw swarms of wildlife, and they rode on horses. But most of all, they joined that great company of North American explorers that, to a man, "almost found the Western Sea." Such a legacy of memories was enough for a lifetime of dreams, and that was a fortune not Maurepas, nor the King, nor anyone else could pry loose from the La Vérendryes. For all their personal losses and family troubles, they had won the day.

Twelve years later, it was Anthony Hendry's turn to visit the plains. Hendry was born on the Isle of Wight, date unknown, and in 1748 was convicted of smuggling and declared an outlaw. In 1750 he entered the service of the Hudson's Bay Company, the directors not knowing about his past. He soon shipped out to Canada, and in 1754 asked if he might explore fur-trapping possibilities in the western interior of Canada. He headed west from the Bay in late June, following the Hayes and other rivers westward to the north end of Lake Winnipeg, then continuing on to The Pas, where he left his canoe and walked overland about to present Saskatoon, then to Battleford, before turning southwest toward present Calgary. He wintered among the Blackfeet on the plains between Calgary and Edmonton, having arrived almost at the base of the Rockies. He hunted, snow-shoed, and lived successfully enough on deer, buffalo, moose, and beaver meat. After breakup the following spring, he canoed down the Red Deer to the South Saskatchewan, then continued eastward to the Bay, arriving there in late June after being gone a year almost to the day.

This journey was highly interesting from several aspects. It was first of all a bold thrust deep into territory so dangerous that no white man had any reasonable right to expect to sur-vive. Hendry's journal also provides the only known early view of the Blackfeet before corrupting white influences began to change their way of life. He was the first white man to travel to the headwaters of the Saskatchewan River system, proving its critical importance to any future commerce or exploration of the interior. And finally, his daily journal is in itself a fascinat-ing piece of descriptive writing on the life style, survival tech-niques, and cultural equipment of the peoples he met. A few scattered entries from his diary provide an interesting glimpse of life on the plains at this time. He was here traveling with a group of about twelve Indian men and women.

"September 10, Tuesday. Traveled none. The young men and I went a hunting, killed 3 moose and 6 Waskesew [red deer]. I killed a Bull Buffalo, nothing but skin and bone. Took out his tongue, and left his remains to the Wolves who were waiting around me in great numbers. They do not meddle with any person. We cannot afford to expend our ammunition on them.

"September 15, Sunday. Traveled 7 miles W.S.W. Level land, no woods to be seen. Passed by a lake. The buffalo so numerous obliged to make them sheer out of our way. Also, Wolves without number, lurking Indians killed a great many Buffalo, only taking what they choosed to carry.

"September 17, Tuesday. Indians hunting. Women drying meat. Two young men miserably tore by a grizzle bear, whom they had wounded. One may recover but the other never can; for his arm is almost tore from his body, one eye is quite out, and his entrails are hanging from his body.

"September 18, Wednesday. Traveled none. One Indian dead and the other in a weak condition. Two Asinepoet natives came to us and informed us the Blackfeet had killed and scalped 6 Indians and that there were a great many nigh us.

"October 8, Tuesday. Traveled 7 miles S.W. [Hendry is now well to the southwest of present Battleford]. Pleasant valleys, hillocks, & ledges of woods. Indians killed a great many Buffalo, took out the tongues and left the remains to be eat by the wolves. I cannot say whether them or the Buffalo are most numerous. Saw several snakes."

This journeying and hunting continued as Hendry and his little company neared the land of the dreaded Blackfeet. By this point in history the Blackfeet had horses, and were mobile, war-like, and powerful in numbers. Nevertheless, Hendry continued westward across the plains of southern Alberta and eventually made contact, which he described as follows:

"October 13, Sunday. Traveled 7 miles S.W.b W. Level land, & ledges of woods, and numbers of buffalo. Indians killed a great many. In the evening we were joined by 7 Blackfoot natives on horse-back, who informed us we should see the Great Leader & numbers of Blackfoot natives tomorrow.

"October 14, Monday. Traveled 4 miles S.W. b W. Then came to us four men on horseback. They told us they were sent from the main body to see whether we were friends or enemies. We told them we were friends . . . our leaders walked in front about 4 miles farther. Came to 200 tents of Blackfoot natives pitched in two rows and an opening in the middle where we were conducted to the Leader's tent, which was at one end, large enough to contain fifty persons, where he received us seated on a white Buffalo skin, attended by 20 elderly men. He made signs for me to sit down at his right hand, which I did. Our Leader set up several grandpipes, and smoked all around, according to their usual custom. Not a word was spoke on either side. Smoking being over, Buffalo flesh boiled was served round in baskets of a species of bent, and I was presented with 10 buffalo tongues. Attickasish my guide informed him I was sent by the Great Leader who lives down at the great waters to invite his young men to see him and to bring with them Beaver skins & Wolves skins & they would get in return powder, shot, guns, cloth, beads, &c. He made little answer, only said that it was far off and they could not paddle. Then they entered upon indifferent subjects until we were ordered to depart to our tents, which were pitched about a full quarter of a mile without their lines."

Next day, Hendry was told the Great Leader of the Blackfeet would not send any of his young men down to the Bay. He said they hunted here and followed the buffalo and never wanted for food. On leaving the camp that afternoon, Hendry made the following notes:

"Their horses are turned out to grass, their legs being fettered, and when wanted are fastened to lines out of buffalo skin, that stretches along & is fastened to stakes drove in the ground. They have hair halters, buffalo skin pads, & stirrups of the same. The horses are fine tractible animals, about 14 hands high; lively and clean made. The natives are good horsemen & kill the buffalo on them. These natives are drest much the same as others; but more clean and sprightly. They think nothing of my tobacco and I set as little value on theirs which is dryed horse-dung. They appear to be under proper discipline, & obedient to their leader who orders a party of horsemen evening and morning to reconnoiter. Saw many fine girls who were captives & a great many dried scalps with fine long black hair, displayed on poles & before the leader's tent. They follow the buffalo from place to place & that they should not be surprised by the enemy, encamp in open plains . . . their cloathing is finely painted with red paint, like unto English Ochre, but they do not mark nor paint their bodies. Saw four asses."

The next day, Hendry and his group took their leave of the Blackfeet, and in parting the Englishman was given a fine bow and set of arrows, and one of his Indians was given two young girls as slaves. Female captives in that northern country were less well treated than in other tribes farther south, and served as chattel property valued somewhat below the level of camp dogs.

With the coming of spring, Hendry and his Indians camped near the Red Deer River in southeastern Alberta and began to make birch canoes. Toward the end of April, with the breakup of ice in the river, they bundled their furs and baggage into the canoes and headed east toward Hudson Bay. The Red Deer tributes the South Saskatchewan, and as both are powerful, full-flowing rivers, Hendry was able to make steady and rapid progress homeward, where he arrived on June 20, 1755. His was an adventure-packed journey, providing the Hudson's Bay Company with ample information about the interior which they did not begin to use effectively for nearly half a century.

The mission completed, Hendry quit the Company and dropped from sight. But Andrew Graham, then secretary at York Fort, gave Hendry the single most important accolade any explorer could ever hope to receive. Writing in the Company's records for the year 1755, he said simply, and with finality: "He was the first person who ventured inland."

CHAPTER 8

The World's Biggest Real Estate Swindle

Thomas Jefferson, third president of the United States, purchased the Great Plains from Napoleon Bonaparte in 1803. History books have gotten in the habit of calling it the Louisiana Purchase, but it was really a very large hoax involving a transfer of title to our Great Plains, plus part or all of seven states bordering on the plains. Neither the French people nor the American people had anything to say about the matter until this largest land swap in history had been consummated. The American Constitution did not allow or authorize such a purchase. Congress had not appropriated money for it. The United States Treasury did not have money to make payment. And the American people generally were unaware such a transaction was even being considered. They were told about it after it happened.

"I stretched the Constitution until it cracked," Jefferson admitted to Congress, " . . . yet the fertility of the country, its climate and extent, all promise in due season important aids to our treasury."

Agreement on the purchase came after only three weeks of negotiations in April 1803. Jefferson and Napoleon simply made a deal at that time, their ministers shook hands, and the agreement stuck. Congress ratified the purchase as a "treaty"—the only legal arrangement they could make under the Constitution—on October 25, 1803.

Most interesting of all, the sale lacked any legal basis whatever, and proved the biggest land swindle in world history. Whole continents have changed ownership through colonization, or been brutally taken as prizes in war, but this was an arrogant marketplace hoax in which the seller didn't own the property, and the buyer had no authority to purchase. That the arrangement held together at all was amazing in itself.

The core of the matter, for our story, is that all subsequent Great Plains history unfolds as it did as a result of the purchase. The land area taken over included all or parts of twelve states, and was 827,987 square miles in size. It nearly tripled the size of the United States, then composed of seventeen states encompassing 456,091 square miles. No one party to the sale had ever seen the lands in question—not Jefferson, nor Napoleon, nor any of their ministers, and in fact not more than a handful of citizens of either country. La Salle, Bourgmond, La Vérendrye, and all the other great French explorers of the early eighteenth century had long since died, and the travel records they left of "Upper Louisiana" were not reviewed before the sale. No one even knew how much land was involved, how far north, south, or west it extended, what its actual use or value might be.

The roots of the story behind the Louisiana Purchase go back to the foundation of the French colony at New Orleans early in the eighteenth century. The French had been there sporadically for a long time, and small settlements had sprung up, then collapsed to be replaced by others. Officially, the region was Spanish, claimed by that country as "West Florida." To break the Spanish hold, the French king, Louis XIV, gave colonization rights to an ambitious but unwary French merchant named Antonine Crozat. Both the King and Crozat knew that the few trappers who cooked their squirrel meat in the lower Mississippi Valley did not constitute French ownership of that land, but they pushed ahead with the colony's plans anyway. Crozat, in short, was authorized by a French king to settle Frenchmen on property that rightfully belonged to Spain. Still, they reckoned if they could make it stick, one would have the trade and the other a new colony.

Crozat received his charter in 1712, but by 1717 the venture was a bankrupt failure. Its death rattle was heard by a brilliant, erratic, troublesome Scot named John Law, then in Paris as an outlaw from England. Law was a financial genius and took over the floundering colony, promoted it as a paradise, and sold thousands of shares of stock in his "Mississippi Company." After cropping all gullible investors, Law pocketed the money and left the colony bankrupt. His scheme now resides in our history as "John Law's Mississippi Bubble." But it had little effect on older residents of the tiny colony, who had by then arranged themselves into a little palisaded village named New Orleans, with ownership after 1728 residing in the French Crown. There it remained for a time, and the colony—being left alone—began to prosper. By the 1750s, it was a busy little port and center for pirates, contraband exchange, river traffic, Indians from the interior, and fur traders. Much of this trade originated farther north in the interior of both the plains and eastern America. France had gained at least nominal hold over the upper Mississippi Valley by that date, which included all the rivers draining into it from the west, plus the rambling Missouri far to the northwest. The edges of the Great Plains were known to many settlers as part of this vast landholding, and a few had even gone all the way to the Rockies. But they had been few indeed, and the land was still almost unknown.

Then the British General James Wolfe came to Quebec with his armies, and resoundingly defeated the French army in 1759. The French maneuvered diplomatically until 1763, but finally signed the Treaty of Paris, giving up all claim to their lands in Canada—nearly all, that is. Three tiny islands remained in French possession at the mouth of the St. Lawrence—and are still in French ownership today, the islands of St. Pierre and Big and Little Miquelon.

Louis XV, smarting from his defeat in Canada, moved to cement relations with Spain, and by the same stroke to thwart British designs on his Louisiana colony. In 1762, he secretly gave the entire Louisiana territory to Spain. That nation then controlled everything west of the Mississippi, from the Gulf of Mexico to a distance fourteen hundred miles northward to the vague frontier of Britain's Canadian colonies.

For a time, a puppet French administration remained at New

Orleans. However, the secret exchange became known in 1768 when a Spanish governor set up offices at New Orleans and for the next thirty-two years, the Spanish flag flew over all that vast western flatland. This accounts for such plains names as Montana, Colorado, New Mexico, and Texas, as well as hundreds of lesser place-names throughout the entire region. The Spaniards, long before controlling the Louisiana country, had moved up along the continental backbone of the Rockies, northward from Colorado, into the Platte River country of Nebraska. After Louis gave them the plains region, they filtered up the Mississippi to St. Louis and farther north. They became active along the Gulf Coast and in eastern Texas, and as far north as the Arkansas. The land between the Arkansas and St. Louis, however, was largely wilderness, known mainly to Indians as a morass of swamps, sandy ridges, spectacular mountains, and finally—beyond to the west—endless miles of dead-level grassland. The Spaniards, despite the promise such land might hold, were for now content to leave it untouched. It had not been, in their thoughts, much of a gift.

In the last ten years of the eighteenth century, however, the Americans pushed west like a band of gypsies into Tennessee and Kentucky and spilled across the Mississippi into those Spanish lands where they settled as squatters. From 1790 to 1800, the combined population of Tennessee and Kentucky increased threefold from 109,000 to 326,000. How many crossed the river into Missouri and Arkansas in that time is unknown.

In any case, the main center of trade for all these people, and others both up and down the Ohio and Mississippi, was New Orleans. These new Americans far outnumbered the Spanish and French, and by their trade and increasing numbers provided a forecast of the future of the Mississippi Valley. The French had given the West to Spain, but the people using it would clearly not be Spanish. Frontiersmen who had attached themselves to the rich bottomlands along these rivers soon produced large amounts of foodstuffs and homemade products. Heavy flatboats laden with potatoes, corn, hides, whiskey, dried meats, cider, homespun, and other commodities became common on the river, all drifting south to New Orleans. Such trade that started as a trickle grew steadily. Soon most affairs of the new little town at the mouth of the river were controlled by it. Faced with this, Spanish authorities tried like aging school-masters to maintain their creaky little bureaucracy.

Meantime, events in Europe were about to change the face of our nation. Napoleon seized power in France late in 1799, and quickly began maneuvering to build his empire. One of his first moves was a brazen attempt to retrieve Louisiana from Spain.

Soon after, Spanish authorities halted American trade at New Orleans, sending talk of war rolling across the frontier and into Congress. President Jefferson, despairing of another conflict so soon after the Revolution, urged his ambassador at Paris to con-duct a fishing expedition through the French government. The ambassador was Robert R. Livingston, and Jefferson asked him merely to secure a United States outlet for trade into the Gulf of Mexico. He was urged to buy a piece of the Gulf Coast, or a thin strip down the east shore of the Mississippi, or the little colony of New Orleans itself. Failing all of those, he was to secure at least the right of American trade through the port of New Orleans.

But Livingston did not content himself with such narrow objectives, and he seems to have been the first to suggest that the French sell to the United States not only New Orleans but Upper Louisiana as well. Upper Louisiana was everything north of the Arkansas River on the west side of the Mississippi. As a land still virtually unknown, it appeared to have little economic or political value. It had proved a commercial wasteland for numerous French ventures and was best known as a wilderness peopled with fiery Indians and strange woolly beasts. Besides, Livingston kept saying, by selling Upper Louisiana to the Americans, the French would have a New World buffer between their holdings on the lower river and those of Great Britain to the north. From November 1801 to April 1803 under orders from Jefferson he kept up this attack. To all his propos-als, however, the French merely turned a deaf ear.

Jefferson meantime had to wrestle with the quandary at home, and he found no way to dislodge the plug at the lower end of the Mississippi. In desperation, after nearly eighteen months of

A troop of American militia under the infamous General James Wilkinson was present to take over New Orleans from the French after the Louisiana Purchase was completed. Here the soldiers fire a salute as the Stars and Stripes is hoisted in the city for the first time on December 20, 1803. (PAINTING BY THURE DE THULSTRUP, LOUISIANA HISTORICAL SOCIETY, NEW ORLEANS)

inaction, he decided on one last attempt to buy his way out of the dilemma. He dispatched James Monroe as a special envoy to Paris to bolster Livingston's work, and he secretly advised the pair they could offer up to $9,375,000 for the purchase of West Florida and New Orleans. Congress had voted that only $2,-000,000 would be available, but Jefferson, the reserved plantation lawyer, decided to gamble a long shot on his own. At that late date, however, his writings still showed no expectation of buying the entire Louisiana colony.

Then Charles Maurice de Talleyrand-Périgord, Napoleon's minister of foreign affairs, surprised Livingston on April 11, 1803, by suddenly asking "what America would give for the whole of Louisiana?" Apparently Napoleon had decided to sell. This opened several days of haggling over the price, which finally stuck at $15,000,000. The United States was to obtain the money from Dutch and English bankers at 6 percent interest and the people of Louisiana were to be admitted to American citizenship as speedily as possible. After Napoleon gave the agreement a cursory review, Monroe and Livingston signed for the United States and André Marbois, one of Napoleon's ministers, signed for France on April 30, 1803. The United States nearly tripled in size by the strokes of three pens.

So the purchase of the Great Plains and the Mississippi Valley states was completed, all very illegally. Because of time and distance and slowness of travel, Monroe and Livingston had to guess that Congress would approve the purchase. They had paid $15,000,000 but were authorized by the President to spend less than $10,000,000—and by the Congress, only $2,000,000! In the same arrangement, Napoleon paid Spain $2,000,000 for the land he did not own, having first sold it for $15,000,000! All these shenanigans raised political objections in America, but on October 28, 1803, a final bill authorizing possession of the new territory passed the House 89 to 23. Jefferson signed the bill on October 31, thus formally concluding the entire transaction.

The Spanish government was furious at Napoleon, but powerless to oppose him. On November 30, the Spanish flag was lowered at New Orleans, and the French ran up their colors. Twenty days later a military contingent arrived, accompanying William C. C. Claiborne, a Virginia planter appointed by Jefferson to serve as first governor. Once again, the flags of ownership were changed. Thus, within one month the bartered and bargained people of Louisiana found their nationality altered from Spanish to French to American.

At St. Louis, the illegality of the purchase hardly bothered the toughened frontier residents, with the change of ownership becoming something of a comic opera. The French did not even have an authorized agent in the area, and their prefect at New Orleans, Pierre Laussat, asked if the Americans could loan him a citizen to act for the French government. Amos Stoddard, a Yankee lawyer turned soldier, was then stationed at Kaskaskia, across the Mississippi from St. Louis. Claiborne appointed him as Frenchman for a day, and the orders went upriver to effect the transfer of land ownership. The American army detachment that would take command of St. Louis left Kaskaskia with Stoddard and traveled to St. Louis. They arrived there on March 9, 1804. Stoddard met the Spanish owners of Upper Louisiana at the old fort, and after appropriate ceremonies and signings, the Spanish flag was lowered and the French flag raised. A sizable amount of frontier liquor was consumed during this celebration, and the guns of the old fort fired off a few erratic salutes, narrowly missing a cow grazing in a nearby meadow. Then the United States troops marched into the fort, and another signing took place with Stoddard again serving for France. The French flag was lowered and the Stars and Stripes was cranked up the fort's little flagpole. One of those who signed for the United States that chill afternoon was a young army captain named Meriwether Lewis, who would soon enough carve himself a sizable notch in American history crossing those very lands he had just helped purchase.

At St. Louis, the land known as Upper Louisiana was transferred from Spain to France, then from France to the United States. The entire transaction took place in one day, March 9, 1804. Meriwether Lewis, soon to explore the Louisiana Purchase, was present that day. (ALFRED RUSSELL, *Louisiana and the Fair*)

With ceremonies completed, Spain, France, and the United States now had to decide how much land actually changed hands. The Great Plains standoff that Spain and France carried on during the eighteenth century, the ferocity of the Plains Indian tribes, the lack of settled establishments or trade routes, and the generally unexplored nature of the entire region all contributed to the doubts and shrouding of the land in question. Napoleon, in fact, had instructed his ministers in selling Louisiana that "if an obscurity did not already exist concerning the borders, it would perhaps be good policy to put one there."

The wisdom of power lay behind that remark, and the treaty that was finally offered called for France to sell to the United States " . . . the colony or province of Louisiana with the same extent that it now has in the hands of Spain, and that it had when France possessed it; and such as it should be after the treaties subsequently entered into between Spain and other states." But of course no one knew the boundaries when France possessed it, and they were as totally undefined during Spanish ownership.

Disputes arose immediately. Jefferson, a very scholarly man with a large personal library, studied the question thoroughly and early in 1804 became convinced from past treaties, occupations, and French travels that the United States purchase included property extending to the Rio Grande, our present boundary with Mexico. The Spanish denied this, saying claims extended only to the Sabine River, about 240 miles west of New Orleans. The Spanish Crown, they said, owned everything west of that line, plus much of the southern plains region and all the west slope of the Rocky Mountains including California, Oregon, and the entire Great Basin. These conflicting claims touched off years of bickering and dispute over who owned much of Texas, Oklahoma, Mississippi, and the Gulf Coast, coloring our relations with Spain and Mexico throughout the nineteenth century. The struggle for Texas, for example, and the many border clashes with Mexico were some obvious aftereffects of this dispute, and even in times of peace, ill feeling remained intense between our two peoples.

At first, this argument was mainly legal. No less than twenty-two border locations were suggested before Spain and the United States could finally agree on a boundary, sixteen years after the sale was completed. In addition at least sixteen different proposals were made for location of a "Neutral Ground" strip of land straddling the border. Both nations would agree not to occupy this strip with settlers or troops, thereby creating a buffer zone to keep disputes at a minimum. The Treaty of 1819 was finally ratified by both nations on February 22, 1821. It provided that the western boundary of the Louisiana Purchase would be located by starting at the mouth of the Sabine River on the Gulf of Mexico, then angling north and west about to the Rockies and northwest from there to Canada. The line followed the present eastern and northern borders of Texas, thereby excluding all of Texas from the purchase, but including among other states the largest portion of the plains states of Colorado, Oklahoma, Montana, Kansas, and North and South Dakota, plus all of Nebraska.

The northern boundary, however, remained to be settled. The original purchase called for the United States to receive all lands drained by the Missouri River. That included 9,715 square miles of Great Plains now lying in Alberta and Saskatchewan north of the present Canadian-United States boundary. However, it left parts of western Minnesota, northern North Dakota, and a small corner of South Dakota in Canadian ownership. In 1818, America and Great Britain agreed to exchange these bits of land, thereby straightening the line and placing the boundary at the 49th Parallel, where it exists today.

Thus by 1821, all looked calm and settled. Unfortunately, however, the treaty with Spain did not erase angers and disputes that arose on both sides. Americans had been allowed to establish colonies in Spanish Texas under local settlement charters. One of these was headed by Stephen F. Austin, a Missourian whose father, Moses, had led a band of farmers to the present location of the city of Austin. A number of similar settlements also were established, so that the Spanish gradually became concerned and finally closed their border to further immigration. Still, in a land of unsurveyed borders and few government officials, Americans continued to drift across in growing numbers. The confusion this caused was compounded by a troubled and fiery Mexican priest named Miguel Hidalgo y Costilla, who arose in his pulpit at Dolores Hidalgo on September 16, 1810, and instead of chanting the 6 A.M. mass, turned his native land around a corner and headed it down the long road toward liberty. "Long Live Our Lady of Guadalupe!" he shouted, "Long Live Independence! Death to the Spaniards!"

Those phrases set off a powder keg, and within days, 100,000 mestizos and Indians rallied to Hidalgo's revolt. Within a year, the little priest had been captured and executed, but another priest took up the fight and carried it forward. He too was captured and executed and for a time the revolt appeared crushed. Periodic flare-ups continued, however, and in December 1820, a Spanish army unit under Agustín de Iturbide was sent into the northern provinces to quell a routine uprising. Instead of fighting the Indians, Iturbide joined them and soon led the Mexicans on a swift campaign to overthrow the Spaniards. Hidalgo's "Cry of Dolores" rallied the countryside and Iturbide's troops captured Mexico City in September 1821.

This turn of events threw the Treaty of 1819 into doubt, and delayed clear understanding of the Mexican-United States border for decades. In February and March of 1836, the problem was compounded when a gathering of 150 frontier-toughened Americans battered a force of 4,000 to 6,000 Mexican troops before being annihilated in the Battle of the Alamo. Antonio López de Santa Anna, the Mexican general who finally captured the embattled little church, also executed 330 other Texans captured in a second campaign nearby. The American settlements were enraged by these actions, and gathered a little army of 800—nearly every able man in the province—under General Sam Houston. Santa Anna, leading a force of 1,500, drove Houston back from the battle region of southern Texas on a long retreat. But the Mexicans became overconfident and during a customary siesta on the afternoon of September 21, Houston's army attacked and in a twenty-minute fusillade wrecked the Mexican force and sent the remnants fleeing. The next day, Santa Anna himself was captured and forced to sign a treaty acknowledging the independence of Texas. This treaty,

The Battle of San Jacinto on April 21, 1836 gave the Texans victory in their War of Independence, but General Sam Houston suffered a Mexican bullet wound in the ankle that day. Here he's been knocked from his horse in the midst of the fray. (C. E. LESTER, *The Life of Sam Houston*, NEW YORK, 1855)

however, remained in dispute for years, so when the Texas government decided to join the Union in 1845, Mexico took exception and declared war. This time facing the United States Army, Mexico again lost, and in 1848 gave up all claims to Texas and parts of New Mexico, Colorado, Kansas, Oklahoma, and Wyoming. The entire Great Plains region south of the Canadian border was now in United States ownership.

In Canada, somewhat later, a curious set of circumstances found the United States momentarily pitted against the Canadian government for ownership of Rupert's Land—including large portions of the Great Plains regions of Alberta and Saskatchewan. Rupert's Land was owned by the Hudson's Bay

Company and included all river basins draining into Hudson Bay. This was part of the Company's original 1670 charter, but in 1869 those lands were sold to the Canadian government. The sale was delayed, however, during a dispute over the price, and several leaders in the American government quietly began preparations to complete the purchase for the United States. Word of this leaked out and caused such alarm in Canada that envoys were dispatched immediately to London to forestall the American purchase. The transfer of Rupert's Land to Canadian ownership was then completed the following year.

Thus was ownership of the Great Plains removed from the hands of Spain, France, Mexico, and Great Britain, and given over to Canada and the United States. The transition started with the Louisiana Purchase on April 30, 1803, and ended with the conversion of Rupert's Land to the Canadian government in 1870. It now remained for the people of the two nations to examine these lands and determine the value—if any—of their purchases. Hardly, in fact, was the ink dry on the first of the transfers before two groups of unusual young men set out for their government to explore the new lands. The first of these journeys proved to be one of the most curious and puzzling in the annals of our history.

CHAPTER 9

The Great
American Desert

Prior to the Louisiana Purchase, only three crossings of the Great Plains had been recorded in history—that of the Mallet brothers in 1739–40, the long western walk of Anthony Hendry in 1754–55, and the several crossings of Pedro Vial late in the eighteenth century. But immediately following American purchase of the vast Louisiana tract, exploration of the Plains moved ahead rapidly and with vigor. In the years 1804 to 1807, five separate crossings were made, four going to Santa Fe while the fifth, the Lewis and Clark expedition, reached the Pacific Ocean. The four going to Santa Fe, or "St. Afee," as it was commonly written, included three junkets by merchant traders, plus the army expedition of Lieutenant Zebulon Montgomery Pike.

The merchant traders included a pair of political innocents named Baptiste La Lande and James Purcell. The third "merchant," Philip Nolan, is a shadowy figure but seems to have been a double agent in the employ of both Spain and the American Aaron Burr conspirators. Nolan traveled extensively on the southern plains and during one crossing was killed in a skirmish with Spanish troops. Other members of his party, however, were captured and taken to the New Mexican capital, then later returned to their Mississippi settlements.

La Lande, a bold, knowledgeable, frontier opportunist, had been hired by William Morrison, a St. Louis trader, to see if he could penetrate that elusive Spanish market by a direct mercantile assault. La Lande left St. Louis in the spring of 1804 carrying a quantity of kettles, knives, cloth, and other valuables, and headed west along the Missouri. He followed the Kansas River to the Republican, angled north to the Platte, then continued on for an unknown distance before turning almost due south to intercept the Arkansas in southeastern Colorado. With him were several Pawnees who led him along this age-old Indian trade route and who agreed to guide him to Santa Fe. Arriving on the Arkansas, however, he was intercepted by a platoon of Spanish cavalry. The dragoons were diplomatic. They had come to accompany him to Santa Fe. Yes, it would be acceptable to sell his trade goods there. He might also like to settle down and stay among the Spanish? No, he thought he'd return to St. Louis. But the governor himself had asked that La Lande remain in Santa Fe for a long visit. After all, he could hardly refuse the governor. Besides, there were all those dangers in crossing the plains, and the Spanish did not want anything ugly to happen to their guest.

So La Lande was made to realize that their polite invitation left him little choice, and he reluctantly agreed to settle down to life as a citizen of the Spanish capital. His hosts made certain his life was easy and pleasant, and he soon used Morrison's trade money to buy a permanent residence. For the Spanish, that was just fine. They did not want to stir any new trouble into the already strained Spanish-American relations. But neither did they want La Lande to return to St. Louis to open a floodgate for Great Plains traders.

The next plains crossing was made the following year by the American, James Purcell, and two French voyageurs named Lacroix and Terien. They also were based at St. Louis, and in the spring of 1805 departed that city to trade with Indians along the Platte. But after arriving at that river, they wandered west, were captured by Kiowas, escaped to the south, were picked up by Apaches, and finally arrived at Santa Fe.

This time the Spaniards were less subtle. The three wanderers were not to return to St. Louis. Neither would they be imprisoned as a drain on the Spanish colony. Instead they would be allowed to work at various tasks of carpentry or manual labor and could thereby earn their fare in this Spanish "outdoor prison."

At the same time, but farther south, Nolan was carrying out his part of the tense drama then growing between Spain and the United States. The tension, of course, was over the purchase of the Louisiana Territory and the disputed boundary between the two nations. The complexity of Nolan's actions during this period have never been successfully unravelled, but it was clear he was playing one side against the other for personal gain. His duplicity, however, may also have been part of the larger scheme of the Aaron Burr conspirators, although that has always remained uncertain. In any case, he was a confidant of Commanding General James B. Wilkinson, then head of the entire United States army. That in itself was enough to cast doubt on any of Nolan's activities. Wilkinson was a renowned scoundrel and traitor, but more crafty and dangerous than the mine run of traitors this country has known. During the Revolution, he served with Benedict Arnold and Aaron Burr in the same command—all three later being tarred with the brush of treason. But for their treasons, Arnold was executed and Burr ruined. Wilkinson escaped both fates and continued in high office to the end of his life.

He accomplished this shady career first by keeping his tracks well covered and second by turning informer against coconspirators when discovery proved imminent. He also made prime use of the difficulties of communication and travel, acting on his own whenever it suited his needs. He was party to the Conway Cabal, an abortive smear campaign against General Washington that developed immediately after the Revolution began. When the seams of that intrigue began to leak, Wilkinson exposed his partners and posed in righteous indignation as a Washington supporter. The trick failed and he had to quit his post as brigadier general. When the heat eased out of that venture, he was able to reenter the army in 1779. Two years later he resigned again to avoid a court-martial over some doubtful auditing reports and missing public property. He went west to Ohio, then to New Orleans. He became a spy for the Spanish and was given a salary of $2,000 per year. By the mid 1780s, he had met

General James Wilkinson (1757–1825), an infamous traitor who took pay from two governments and plotted to create a third while serving as chief of the American army. He assigned Lt. Pike to conduct the western expedition. (Painting by James Sharpless, Independence Hall, Philadelphia)

Nolan and the two were conspiring to obtain frontier information for sale to the American government. In 1791, President Washington was desperately in need of trained officers, and appointed Wilkinson a lieutenant colonel in the frontier army. It was a move that nearly led to destruction of the Union.

Wilkinson rose steadily and soon found himself second in command to General "Mad" Anthony Wayne. Pushing hard, he started a campaign to discredit Wayne, and when Wayne conveniently died in 1796, Wilkinson became commanding general of the American army. He was still in the employ of the Spanish government at the time, serving as a spy. When Jefferson purchased the Louisiana Territory in 1803, Wilkinson arranged to have himself lead the army unit that took over the seat of government at New Orleans. While there, he also collected his spy's pay from the Spanish.

Another of his opportunities arose with the Burr conspiracy. The chance came when Thomas Jefferson and Aaron Burr, both members of the Democratic-Republican party, became locked in a battle for the presidency. The popular vote in 1800 had been close and the House of Representatives gave each man

73 electoral votes. The House then labored through 36 dead-locked ballots to select one or the other as president. Alexander Hamilton, highly regarded and then in retirement, finally threw his prestige behind Jefferson. This caused an uproar, gave Jefferson the presidency, and forced Burr to accept the vice-presidency. Matters worsened steadily until 1804, when Burr killed Hamilton in a duel. Indicted for murder and ruined politically, Burr went west to Ohio where he met Wilkinson, his old comrade in arms. The conspiracy they hatched was a plan to split the Union and establish a separate nation in the West, composed of lands then in dispute between Spain and the United States, but including Mexico as well. Burr, very popular in the West, would be emperor of the new nation—just as Napoleon had recently proclaimed himself emperor of France.

Into this heady alliance stepped Lieutenant Zebulon Montgomery Pike, a raw young infantry officer serving at a tiny army post near present Cincinnati. Wilkinson had known Pike's father in the Revolution, and he now transferred the young lieutenant to Kaskaskia in southern Illinois, along the Mississippi, with instructions to prepare himself for expeditions into the wilderness of the Louisiana Purchase.

Pike's place in the whole conspiracy has never been adequately understood, and remains essentially unmeasurable, primarily because he was an army officer acting under orders from a superior, but also because the conspiracy never reached a point where he was forced to decide his allegiances. Furthermore, Pike never exhibited a conspiratorial nature, being much too direct in temperament and personality, and too wedded to his uniform. He was a strong-willed man born of poor circumstances who believed the path to glory lay in super-soldiery. He idolized Wilkinson as a great leader, and the general used this subservience to mold Pike into one of his conspiratorial tools. But Pike himself, while proud, naive, and prudish, was probably not privy to the main conspiracy. He was perhaps a foolish man who allowed self-seeking ways to overcome reason and good sense. He was also a very courageous man—foolhardy some have said—but if for no other reason, his place in American history is held secure by the one difficult and dangerous journey he made across the Great Plains.

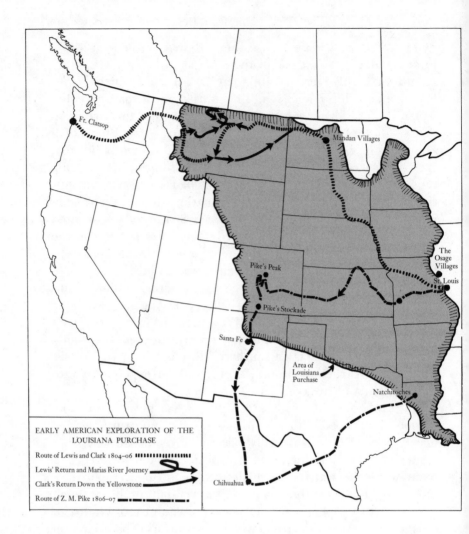

EARLY AMERICAN EXPLORATION OF THE
LOUISIANA PURCHASE

Route of Lewis and Clark 1804–06 ▪▪▪▪▪▪▪▪▪▪▪▪▪▪
Lewis' Return and Marias River Journey
Clark's Return Down the Yellowstone
Route of Z. M. Pike 1806–07 ▬ ▬ ▬ ▬ ▬

Ft. Clatsop

Mandan Villages

The
Osage
Villages

St. Louis

Pike's Peak

Pike's Stockade

Santa Fe

Area of
Louisiana
Purchase

Natchitoches

Chihuahua

Wilkinson had ordered Pike to Kaskaskia in 1804. In 1805 the general sent his protégé to find the headwaters of the Mississippi, and while there to warn British traders not to venture onto American soil. The headwaters mission was a convenient smoke screen, designed supposedly to accommodate President Jefferson's expressed interest in exploration of the Louisiana Purchase. But Wilkinson's real reason was to scare British fur traders out of the North. The many-sided general had entered the fur trade himself, and was on a campaign to eliminate competition. His position as commander of the American Army included authority to issue fur-trade permits. He pressured the prominent Chouteau family, renowned St. Louis fur traders, into helping with his designs. As trader-traitor, Wilkinson now found himself with income from the Spanish government, the American army, and the commercial fur trade. Despite all this, and while continuing to serve as commander of the army, he was appointed governor of the Louisiana Territory in 1805, thus becoming the most powerful figure in western America. No wonder Pike, a lowly frontier lieutenant, was flattered to carry out the great leader's slightest wish.

In the spring of 1806, shortly after Pike returned from his junket up the Mississippi, Wilkinson ordered him to prepare for an expedition to the headwaters of the Arkansas and Red rivers. Lewis and Clark were just then heading back down the Missouri at the end of their long journey to the West, and Wilkinson's sense of timing drove him to get Pike's trip underway before they returned.

Pike's written orders from Wilkinson were lengthy and detailed. He was first to return a group of Osage Indians to their village on the Osage River in eastern Kansas. He was then to proceed farther west and seek an understanding with the Comanches. "As your interview with the Comanches will probably lead you to the head branches of the Arkansas and Red Rivers," the orders continued, "you may find yourself approximated to the settlements of New Mexico. There it will be necessary you should move with great circumspection, to keep clear of any hunting or reconnoitering parties from that province, and to prevent alarm or offense; the affairs of Spain and the

United States appear to be on the point of amicable adjustment, and moreover it is the desire of the President to cultivate the friendship and harmonious intercourse of all nations of the earth, particularly our near neighbors the Spaniards."

Such phrasing was written almost as though Wilkinson expected it to be read by the Spaniards. Throughout the remainder of the long set of written orders, he was equally careful and proper, so that anyone who read the document could find no fault with it.

It was the *unwritten* orders that have fascinated scholars of the Pike expedition. Wilkinson probably sensed that Pike was too much a patriot, too proud of his uniform to ever join a direct conspiracy against his country. He therefore apparently asked Pike to go to New Mexico as a spy, and out of patriotism Pike agreed. It would be a difficult and dangerous mission to be carried out in the service of his homeland. In fact, however, if Pike succeeded at all, he would pioneer a trail that might be followed by an invading force of western American malcontents— with Aaron Burr as their leader and James B. Wilkinson as their general. That at least looked like the plot being hatched, and Pike would be its lead scout, whether he knew it or not.

And so, on July 15, 1806, Pike and his little detachment loaded into two keelboats and set off up the Missouri from an army encampment north of St. Louis. The party included Lt. Pike in command, with Lt. James Biddle Wilkinson, son of the general, as its second in command. There was a sergeant, 2 corporals, 16 privates, a somewhat mysterious surgeon named Dr. John Hamilton Robinson, the interpreter Antoine Vasquez, and 59 Indian men, women, and children. Hardly had they put paddle to water, however, before an express canoe containing two patriot Spaniards pushed off silently from below the encampment and headed down the Mississippi at top speed. Tucked in the duffle of one was an urgent dispatch addressed to General Don Nimesio Salcedo at Chihuahua, Spanish governor of the northern provinces of Mexico. He was to learn the size, direction, and armament of Pike's expedition before it was well started, and he would have a troop of cavalry riding hard for the north long before Pike had entered Spanish territory.

Pike's little force pushed up the Missouri slowly, finally arriving at the Osage villages in central Kansas in a state of nervous exhaustion. In a month, they had traveled five hundred miles through dangerous Indian territory. At the villages, Pike delivered the freed Osages to their tribal bosom amid great outpourings of joy, weeping, embraces, and festivities. "The whole ensemble," Pike wrote in his prudish tones, "was such as to make polished society blush, when compared with those savages, in whom the passions of the mind, either joy, grief, fear, anger, or revenge, have their full scope: Why cannot we correct the baneful passions without weakening the good?"

Next day, however, the Indians' joy gave way to their cannier senses of profit, and Pike was allowed to purchase only 37 horses, at exorbitant prices, and at that the scraggliest of the 700 to 800 owned by the Osages. He needed many more. He tried patience and threats. He appealed to their honor. He told them the Great White Father in Washington would be displeased and would not free others of their tribe. But nothing worked. Thirty-seven bony hay-burners were all they'd sell. Pike was forced to pull together what he had and on September 1, 1806 headed west into the Great Plains—part of his troop moving along on foot.

For three weeks, the little band of 23 whites, 30 Osage warriors, and one Indian woman drifted west. It seemed a ludicrous little column. Yet the future public image of the Great Plains was being shaped during this time by observations taking form in Lieutenant Pike's brain, and this image would endure in America for the next fifty years. His thoughts about the plains, in fact, soon drove Pike to write the following unfortunate passage in his journal:

"Numerous have been the hypotheses formed by various naturalists," he wrote, "to account for the vast tract of untimbered country which lies between the waters of the Missouri, Mississippi, and the western Ocean, from the mouth of the latter river to the 48th degree north latitude. Although not flattering myself to be able to elucidate that, which numbers of highly scientific characters have acknowledged to be beyond their depth of research; still I would not think I had done my country justice did I not give birth to what few lights my examination of those internal deserts has enabled me to acquire. In that vast country of which we speak, we find the soil generally dry and sandy, with gravel, and discover that the moment we approach a stream, the land becomes more humid with small timber; I therefore conclude that this country never was timbered, as from the earliest age, the aridity of the soil having so few water courses running through it, and they being principally dry in summer, has never afforded moisture sufficient to support the growth of timber. In all timbered land, the annual discharge of the leaves, with the continual decay of old trees and branches, creates a manure and moisture, which is preserved from the heat of the sun not being permitted to direct his rays perpendicularly but only to pass them obliquely through the foliage. But here a barren soil, parched and dried up for eight months in the year, presents neither moisture nor nutrition sufficient to nourish the timber. These vast plains of the western hemisphere may become in time equally celebrated as the sandy desarts of Africa; for I saw in my route in various places tracts of many leagues where the wind had thrown up the sand, in all the fanciful forms of the ocean's rolling wave, and on which not a speck of vegetable matter existed."

Thus it was that the first inkling of a "Great American Desert" came into being. Stephen H. Long, during his western travels in 1821, added to Pike's observations on this point and intensified the belief. Soon the name itself, Great American Desert, was allowed to sprawl in large type across all maps of the Great Plains region, there to remain for the next half century. But Pike started that vision with his journal passage. The Great American Desert marked the limit of west-bound agriculture, the wall through which settlers could not penetrate nor enemies attack. It frightened off unknown thousands who felt wiser staying east of the region, rather than attempt the dangerous passage to Kansas or Colorado. Instead they opted for a straight-line passage to Oregon and California and in the process changed our national direction entirely. The desert concept brought introduction of both camels and the westering wagon caravan—adaptations drawn directly from the Arab approach to desert travel.

Of course the plains were one of the world's richest grazing lands, the buffalo had proved that, and barely two pages earlier in his journal, Pike himself commented that the region was rich with grass eaters. "Of all countries ever visited by the footsteps of civilized man, there never was one probably that produced game in greater abundance. . . . I believe that there are buffalo, elk, and deer sufficient on the banks of the Arkansaw alone if used without waste, to feed all the savages in the United States territory one century." The connection between agriculture and vast grazing lands had not at that time been established, how-ever, hence farmers saw little future in the plains. There were as yet no railroads, barbed wire, slaughterhouses, or refrigera-tion. If the plains couldn't be plowed, they were worthless. That in essence was what Lieutenant Pike told his countrymen. Far from "doing his country justice" by his comments, he delayed settlement of the Great Plains for more than half a cen-tury, and marked it a certainty to be the last west of our conti-nent.

Lieutenant Zebulon Montgomery Pike, who led a small band of American sol-diers across the central plains and into Spanish-held territory in 1806–07. He probably knew nothing of the Burr-Wilkinson conspiracy. This painting was made after Pike became a general, and shortly before his death in the War of 1812. (PAINTING BY CHARLES WILLSON PEALE, INDEPENDENCE HALL, PHILADELPHIA)

Pike's little troop marched on, finally arriving at the Pawnee villages on the Republican River, somewhere near the present Kansas-Nebraska border. The Pawnees were friendly, very numerous, and great lovers of ceremony. Pike proved himself equal to their welcome and the first evening was guest at a grand dinner. At least it all looked welcome enough until trouble almost overcame the festivities. The Pawnees had become allies of the Spaniards in recent years, and now a flag of Spain flew on a staff before the door of the Pawnee chief. Pike, the patriot, was stunned when he saw it there, on this new American soil. In fact, the large force of Spanish cavalry sent to intercept Pike had been at the same village only a week before under leadership of Lieutenant Don Facundo Melgares. Undaunted, Pike demanded that the Pawnees remove the Spanish flag and replace it with the American flag. He told them this was United States territory and their father was now in Washington, not Mexico City. This brought on a sudden stiff silence, broken only by the heavy breathing of several hundred well-armed, and now angered Pawnees. They knew where their allegiances lay, and they would not be moved to change them without cause. So Pike carefully explained again that their new leader was President Jefferson, and that the Spanish flag must be removed. Another heavy silence. Finally, one of the old chieftains rose slowly, lowered the Spanish flag, and laid it at Pike's feet. He then took the American flag and raised it slowly, while all the Indians stoically allowed this solution.

For his side of it, Pike also found a solution. He took up the Spanish flag and presented it to the old chief. "I did not wish to embarrass them with the Spaniards," he wrote, "for it was the wish of the Americans that their red brethren should remain peaceably around their own fires, and not embroil themselves in any disputes between the white people; and for fear the Spanish might return there in force again, I returned them their flag, but with an injunction that it should never be hoisted during our stay." This gave the Pawnees an acceptable solution, and the banquet ended in a contented mood.

Next day, however, the old chief tried to prevent Pike from going farther, saying he had stopped Melgares from pushing eastward, and had promised the Spaniard he would also make Pike turn back. But Pike would not turn back. His little force headed out of the village under menacing conditions, all the Pawnees well armed and on the move. Pike kept his party compact, and "marched on by a road round the village, in order that if attacked the savages would not have their houses to fly to for cover. I had given orders not to fire until within five or six paces, and then to charge with the bayonet and sabre, when I believed it would have cost them at least 100 men to have exterminated me—which would have been necessary." The determination of the little force was too much for the Indians, and they gradually pulled back and let the troop climb a nearby slope and continue on their way.

Pike was now far out on the open plains and attempting to follow Melgares' track. From the nightly campsites, he estimated Spanish strength at 350 to 400 men. He had decided to follow them, he wrote, "because they had competent guides." But the tracks of the Spanish horses blended into a maze of buffalo tracks, and then the little column was thoroughly lost. Pike and Dr. Robinson rode ahead to search it out, but the sea of grass on the endless plains was too much—and shortly they were both lost from the main column. For four days they wandered about in a tangle of tracks, trying to find a way back to their troop. On October 17 Pike wrote: "Our own situation was not the most agreeable, not having more than four rounds of ammunition each, and 400 miles in the nearest direction from the first civilized inhabitant; we, however, concluded to search for them on the morrow, and if we did not succeed in finding them, to strike for the Arkansaw, where we were in hopes to discover some traces, if not cut off by the savages. ..." Next morning, they saw two riders approaching, who turned out to be members of the main party. The troop was only three miles away, camped on the Arkansas.

Here they rested for nine days, hacking a dugout from the only tree they could find, and building a second boat of buffalo skins stretched over a wooden frame. They also held a shooting match, aiming at a target on the stump of the tree. This excited the interest of the lone dog that had been lapping along at the feet of the troopers, and when Bowser went to investigate the target, "one of the balls struck him on the head and killed him."

The delay here was costly. The soft fall days that called the troopers to play were fading, and every hour lost would exact its toll in the weeks ahead. Finally, on October 28, Lieutenant Wilkinson, the general's weakly son, started downstream with his six men to explore the Arkansas. They went in the two makeshift boats, young Wilkinson grumbling at the limited supplies and little ammunition he was given. "My son," the general had written Pike, "has the foundation of a good constitution but it must be tempered by degrees—do not push him beyond his capacities in hardship too suddenly. He will I hope attempt anything, but let the stuff be hardened by degrees." Now young Wilkinson was headed down the river, back toward his father's command, supposedly to explore the course of the Arkansas. It would be the most dangerous adventure of his life, and he would nearly perish. Later he complained bitterly of Pike—who was however now faced with far greater problems of his own.

After sending Wilkinson on his way, Pike headed west against all reason into a Great Plains winter. He had no tents, little ammunition, not enough bedding to provide one blanket for each man, and a paucity of clothing. The least sensitive of practiced plainsmen, even well equipped with all these items, would have holed up under a protective bank of the river, stored a great pile of jerky and buffalo chips, and there awaited the coming of spring. But Pike had no appreciation for the plains, and knew nothing of the winters there. So late in that October, with a harsh wind blowing and snow on the ground, he headed west with his sixteen men to cross the plains.

Pike's group did not lack for food, at least not immediately. One afternoon in early November, the north shore of the river was ". . . covered with animals; which when we came to them proved to be buffalo cows and calves. I do not believe it an exaggeration to say there were 3,000 in one view. . . . I will not attempt to describe the droves of animals we now saw; the face of the prairie was covered with them . . . their numbers exceeded imagination." He commented on buffalo, deer, elk, antelope, wild horses, coyotes, cougars, and bands of wolves as well as masses of large birds. The feral horses (he called them wild) were exceedingly curious and galloped up to look the group over. In the chases that followed, none was caught, but both men and horses appeared to enjoy the frolic.

Slowly, however, game animals began to thin out as the tiny squadron pushed west and the bitterness of winter settled in. The men began to suffer chills and fevers in their cotton uniforms. Their shoes had fallen apart long since, and makeshift moccasins barely protected their feet. The blistering heat of August was replaced now by a bruising cold and a wind they could lean their rifles against. One day a marauding band of several hundred Pawnees intercepted them in a cottonwood grove, suddenly, and demanded presents. As the Indians milled around his mounted men, Pike called for a smoke of peace. The ruse worked, and the temper went out of the encounter as everyone sat down to a council. Pike talked long about the new white father who was coming to help them with peace and presents, and to show them he meant what he said, he gave them such small gifts as he had. Some of the group were satisfied while others scorned the gifts and cast them aside. Pike called for his men to mount up. When one of the Indians tried to seize his pistols, he shouted that he would shoot the first man who tried to stop him. His men were able to separate themselves from the tribe in a wild melee of shouts and milling horses. Miraculously, no shots were fired, an act that would have ended the expedition on the spot. They kept on up a slight rise and out of danger, losing some small items of equipment to the angry tribesmen.

On November 15, Pike spotted "a small blue cloud" far ahead on the horizon. As he looked through his spy glass, his hands numb with cold, he gradually realized it was a mountain —snow capped, low, and dead ahead. He immediately named it Grand Peak. A little later that day they could see it clearly and decided they had arrived at "The Mexican Mountains." In fact, they were still one hundred miles east of the present Front Range, the beginning of the Rockies, but the immensity of that massif and the clear air of eastern Colorado deceived them all

—as it would countless other travelers who followed. On November 24, they arrived at what Pike believed was the base of his Grand Peak, and leaving most of the troop below, he and three others started to climb. Three days later, after nearly freezing one night in a small cave, they gave up the climb only a short distance up the side of the formidable mountain. Wind, snow, and bitter cold slashed the foursome, driving them back.

Pike consequently never did reach more than a short distance up the slope of his Grand Peak. Nonetheless, the great mountain was indelibly marked by this little excursion, and the name that stuck to it in later years would not be Grand Peak, but Pike's Peak, a 14,110-foot block of Rocky Mountain granite that is one of the scenic wonders of this continent. Many, many others had seen it before Pike—countless Indians, hundreds of Spaniards, and a sizable number of wandering, unknown French traders. The Spaniards, in fact, had been there two hundred years before Pike. But it would become Pike's Peak to the thousands of new Americans who were soon to trace his footsteps across the plains. It was in fact his only encounter with the mountain, and the weather quickly drove him south, away from it, in search of food and shelter.

The thermometer he carried was registering subzero temperatures and several of his men were suffering now from frostbite. A blizzard struck, and the horses had no food except such miserable scratchings as they could obtain through the snow. While fording a river, two men had their feet frozen. One of the horses, crazed with hunger and cold, went berserk and ran off down a valley. Another had to be shot for food. On December 5, they were near present Canon City, Colorado, where they built a makeshift camp to wait out another storm. Soon they were out again, and for the next three weeks plowed back and forth along mountain valleys searching for the headwaters of the Arkansas and Red rivers. They were, of course, nowhere near the Red, but they did find a river flowing northeast. "Must it not be the headwaters of the Platte?" Pike wrote. This time he guessed correctly, though he was some distance from its headwaters.

Christmas was spent in camp, with plenty of buffalo meat and roaring fires, but in the two weeks that followed, they survived for days without food, froze their feet, lost horses, were lost themselves, and became separated from each other. In mid-January, they went four days without food before killing a buffalo. Two of the men could no longer stand, their feet were so injured by frostbite. They had to be left behind, fortified by piles of firewood, as much food as could be spared, and enough ammunition to sustain themselves if game passed nearby.

Pike and the others straggled south, searching for the Red River—at least that was his claim and his journal entries follow that line of thought. But rather than finding the Red, they stumbled onto the headwaters of the Rio Grande, deep in Spanish-held territory, and about one hundred miles north of Santa Fe. Here they built a small fort, raised the American flag, and tried through hunting and rest to regain their strength.

More was now taking place in this little camp than met the eye, however, and the first moves in a new game were soon to be

Lt. Pike's stockade in Spanish territory is believed to have looked like this. A replica has been constructed near Alamoso in south central Colorado. The cottonwood-log stockade measured thirty-six feet square and twelve feet high. (DENVER PUBLIC LIBRARY)

played. Though there is no written evidence to prove it, Pike must have known he was in Spanish territory. He knew, for example, that the Louisiana Purchase extended only to the Rocky Mountains—not into them. Yet here at his little fort he had passed across the plains and was into the mountains. If he knew of this "error" he of course also realized that his presence represented a military intrusion during a time of tension between the United States and Spain.

However, the major thrust of Pike's unwritten orders, so critics say, could only be accomplished by getting himself captured by the Spanish. They would then take him to Santa Fe for questioning. During this visit to the Spanish capital, Pike would have opportunity to observe the strength and disposition of enemy forces, and would gain firsthand knowledge of the country to be traversed. The Spanish, however, would have to release him, both for lack of evidence that he actually was spying, and because jailing him would severely increase tension between the two nations. With the northern Spanish colony lying at the far end of a 2,000-mile supply line, and with American strength at midcontinent increasing steadily, conflict along this border could only be decided in favor of the United States. Both the Burr conspirators and the Mexican governor at Chihuahua knew this. And Pike had now interjected himself in such a way that he could serve as the pawn to be maneuvered.

The Spanish, when they found him, which was soon, chose diplomacy. They arrived on the morning of February 26, a force of one hundred dragoons in charge of Lieutenant Bartholomeo Fernandez, who courteously sat down to breakfast with the American leader. The breakfast settled into a sparring match:

Fernandez: "Señor Pike, we would like to show you to the headwaters of the Red River, if that is what you seek."

Pike: "What, you mean this is not the Red River?"

Fernandez: "Ah, no. This is the Rio Grande. You see you are in Spanish territory."

Pike: "Are you positive of this?"

Fernandez: "Yes, of course, this has always been Spanish territory."

Pike: "Sergeant! Lower our flag at once. I deeply regret this intrusion into your lands, Lieutenant. Please forgive me. I was looking for the Red River, and having never been here, I sought a river flowing southward."

Fernandez: "Yes, Lieutenant, the Rio Grande does flow south. To Santa Fe. Our governor would like you to come to visit him there. He thought perhaps I would find you here."

Pike: "You knew I was here? But how could that be? I did not know myself I would be here."

Fernandez: "We received reports, Lieutenant. We rather expected you. May we leave for Santa Fe this morning?"

Pike: "But of course, Lieutenant. I would be pleased to offer my respects to your governor, and my apologies as well. But some of my men have been left behind. I will need to bring them out of the mountains before leaving this post."

Fernandez: "My men will attend to them today, and we can leave in the morning."

So the second half of Pike's mission would now be accomplished. The journey was delayed, however, until February 28, when Pike and his little band were shepherded south toward the Spanish capital. Part of the Spanish force and a few Americans stayed behind to rescue the men with frozen feet, who survived but were crippled. Meantime, the main force arrived in Santa Fe on March 3, 1807, and became "guests" of the Spanish for the next four months. During that period they were taken on the long overland journey to Chihuahua to see the governor. The Spanish tried several times to trick Pike into an admission of spying, and the lieutenant was "interviewed" by Spanish authorities on a number of occasions. Each time he stuck to his story that he became lost while searching for the Red River, and that he was on a scientific and geographic expedition. Finally they agreed to return him to Louisiana and after a sandy, dry-spit journey over the southern plains, he entered the Mississippi River village of Natchitoches on July 1, 1807, ending a journey just two weeks short of a year in length. The Spanish had kindly sent a cavalry column to accompany the little troop back to the United States—and carefully saw that the lieutenant didn't tire himself making notes.

Pike found his country in an uproar over the Burr conspiracy. During the young lieutenant's absence in the West, some thorny official suspicions had begun to sprout around Wilkinson and Burr. To save his own skin, Wilkinson exposed the plot. He reported to his superior, Secretary of War Henry Dearborn, that Burr had collected men and supplies on the Ohio River and had then headed southward down the Mississippi, stopping frequently to gather personal support. Wilkinson said Burr was waiting for an incident to arise between Americans and Spanish along the Sabine River border, then still in dispute. Whenever the incident occurred, Wilkinson claimed Burr would raise his army of indignant westerners, march west, thrash the Spanish, take over their territory, and form it into an independent nation. To prove his innocence, Wilkinson had hustled off to the border himself, made a stab at working out a neutral ground treaty—what we might call a demilitarized zone—then scurried back to New Orleans to repel Burr's "invasion." Burr was arrested in Mississippi shortly before Pike returned to Natchitoches. That fall, the sensational Burr trial took place in Richmond. Wilkinson, too, was later court-martialed, and though both men were acquitted, they did not escape severe public censure. Pike, because he was involved with Wilkinson, suffered this rancor as well and long felt he deserved more generous treatment than he received from his government. Perhaps his greatest irritation was against those countrymen who dubbed him with the wry title "The Lost Pathfinder." The name stuck, however, and he carried it to the end of his life.

Pike remained in the army and eventually rose to the rank of major. General Wilkinson, being acquitted during his court-martial, remained in command on the Mississippi and tried to elevate his young protégé to the post of Indian agent for the western territories. The government, however, refused to confirm the appointment. When the War of 1812 broke out, Pike was commissioned a brigadier general and on April 27, 1813, led a 1,500-man landing force in an assault on York, Ontario, now Toronto. The fighting was sharp, and heavy casualties resulted on both sides. As the British retreated, they fired a powder magazine left behind. It exploded and mortally wounded the thirty-four-year-old general. He died the next day.

Pike's life will forever be shaded by the question of his involvement with the Burr conspiracy, and the value of his travels will likewise remain marred by an overzealous desire to please his commander. General Wilkinson's scheming had driven him onto the plains with insufficient planning, little equipment, and a vague or shrouded purpose. All that seriously undermined the value of the expedition. But Pike was exceptionally brave, and a disciplined leader who carried his men to the ends of their endurance and then brought them back again. He showed that he cared for them when it counted, and by his unflinching courage saved them on two occasions from certain massacre by Indians. It is also of singular interest that he led his tiny contingent of infantry through a vast region of hostile Indian country without ever firing a shot against anyone, either in defense or offense. He lost one man through desertion and two others during an incident near Santa Fe, for which he was blameless. His journals record only one instance when he had to mete out discipline—a severe tongue-lashing given one man who spoke of sedition toward the bitter end of the Great Plains journey.

Most of Pike's papers were kept by the Spanish for many years, but shrewdly—and dangerously—the young lieutenant rolled some of his written observations into his soldiers' gun barrels and so brought them back to be read by his countrymen. Had the Spanish discovered the trick, he might have been shot as a spy; yet he felt those papers of enough value to take the risk. They proved of great interest to the public, but unfortunately for Pike, they also served to raise suspicions about his involvement as a spy for Wilkinson and Burr.

It is now interesting to compare aspects of the much more widely known Lewis and Clark expedition with those of Lieutenant Pike. Back to back, the two journeys provided the American people with their first solid knowledge of the trans-Mississippi West. Yet despite many similarities between the two expeditions, there are several key points of contrast to observe as this gradual unfolding of the Great Plains continues.

CHAPTER 10

Pathfinders Across the Northern Plains

A tiny snow-fed mountain stream known as the Gallatin River rises at the western base of the Gallatin Range in southwestern Montana, threads its way northward, and at the town of Three Forks, Montana, joins the tumblings of two other young rivers, the Jefferson and the Madison. Together the three form the headwaters of the Missouri River. Adopting the direction of its parents, the Missouri continues along the western base of the Big Belt Mountains, but soon skirts their northern edge and breaks through onto the Great Plains. After spilling over a series of rock shelves at Great Falls, the now mature river turns due east and heads toward the Dakotas through gently rolling, treeless grasslands. As it travels, it gathers tribute from a series of smaller creeks and flowages, and by the time it arrives at the Dakota border, it is a very powerful river. The Yellowstone joins it at this point, having selected its own route eastward after rising in Yellowstone Lake along the other side of the same mountain range that creates the Gallatin. In short, the Missouri and the Yellowstone hold a large part of central Montana cradled between them, like an almond in a pair of pincers.

It is this piece of the Great Plains that Lewis and Clark examined as the first white travelers to the region, going west to the Pacific in 1805 and returning eastward in the summer of 1806. Their expedition was highly important to our history for many reasons, of course. But for the moment let us consider merely the Great Plains portion of that great adventure.

The three rivers that give rise to the Missouri were named for President Jefferson, Secretary of State James Madison, and Secretary of the Treasury Albert Gallatin. Aaron Burr as vice-president had defected from the government by this date and thus lost his chance to be remembered in American geography. Jefferson and Madison are understandable figures for a river-naming project, while Gallatin, at the strings of the American purse, may have been included out of a shrewd sense of expedition economics. But Gallatin was also very learned in western Indian cultures, and one aim of Lewis and Clark was to record in depth their impressions and observations of Indians met along the way. Thus, Gallatin's hand is seen resting lightly on the journals as the expedition fared across the continent, and such influence added inevitable zest to some of the most profoundly moving pieces of natural history in our literature.

Every day of the entire journey seemed to bring some new adventure to Lewis and Clark. Through the plains portion of the journals runs a thread of excitement, of new discovery, of men in contest winning victories day after day. Only one member of the group died during the entire expedition, Charles Floyd, who succumbed to a ruptured appendix near present Sioux City, Iowa. That record, however, leaves a false impression. Time after time, members of the expedition came within inches and seconds of death. Their survival in fact was based almost daily on quick thinking, tough frontier wisdom, and plain luck. As with the Pike expedition, they had frequent dangerous brushes with Indian tribes, who nearly always outnumbered them overwhelmingly. Pike came through without shooting or being shot at during his entire yearlong journey. Lewis and Clark were almost as sensible, though their expedition was marred by one encounter that left one Blackfoot dead and another at least sorely wounded. Considering that an almost constant state of warfare then prevailed between local Indian tribes, it is all the more remarkable that Lewis and Clark could pass through safely.

One reason was their native respect for the several Indian cultures they encountered. They willingly accepted the hierarchy of social values and customs they found. They seemed to see themselves as equals, and became friends with many Indians they met. The vision lingers of Captain Clark returning to Fort Mandan after a hunt along the Missouri River one bitterly cold December afternoon, then turning aside to stop and enjoy a pipe and a chat with Chief White Cloud before continuing on to his camp. It was the action of a friend in search of a moment of human companionship, nothing more. Lewis and Clark routinely invited the Mandans to visit the expedition's camp during evenings of fiddle playing, dancing, and general merriment—and the courtesy was returned. At first encounter, they also met on even terms with the Teton Sioux, though matters worsened later. And the encounter with the Blackfoot war party could only have been avoided had Lewis been less trusting and suspicious enough to stay clear of them.

The expedition, known as the Corps of Discovery, had been created by President Jefferson to examine parts of the new Louisiana Purchase, and also to search for a land route to the Pacific. Meriwether Lewis, an army captain, was chosen to lead the expedition. Born in Virginia in 1774, Lewis early came to Jefferson's attention and in 1801 became the President's private secretary. To share leadership duties, Lewis chose William Clark, born in 1770 as the younger brother of the famous Revolutionary War hero, George Rogers Clark. The choice was excellent. Where Lewis was quick, brilliant, and well educated, Clark was a solid, practical frontiersman. Both men were born leaders and outstanding intellectuals. They shared a deep and abiding curiosity, a gem-hard persistence in purpose, superb judgment, and a truly objective sense in observations. The two men quickly fell into an easy, workable relationship and though Lewis was the nominal leader, both exerted equal authority during the journey.

On May 21, 1804, the expedition set off without fanfare from St. Charles, Missouri, north of St. Louis, traveling up the Missouri in a keelboat, two pirogues, or dugouts, and six large canoes. The keelboat was fifty-five feet long and had a three-foot draft. It was driven by twenty-two oars, plus a square sail set on a stubby mast, used when the wind allowed. The dugouts were of six and seven oars respectively, and two men were assigned to each canoe. Travel was slow and tiresome against the current, but they kept moving steadily forward. In forty-four days the group of forty-eight soldiers and hired civilians crossed the present state of Missouri, and on July 4 camped at a site they appropriately named Independence—later to become Independence, Missouri.

Seventeen days later they had arrived at the mouth of the Platte and were still making steady progress. However, from the Platte north to the mouth of the Teton River, a distance of four hundred miles, their progress slowed, and they did not arrive at that stream, now known as the Bad River, until September 25, more than two months after leaving the Platte. Several villages of Teton Sioux were settled at the mouth of the Bad, and when the boats arrived, Indians crowded both shores. The boats tied up at an island in the river and at first all went well. The Sioux chiefs came on board the keelboat and received the American presents and a small glass of whiskey. But when they were taken ashore in the pirogue, the mood suddenly turned ugly. One of the chiefs staggered against Clark in feigned drunkenness, and several young Indian braves held the towline of the boat. Clark drew his sabre and called his men to arms. Instantly, the keelboat bristled with rifles, and the other pirogue headed to shore to help Clark.

"I felt My Self warm & Spoke in verry positive terms," Clark later wrote in his journal. After some brusque talk on both sides, Clark's reinforced shore party wrestled the pirogues away from the Indians and headed back to the keelboat. Clark had kept his head, for any bloodshed at that moment would have meant instant battle and almost certain destruction of the entire expedition.

Three days later, trouble arose again at the same location. Some of the Sioux chiefs had come on board to negotiate with the captains. Again a dispute arose, this time over tribute. It was expected that any white man who traveled this route must pay the Sioux. Sergeant John Ordway, who also kept a journal, tells what happened:

". . . Some of the chiefs were on bord insisting on our Staying until the others came. We told them we could not wait any longer. They then did not incline to let us go on. They Sayed we might return back with what we had or remain with them, but we could not go up the Missouri any further, about 200 Indians were then on the bank. Some had fire arms. Some had Spears. Some had a kind of cutlashes, and all the rest had Bows and steel or Iron pointed arrows. Several of the warriors Set by the chord where our boat the big Barge was tied. The 2 pirogues were tied on the outside of the Barge. Capt. Clark was Speaking to the chiefs in the cabbin. Capt. Lewis asked the chiefs if they were going out of the boat. They did not incline to. Then Capt. Lewis came out and ordered every man to his place, ordered the Sail hoisted, then one man went out and untied the chord, which the warrier had in his hand, then 2 or 3 more of their warriers caught hold of the chord and tyed it faster than before. Capt. Lewis then appeared to be angary, and told them to Go out of the Boat and the chief went out and Sayed we are sorry to have you go. But if you will Give us one carrit of tobacco we will be willing for you to go on & will not try to stop you. Capt. Lewis Gave it to them. The head chief Sayd then that we must Give him one more carrit of tobacco more for his warriers who held the chord and then we might go, boath of our Captains told him that we did not mean to be tri-fled with. Nor would not humer them any more, but would give him 1 carrit more for the warriers, if he would be a man of his word and Stand to his word like a man. The chief Sayd he was mad too, to see us Stand So much for 1 carrit of tobacco. If we would Give it we might go on. Capt. Lewis Gave it to him. He then took the chord in his hand & Gave it to us. We then set off under a gentle breeze which happened to be favourable.''

So it was a standoff. The Sioux received a token tribute of two "carrits"—dried tobacco twisted into a carrot shape—and the two groups parted company with a healthy respect for each other. That ended a four-day miracle—no one had shot at anyone.

The expedition continued on to the Mandan villages, located at that time about fifty miles above present Bismarck, North Dakota, well out onto the Great Plains. Two markers stand

This painting, "The Interior of the Hut of a Mandan Chief," shows the high, heavy-pole construction of the bark-covered lodges. Lewis and Clark spent many hours visiting such chieftains during their winter among the Mandans in 1804–05. (PAINTING BY CHARLES BODMER, *Travels in the United States*)

today on a high, windy slope overlooking the Missouri, but the actual site of the villages and the winter quarters the expedition occupied are now believed to be under the thread of the Big Muddy.

The Mandans had long been known as peaceable middlemen both in times of trade between Indian tribes, and later when the white men arrived. The Corps of Discovery arrived here on October 24 and immediately began to seek a favorable site for winter quarters. Winter months among the Mandans would prove a pleasant but adventuresome stay, with a few dangerous moments. On October 29, for example, a grass fire swept past the Corps' temporary riverside camp and Clark wrote the first

account in English of the dread speed of these Great Plains hol-
ocausts, later to prove so fearsome to our westering pioneers:

"The fire went with such velocity that it burnt to death a
man & woman, who Could not get to any place of Safty, one
man, a woman & Child also much burnt and Several narrowly
escaped the flame." One boy was saved when his mother in desperation flopped a heavy green, or fresh untanned elkskin over
him which prevented his patch of grass from burning.

"This fire passed our Camp last night about 8 oClock P.M. It
went with great rapitidity and looked Tremendious." Clark's
exuberant spelling should be approached for the bright sounds
it provides. Noah Webster's first dictionary, *The Compendious*,
was not published until 1806, and the general practice in American schools when Lewis and Clark were young was either to use a
stifling, academic, and much-overlooked English dictionary or
none at all. In fact, the many wonderful, varied, and delightful
ways Clark and several of the soldiers spelled their way west is
fascinating. It displayed acute ears and observant and creative
minds in a day before spelling was standardized.

Soon after the incident of the grass fire, the Corps found a
grove of cottonwoods below the Mandan villages and there
began construction of an L-shaped set of log dwellings. A stockade was built to complete the square and the whole troop
moved into the unfinished buildings on November 16. Clark
pronounced the work completed on November 20.

Now began a series of disputes that continued all winter
between and within local Indian factions. Lewis and Clark were
called time after time to judge and settle these arguments. As
one aim was to assure the future of United States commerce by
promoting an Indian peace, they obliged these requests as a
normal practice. In addition, they hunted steadily for buffalo
and elk, they kept their winter fires burning, and they kept
their guard up. At times the temperature dipped to forty below,
and frostbite was common. But all was not strictly business.
Clark's journal entry for January 5, 1805, describes in his blunt,
forthright manner a buffalo dance as practiced by the Mandans:

"I imploy my Self Drawing a Connection of the Countrey
from what information I have received. A Buffalow Dance for 3

nights past in the 1st Village, a curious Custom. The old men arrange themselves in a circle & after Smokeing a pipe which is handed them by a young man, Dressed up for the purpose, the young men who have their wives back of the Circle go each to one of the old men with a whining tone and request the old man to take his wife (who presents herself necked except a robe) and (to Sleep with her). The Girl then takes the Old Man (who verry often can scarcely walk) and leades him to a convenient place for the business, after which they return to the lodge; if the old man (or a white man) returns to the lodge without gratifying the Man & his wife, he offers her again and again; it is often the Case that after the 2d time without Kissing, the Husband throws a new robe over the old man &c. and begs him not to dispise him & his wife. (We sent a man to this Medisan Dance last night, they gave him 4 Girls). All this is to cause the buffalow to Come near So that they may Kill them."

Lewis had received some medical training prior to the expedition and he served as physician and surgeon for both his command and the local Indians. Sacajawea, the Snake Indian woman who would prove so valuable as guide and interpreter, gave birth to her first son at this camp on February 11, 1805. She was one of the wives of Toussaint Charbonneau, a Canadian frontiersman, and Lewis hired him into the party as a cook as soon as he learned of Sacajawea's nationality. Charbonneau was to prove as much a sniveling nuisance as she was a staunch and courageous aide. She carried her infant son on back and hip for more than three thousand miles with never a whimper and earned the undying respect and admiration of the entire command.

In mid-February, four members of the expedition were returning to camp with a load of buffalo meat on a horse-drawn sleigh when a band of about one hundred Sioux suddenly fell on them, stole two horses, caused an uproar, and dashed off. Next day, Lewis set out with twenty-four men to hunt them down, but they escaped across the plains.

In March, with winter softening, the troop began hacking away at some dugouts, and by the end of the month, ice was out of the river. In early April, the entire command packed and

made ready to go, and on April 7 at four in the afternoon everyone set out on the river. The keelboat was dispatched downstream to St. Louis in charge of six members of the Corps, plus
four French traders, carrying messages, pressed plant specimens,
journals, and animal hides to President Jefferson, also certain
baggage no longer needed. At the same moment, the main body
of the expedition pushed off upstream in the two pirogues and
six small canoes.

"This little fleet," wrote Lewis, "altho not quite so rispecta-
ble as those of Columbus or Capt. Cook, were still viewed by us
with as much pleasure as those deservedly famed adventurers
ever beheld theirs; and I dare say with quite as much anxiety
for their safty and preservation. We were now about to penetrate a country at least two thousand miles in width, on which
the foot of civilized man had never trodden. The good or evil it
had in store for us was for experiment yet to determine, and
these little vessells contained every article by which we were to
expect to subsist or defend ourselves."

The troop now consisted of 34 members, including the 2 captains, 3 sergeants, 23 privates, Lewis' black slave York, a tough
weathered hunter and interpreter named George Drewyer,
Charbonneau, Sacajawea and her infant son, and one unnamed
Mandan. In addition, Lewis' Labrador dog Scammon trotted at
the captain's heels—Lewis had elected to walk the first distance
—and Scammon would himself become a most weathered and
durable member of the troop.

For the next ten weeks, the expedition would pass through
the Great Plains on its way to the Great Falls of the Missouri,
just at the base of the Rockies. This period would prove by far
the most interesting and varied of the entire journey—at least
so far as American natural history is concerned. The toilsome
upriver progress was slow going against the turbulence of the
spring runoff, a circumstance that proved lucky for us as latter-
day readers. It prevented Lewis and Clark from moving too rapidly across the plains. It provided them ample chance to observe
and record the magnificence of the Great Plains in the spring-
time, on this first known occasion of a white man's presence
upriver from the Mandans.

Meriwether Lewis, 1774–1809. (Cor-
coran Gallery of Art, Washington)

William Clark, 1770–1838. (Charles
Willson Peale, Independence Hall,
Philadelphia)

It was for all hands clearly an exciting experience. The troop apparently was never out of sight of large numbers of large wild animals. They took their meat supplies almost at will. From their departure of the Mandans on April 7 to the beginning of their Great Falls portage on June 21, a period of seventy-five days, they reported killing more than 100 large game animals, including 29 American elk, 28 deer of three types, 17 buffalo, 15 black and grizzly bears, and a variety of other animals including antelope, bighorn sheep, mountain goats, beaver, one wolf, and one "panther" or mountain lion. But animals actually noted in the journals were only a portion of the total kill. A number of entries tell of expedition hunters taking "several deer," or "several buffalo" on a given day. Journal entries regarding this hunting have proved critically important in present-day understanding of many of these species. The American elk, for example, is today known as a native only in our western mountains. It migrates down to foothills and mountain edges in the winter, but returns to high meadows during summer months. Yet in their crossing of the Great Plains—always proclaimed as buffalo country—Lewis and Clark bagged more elk than any other animal, and buffalo were third after deer in order of total numbers killed. Partly this was because the expedition often hugged the shores of the river where frequent groves of trees beckoned elk to linger. But the discoverers also ventured onto the open plains and found elk there as well. Likewise grizzlies, black bears, bighorn sheep and goats are today all mountain species. The mountain lion and the mountain goat, it should be added, were merely panthers and goats to Lewis and Clark. Later generations have been forced to add the word "mountain" to the names of these animals. Clearly, too much civilization has driven them from the plains since the time of this expedition.

On April 22 they were still in North Dakota, and Lewis wrote: "I ascended to the top of the cutt bluff this morning, from whence I had a most delightfull view of the country, the whole of which except the valley formed by the Missouri is void of timber or underbrush, exposing to the first glance of the spectator immence herds of Buffaloe, Elk, deer, & Antelopes feeding in one common and boundless pasture. We saw a number of bever feeding on the bark of the trees alonge the verge of the river, several of which we shot, found them large and fat. Walking on shore this evening I met with a buffaloe calf which attached itself to me and continued to follow close at my heels untill I embarked and left it. . . . Capt Clark informed me that he saw a large drove of buffaloe pursued by wolves today, that they at length caught a calf which was unable to keep up with the herd. . . ."

On the twenty-fifth, they arrived at the mouth of the Yellowstone, and it was more of the same: "The whole face of the country," wrote Lewis, "was covered with herds of Buffaloe, Elk & Antelopes; deer are also abundant but keep themselves more concealed in the woodland. The Buffaloe, Elk and Antelope are so gentle that we pass near them while feeding, without appearing to excite any alarm among them; and when we attract their attention, they frequently approach us more nearly to discover what we are, and in some instances pursue us a considerable distance apparently with that view. . . ."

Grizzlies now began to give the expedition pause for thought. One which did not attack took ten musket balls before it died. It measured 8 feet 7½ inches from nose to hind feet and weighed 500 to 600 pounds. Another was found lying asleep in a field, and six of the best hunters crept to within forty paces. Four fired at one time while two held their fire. All four balls hit the grizzly, but instead of rolling over dead, it rose out of the grass in a blind fury and charged. The other two hunters fired their muskets and both balls also hit the bear. That only seemed to madden it more, and the enraged bear scattered the six hunters in all directions, fleeing pell-mell across the plain while they desperately tried to load their muskets on the run. One man dashed into a willow thicket, got his gun loaded and let fly. The bear turned and galloped after him. Then another fired from another direction and the bear turned after him. Seeing two others, he chased both toward the river and they were forced to drop their flintlocks and jump off a twenty-foot embankment into the Missouri. The bear followed, and was just a few feet behind one water-flailing member of the Corps of Discovery when another hunter finally killed the animal with a shot in the head. When they cleaned him out, they found eight lead balls. About this time, while the talk about bears persisted, someone asked Drewyer how to tell the difference between grizzlies and black bears. The woodsman, who had experience with both species, suggested the way to tell was to climb a tree. "If the bear comes up after you," he said, "it's a black bear."

A short time later, Lewis was chased into the Missouri by another grizzly which caught him with an unloaded musket. But when the captain turned to give battle with his short walking stick, the bear stopped at the river's edge, turned, and inexplicably dashed off at top speed across the plains.

The boats, too, gave continuous problems. The Missouri in places was four hundred to five hundred yards wide, deep, and treacherous. The current and prevailing westerlies worked against them. They used square sails on the large boats, but where valley walls were high, the following winds were gusty and uncertain. On May 14, the large pirogue was hit suddenly by a crosswind and flopped onto its side. It was two hundred yards from shore at the time, loaded with nonswimmers, the waves were high, and that particular boat contained all the journals, maps, compasses, and sextant, much of the ammunition, medical supplies, and other absolute essentials. Charbonneau was at the helm and had made the mistake that caused the capsizing. He immediately dissolved into cries and prayers. Pierre Cruzatte, tough and sensible, pulled a pistol and threatened to shoot Charbonneau if he didn't take the rudder instantly. Cruzatte then pulled in the sail which allowed the little craft to right itself drunkenly, the rails barely above water. Cruzatte immediately grabbed several kettles and passed them out and all hands began to bail furiously. The waves were high and breaking, but by paddling and bailing they somehow kept it afloat until it reached shore. Sacajawea in this moment of near disaster rescued most of the medical supplies, which had broken free and were scattering on the waves. Had the boat sunk, it almost certainly would have ended the expedition then and there. Loss of the navigation instruments alone would have stopped all progress.

A few nights later, a large bull buffalo swam the river and stumbled out on shore in the middle of the sleeping camp. It clumped over one of the pirogues in leaving the water, smashed a rifle and some other equipment, thundered through the camp, headed directly for the captains' tent, and would have bolted straight through had Scammon not risen, barking furiously. The buffalo turned aside in the nick of time. Next morning they found he had galloped down a narrow pathway between two rows of sleeping men, hooves pounding along the ground narrow inches from their heads, yet touching none of them.

On June 7, Lewis slipped on a cliff and nearly dropped ninety feet into the river. He was able to pull himself up, but Richard Windsor, one of the privates who was following, also slipped and was left hanging by only his left arm and leg, while slowly sliding off the ledge. Lewis, levelheaded, told him to pull his knife with his right hand and dig it into the bank for a stronger hold. After several anxious moments, the man slowly eased himself out of trouble.

And so it went. Battles with bears, nighttime escapades, near drownings, sudden violent storms, sandbars and snags, and a constant struggle with the boats. But despite an almost daily chain of such incidents, the party somehow arrived at the base

The Mandan villages in North Dakota probably looked like this when Lewis and Clark visited there in the winter of 1804–05. Though these Indians were friendly, the American expedition built its own stockade and camped downstream. (GEORGE CATLIN, *North American Indians*)

of the Rockies well fed from their spring hunt, and in sound spirits for the trials that lay ahead.

The course of their full journey is well known, and from this point is of less interest to our Great Plains story. The group entered the Rockies and went to the headwaters of the Missouri. Sacajawea helped the captains buy twenty-nine horses from her native tribe of Snake Indians, and after a few mistaken turns, they finally arrived at the Clearwater and dropped down that beautiful stream to the Columbia, thence on to the Pacific, arriving at Cape Disappointment on November 15. Their winter on the shore of the Pacific was mostly wet and miserable. It was here that Clark carved on a large pine his famous legend: "William Clark December 3rd 1805. By land from the U. States in 1804 & 1805."

By January 1 they had moved inland from the shore and were able to build Fort Clatsop south of the Columbia on the present Lewis and Clark River. Clatsop was named for a local Indian tribe and proved a relatively secure haven. The fort was a log stockade surrounding two rows of cabins, four on one side and three on the other, with a small parade ground between.

On March 26, 1806, they started for home, noting that they had managed three meals each day during their stay at Fort Clatsop, though they were reduced to roots and poor elk meat when the hunting and fishing proved thin. It rained every day of their stay and they were wet to the bone on every venture outside the stockade. Their return up the Columbia and through the Bitter Roots to the Missouri was the most trying portion of the journey, and they were frequently stopped by deep snow, worn-out horses, exhaustion, and a lack of food. On July 3, they split into two groups, Lewis taking a shortcut across northern Idaho to the Missouri while Clark went south to the headwaters of the Yellowstone. The plan was for Lewis to locate the short route through the mountains while Clark returned down the Yellowstone. They hoped to meet at the junction of the Missouri and Yellowstone, or failing that, at the Mandan villages.

Only one incident marred this period—Lewis' brush with the Blackfeet just east of the Rockies. He had found the shortcut overland to the Missouri, but decided to investigate the Marias River, which flows into the Missouri from the north. Lewis in fact named the Marias in honor of a lady friend, Maria Wood. This river was important because the Louisiana Purchase gave the United States the entire Missouri River drainage. The Marias was seen to be a large river when they had passed it going west, and a tributary of the Missouri. If it extended some distance north into present Alberta, that meant the United States owned all that northern drainage basin as well.

With three men, Lewis followed the Marias upstream about a hundred miles looking for its source. One afternoon eight Blackfeet approached warily. Lewis made signs of friendship, and that night the two groups camped together. Just at dawn, the Indians grabbed all the muskets of the troop and several of the horses and tried to run off. The guard then on duty had

This fanciful depiction shows Lewis and Clark meeting with a group of Indians during their historic trip west. But the Americans dressed for the most part in frontier leather, not Continental Army cotton. (*Patrick Gass' Journal*, 1807. ARTIST UNKNOWN)

leaned his weapon against a rock momentarily and they grabbed that first. He raised the whole camp with shouts and in an instant the troopers were wrestling for their lives. Private Reuben Fields stabbed one of the Indians in the heart and killed him. Lewis got his musket back and then pursued two of the Blackfeet down a trail to some rocks. He shot at one, saw him clutch his stomach and crawl behind a boulder. The other returned Lewis's fire but missed. The men had by then recovered their muskets and enough horses to ride. Everyone grabbed what he could and they rode hell for leather back toward the Missouri. They traveled both day and night, thus escaping pursuit and any further contact. The Blackfeet had always been a tough and determined tribe, and this incident probably became widely known throughout the region, no doubt strengthening their resolve to oppose all white men. In any case, the Blackfeet remained a steady source of danger to travelers through that region for more than half a century.

When Lewis and his band reached the Missouri, by a lucky accident they immediately met the other half of their group coming downstream in canoes. The date was July 28. They unloaded the horses, switched them across the rump, and climbed aboard the canoes for the trip home.

The downstream journey was uneventful and rapid. On one day, current hurried, they traveled eighty-three miles. On August 7, they reached the mouth of the Yellowstone to find a note from Clark that he had passed downstream from there several days earlier.

On August 11, the only serious injury of the entire journey occurred. Lewis and Cruzatte had gone ashore to kill some elk for dinner. They downed one and wounded a second. Plunging into the brush after the wounded animal, Lewis was searching through a patch of willows when he was hit in the thigh by a musket ball. Cruzatte had mistakenly shot him, but fortunately no bones or arteries were broken. Cursing with pain, he hobbled back to the boat for help. The wound flattened him for several weeks and put an end to his shoreside exploring.

When the party had split in two back in July, Clark with his group headed southeast to the headwaters of the Yellowstone in what is now Yellowstone National Park. There, after making a pair of dugout canoes, he and his men headed downstream. Travel was easy and comfortable, and he loafed along, feeding on buffalo. He passed the mouth of the Big Horn on July 6, and arrived at the Missouri on August 3. Finding he was ahead of Lewis, and with "Musquetors" outweighing local game supplies, he drifted slowly ahead. The two groups made contact on August 12 a short distance upriver from the Mandan villages. From here it was all downhill, and travel was easy. Without further incident, the Corps of Discovery arrived at St. Louis Tuesday afternoon, September 23, 1806, ending a journey of twenty-eight months and two days. That night the captains went to a local dance.

The expeditions of Lt. Pike and the Captains Lewis and Clark probably placed a decisive bend in the course of this nation's history; at the very least they served to hurry it along its way. They were expeditions with a new approach. The Span-

iards sent their military columns into northern Mexico and
Texas and New Mexico to clear away Indians so Spanish colonists could settle the new lands. The Spaniards were primarily
interested in converting or killing Indians and in settling farmers on the land, and their commercial interests were stifled or
muted.

The French approach was different. The French worked as
individual trappers and traders who sought Indian friendship as
the basis for their nation's commerce and colonization. French
traders moved into the plains one by one, lived by their wits,
took Indian wives and, without using force, infiltrated their
western commerce into the Indian economy and culture. When
disputes arose, the Indians seldom lost.

After the Pike and Lewis and Clark expeditions, however, a
third approach became possible. In a sense, this was a combination of the most useful elements of both Spanish and French
methods. Military columns would advance through Indian
lands urging peace and spreading the word of American power
and control. This would be followed by assorted commercial
interests. When traders and Indians disagreed, as they frequently did, American military forces were called in to deal
with the opposition. Otherwise peace was urged as a necessary
condition of successful commerce. The power of the government, in short, became a club wielded primarily to develop
commercial objectives of our citizens. Commerce could precede
settlement because its purposes were extractive; first it was peltries and then minerals, with these values being carried away
from the frontier for use elsewhere. A settled population of
Americans therefore was not needed locally for these tradesmen;
that could come later. In a very definite way, this approach set
the course of western American history.

The two expeditions in themselves also provide an interesting
comparison. One was well advertised, the other proceeded in
secrecy. As early as 1803, President Jefferson had asked both the
French and Spanish ministers their opinions regarding the proposed Lewis and Clark expedition while the Pike expedition
was carried out subrosa. Where Lewis and Clark crossed the
continent following water routes, Pike's was primarily a land

operation. Both columns were small; Pike had fourteen men at the end and Lewis and Clark thirty. The Lewis and Clark expedition was well planned and thoroughly organized; Pike's was hurriedly patched together with almost no planning and a paucity of equipment. Both expeditions came through unscathed by Indian encounters. And both were led by unusually courageous and resourceful men.

Their expeditions, as we shall see, had the effect of pulling a continental plug and opening the entire West to rapid new migrations. The plains were soon to see thousands of new travelers.

CHAPTER 11

The Rise of the Merchant Plainsmen

One afternoon in the fall of 1833, a roaring drunk was begun in a mud castle beside a sandy river eight hundred miles west of St. Louis. On the same afternoon an elegant gentleman in London bought a new silk hat, perched it on his carefully coiffed head, and marched out for a promenade on Chatham Reach. The two events, ineluctably tied, might be described as the brandy time at the end of a vast continental feast, the prime roast of which was skinned and stuffed *Castor canadensis*, that water worrier, the North American beaver.

The boys in the adobe castle who danced their way through a barrel of Taos lightning that fall afternoon were led by a wiry little frontiersman named William Bent, late a muddy-toed lad along the St. Louis waterfront. Now at age twenty-four he was one of the toughest trapper-traders in a land of very tough or very dead men. The occasion for his fandango and the free whiskey was the opening for business of a large, rectangular high-walled adobe garrison and trade post beside the Arkansas River, a Great Plains bastion and haven, to be known from that day forward as Bent's Fort, and now known as Bent's Old Fort. The occasion for the gentleman strutting the streets of London under his new hat was a change of English fashion from beaver to silk, a mere whim of taste really, a fad wafted hither on trade winds from the Orient. Silk was fine, and new, and expensive, and besides, nearly everyone had a beaver hat or two. Fashion, the lady said, is a cruel master. That summer of 1833, the price of beaver pelts on the dock at St. Louis plummeted from $6 to $2.50. What the Comanches and Apaches and Pawnees had been trying to do for thirty years was now done. The plains and mountain men were bested. The beaver trade was finished. Its death rattle would last another ten years, killing whites and Indians in a desperate dying quest, but in 1833 for all real purposes it was finished. Those who had foreseen the end, like John Jacob Astor, were getting out.

It had been a glorious time. It was that period of our western growth longest on nerve and shortest on firepower. For North American history that's saying a lot, but it was true. It was the time of beaver, and beaver all the way. Beaver was the coin. Beaver built the trade and called the traders. The rewards were a lot of flayed and flattened heroes, both red and white, plus mental warehouses stored with bales of memories for those that survived. A few immortals got rich, but most wound up dead broke, or worse, just dead. And meanwhile, somewhere in that mix, was an answer to who owned the Great Plains—alias Great American Desert. That chunk of real estate may have been purchased from the French in 1803, but ownership didn't transfer with the title. It had to be won.

The struggle for that ownership got underway at St. Louis at about two on the afternoon of September 23, 1806. That was the hour on which Lewis and Clark returned from their twenty-eight-month journey to the Pacific. Many notable figures in later western history greeted the Corps of Discovery that afternoon, and among the smallest viewers was a goggle-eyed youngster named Charley Bent, age seven, and William Bent's older brother. Charley was a lad who could instantly recognize a pack of heroes when he saw them, and his eyes drank in the scene with the thirst of a Saharan bedouin. There were the weathered faces, the worn flintlocks, the leathern clothes and battered baggage, all lean and tough and perfumed with a heady mix of sage, Missouri mud, and grizzly grease. It was the smell of the West and it caught and clung. Who wouldn't be excited? These were the physicians who had delivered this whole newborn land! Captain Clark, tall and rugged with long red hair, Lewis still hobbling from his hunting wound, the men trim and tough, their canoe paddles still dripping from the final stroke of that fantastic voyage. There is no knowing what dreams were planted in a young head that afternoon, but as Charles Bent's life began to unfold, it is not difficult to guess.

The following year, 1807, Lt. Pike returned with his battered batch of durables and sent yet another gypsy call to those dreamers who lived along the Mississippi. The lieutenant's course, as everyone knew, had been overland from St. Louis to Santa Fe. He hadn't stuck to the river. He made it to that fabled far-off Spanish city and returned, all in less than a year. Take away the four months the Spaniards held him in prison and that makes a round trip from St. Louis to Santa Fe of eight months, maybe less, the span of one warm season. That was the message that struck home in the valleys of the Ohio and Mississippi that summer, not Pike's so-called treachery.

The door to the West had been opened, they knew, straight through St. Louis. Lewis and Clark pioneered the northern route, Pike the southern route. Their adventures were numerous and they all came through alive. Beaver prices in 1807 were high. Profits were unbelievable. An axe that cost a dollar in St. Louis could sell to the Indians for $20 worth of beaver pelts. A man with a rifle and $500 in trade goods and enough guts could make himself rich in a single season. Out there, everyone lived off the land, on buffalo mostly. Weeks and months and even years of grubbing stumps and planting corn and swatting mosquitoes in eastern river bottomlands could never extinguish such thoughts in young minds. Charles Bent and later his brother William were members of that generation, and they were destined for excitement. They had to be. And what Charles saw in person that day in St. Louis was easily being imagined or transferred to other young impressionables throughout the East.

So they were soon filing West. Not in packs but as lone, resolute, unanchored wisps of history. They would halt momentarily at St. Louis, each in his turn over the next three decades, gather a sack of possibles and some trade goods and maybe a trapper's contract, then drop below the western horizon. They

said they sought their fortunes, and to go West up the Missouri
in keelboats and dugouts in those years was excuse enough.
Charles and William Bent did it too, but not until some years
after Lewis and Clark had returned, so while they and the main
figures in this yarn season through some green years, consider
for a moment the case of one Manuel Lisa, Spanish merchant
and social outcast at St. Louis, the year, 1807.

Lisa was a worried-looking little man, not physically equipped
to wrestle very successfully against the physical life of the frontier. He had a rat's sense for survival, however, and he was durable, and in the crucial first two decades of the nineteenth century those were the only critically necessary qualities. Lisa,
though not the founder, was the chief exponent of the Company
of Explorers and Adventurers of the Missouri, always known
loosely as the Missouri Fur Company. This firm was an aggrega-
tion of well-anchored St. Louis merchants who served as middlemen between eastern manufacturers and western beaver skin-
ners. Getting trade goods to St. Louis was a tough, lengthy
struggle. Getting them to the plains and mountains was brutal,
exhausting, dangerous, and about 40 percent fatal. Lisa was the
link. He covered this ground annually from the year Lewis and
Clark returned in 1806 until his death in 1820, seeding the
entire northern plains and mountains with trappers and traders.
Hudson's Bay Company trappers repeatedly moved into North
Dakota, Montana, and Idaho during that period. Lisa was the
key American figure who blunted that British thrust.

When the War of 1812 broke out, Congress created the new
Missouri Territory and named William Clark its first governor.
Clark immediately called on Lisa to go upriver and, as Indian
subagent, to prevent British intrigues among those resident
tribes. Lisa's success in this was based purely on his personal
prestige. He was in fact able to raise the Sioux, Omahas, and
Poncas into war against the British and their allies. Peace in the
East at the end of the war meant little in the West where a
boundary settlement still had to be made. For years afterward,
struggle for control of that region continued unchecked. The
British knew as well as the Americans that a boundary would be
chosen based on prior occupancy, so they pushed hard for con-

trol of the region. But the Americans pushed too, and more than any other single man Manuel Lisa created the condition that led in 1818 to placement of the present boundary at the 49th Parallel.

He was a curious figure. Dark hued, explosive, noted for sharp dealings, he nonetheless had a generous side so large it seemed ill fitting. Of his early life little is known. He was born at New Orleans on September 8, 1772. His father may have been a Spanish customs official, but the family apparently had no money. Young Lisa learned his merchant's trade in the rough-and-tumble of the riverfront, and in 1796 moved up the Mississippi to Vincennes and St. Louis. While in Indiana he met Mrs. Polly Chew and her infant daughter, recently ransomed from a band of local Indians. Her husband had been killed on the frontier and she had been held prisoner. Lisa reportedly married her out of pity and the young family moved to St. Louis.

The first mention of his presence in that city was in 1798 when he was embroiled in a lawsuit to recover funds given in a loan. He tried various trades, gathered some land from the Spanish authorities, and became a quarrelsome minor merchant of the city. He was present in 1803 when the Louisiana Purchase passed into American hands, and he expected his Spanish fortunes to suffer severely. But when Lewis and Clark returned from their great voyage in 1806, Manuel Lisa saw his future unfold before him. It lay to the west, up the Missouri, in the fur trade. By the spring of 1807, Lisa had created the first of his many fur companies and was pushing an expedition of about sixty men upriver toward the Rockies. His chief lieutenant was George Drouillard, lately a sergeant in Lewis and Clark's Corps of Discovery. Several other Corpsmen were also in the crew. While headed upriver, they met John Colter coming down, alone, in a canoe, and here now with Drouillard appear the first pair of true mountain men of the northern plains and Rockies. Colter had left the Lewis and Clark expedition at the Mandans the year before and had spent the winter trapping in the mountains. He immediately threw in with Lisa's group and together all headed upriver.

The thrust of this expedition was to penetrate to the heart of the northern plains. From there, small parties of trappers could fan out along the rivers and into mountains of the entire region. Lisa therefore pushed boldly up the Missouri, then up the Yellowstone, all the way to the mouth of the Bighorn in southeastern Montana. Here in November the group built Fort Raymond and settled down for a winter of trading. But first there had to be Indians to trade with. So Lisa sent Colter off on a grueling winter expedition to announce the new post, and to urge Indians to come and swap their furs for kettles, calico, guns, and powder. Colter met the Crows, then crossed the Wind River Range, continued on to Jackson's Hole, and saw the Tetons. Returning, he made the mistake of reporting some unusual geothermal activity in the Yellowstone region. Actually, he told them, it looked like the fires of hell were seeping out of the ground over there near Yellowstone Lake. A few of his listeners might claim they knew what the inside of a church looked like, but most had no authority on the subject. Yet what Colter was describing sounded ominously like preachment, and one raunchy leather pants, who said he'd grown up downwind of a Puritan minister, proclaimed it downright sermonish. Accordingly, Colter was made to suffer through the winter for his supposed big lie, and when word of it seeped back to St. Louis, laughably enough, "Colter's Hell" began to appear on what was, of course, the site of Yellowstone National Park, home of Old Faithful and many other thermal hot pots—none of which eased Colter's suffering during those long gray winter afternoons.

Lisa's expedition that year proved successful, and he headed home in 1808 with a sizable collection of furs. The summer proved uneventful, but that fall Colter became involved in an incident that immortalized his name among his wandering kind. He was canoeing up the Jefferson River one morning with John Potts, an old comrade from the Lewis and Clark days, when they suddenly heard a trampling of horses and found themselves facing about six hundred mounted Blackfoot warriors. The Blackfeet hated Americans and Colter and Potts reckoned rightly that their time had come. The Blackfeet beckoned them ashore where Colter got out. Potts, however, stayed in the canoe and when it swirled away from shore one of the Indians hit him with an arrow. "Colter, I'm wounded," he yelled, and at the same instant raised his rifle and shot an Indian dead on the spot. Others standing nearby then riddled him with arrows. Potts perhaps knew that would happen. In any event he spared himself a slow death by torture, for which the Blackfeet were famous.

Attention now turned to Colter, and the question of how he should die. He had learned enough Blackfoot language from the Crows so he could converse, and leaders of the group now suggested some grim ways of ending his life. One suggestion was to set him up as a target. That method didn't prove so popular, as it would exclude too many from the game. Then an old chief came forward and asked Colter if he could run. He answered that he was only a poor runner. "Good," said the chief, "we will see. We will give you one chance. You can run for your life."

They took him out on the open plain, stripped him naked, and the chief then walked ahead with the unfortunate trapper. They kept going for a distance of about three hundred yards, before he was told to start running and save himself if he could. Colter began to run, and at that instant a horrible howl rang up behind him as six hundred frenzied Indians started in pursuit. Colter was in fact an excellent runner and in fine physical condition. But he was naked, and was running across a plain covered with burrs and thorns which cut his feet at every step. About six miles across the plain he knew there was a bend in the river, and he headed for that. He began to gain ground on the howling pack, and his hopes began to rise. However, when he chanced a look over his shoulder, he could see that one warrior was far ahead of the others and was gaining. He had hoped to ease up when he saw he could outdistance most of the tribe, but now he had to redouble his efforts.

On and on they ran for nearly half an hour, but the lone Indian continued to gain. Blood was now spraying from Colter's mouth and nose, and covering his chest. The pace was terrific. When Colter chanced another look, the warrior was only forty yards back, and soon another look showed he was almost close enough to hurl his spear. To save himself, Colter suddenly stopped and turned around. This so confused the Indian that he

Here's John Colter, running for his life across the southern Montana country-side. The artist who drew this sketch is unknown. (AMERICAN ANTIQUARIAN SOCIETY, WORCESTER, MASS.)

turned off balance and hurled his spear, which missed Colter and broke on a nearby rock. The Indian, exhausted, stumbled and fell, and Colter swooped up the spear and pounced on him, pinning him to the ground with one thrust. Immediately, he turned and raced off again. He was now only a mile from the river, and the Indians were nearly a quarter of a mile back. When they came to the Indian he had killed, their fury rose to new heights, and after a pause they charged on again in pursuit.

Arriving at the river, Colter saw only one chance. An island had snagged a tangle of broken trees and brush on the upstream end, and these formed a dense raft of vegetation floating in the

river. He dived in, swam furiously to this tangle, and dove
under. Coming up somewhere in the center, he searched under-
water until he found a well-covered place to push his head
through, and there he made his stand. In a few moments the
tribesmen reached the river. Dozens dove in and swam across.
They scoured the island and the far shore. They tramped back
and forth across the raft above his head and spent most of the
day searching nearby. Amazingly, they failed to find him and
that night he eased out from under the raft, swam softly downstream a considerable distance, came out on the far shore, and
traveled all night.

By morning he was miles from the scene, but his situation
was still desperate. He was alone, naked, his feet were inflamed
and sore and his legs cut by thorns, he had no food or weapons,
and was in hostile country. The weather was turning cold and it
was six days distance to Fort Raymond, even under the best of
conditions. A lesser man might soon have perished, but Colter
was not a lesser man. He began to search for a food staple that
Sacajawea had shown Lewis and Clark. It was a root plant
named *Psoralea esculente*, and called by the French *Pomme de
Prairie*, or breadroot. It was fairly common in the Missouri
region, and he found enough along the way to sustain himself.
He headed east toward the fort, and after seven days of painful
but steady travel he took the halloos from the guard and staggered in to an amazed company of trappers.

Unlike most later trappers, Colter stayed in the mountains
only two more years, returning to St. Louis in 1810. He had not
been to that city since leaving with Lewis and Clark in 1804. He
stayed downriver thereafter and died at St. Louis in 1813 at the
age of forty-three.

Colter's friend Drouillard, meanwhile, suffered a terrible fate.
Leading a small party of trappers, he headed west from Fort
Raymond into Blackfoot country in May 1810. Such a band of
trappers would normally move as a group, and by concentrating
their firepower they could present a severe obstacle to approaching Indians. Meeting no opposition, however, they decided to
chance their work in units of two. They could cover more
streams and trapping would be far more effective. But Drouil-

lard was not content even with this and soon chose to go out
alone, against all advice. One evening he failed to return to
camp. The next day the entire crew set out in search and soon
found his remains beside a beaver creek, his head hacked off, his
entrails ripped from his body, and his limbs cut apart. Caught
by Blackfeet, he had paid the final price of invading their territory, a fate that would prove all too common for trappers in the
years ahead.

But all their work was not grim. For years after Colter's long
run for life, his tale was told round buffalo chip fires and in the
pine knot smoke of mountain warmers, always of course being
exuberantly edited to include the narrator in place of Colter.
This sort of thing went on for a decade or more until Jim
Bridger got hold of the yarn and added one final variant. The
outrage of Bridger's famous lies was only exceeded by the truth
of his own exploits, which spanned forty years of raised hair as
plainsman, mountain trapper, guide, wanderer, and professional
frontiersman. Bridger first used his variation of the Colter story
on a pair of eastern greenhorns one fall evening around a campfire, starting festivities solemnly enough with a bit of instruc-
tion to them about the Marias River and its dangers. This
drifted easily into a memory of the time he stirred a nest of
Blackfeet while trying to trap the upper reaches of that river.
Those Blackfeet chased him, he said, and chased him so he had
to run all afternoon, for about twenty miles, till he was so near
tuckered out he reckoned he had to drop his pack of furs if he
was ever going to get away. "Hundred pounds worth, too," he
recalled sadly. "Hated to leave 'em, but them Blackfeet was
a'gaining on me, you know. After I dumped the pack, they just
kept right on a'chasing anyway, and we ran all night and half
the next day too, and finally I wasn't watching jist close enough
and run myself up a box canyon. Well, since I seen they was no
way out, I jist turned around and started potting at 'em, and I
killed six afore they caught me."

"They caught you?" says one astonished fuzzy cheek, his
mouth open. "Then what happened?"

"Why," says Bridger, "they killed me. Cut my head off and
ate my heart, saying I was the bravest they'd ever seen. Another
time I was headed up the Green when a band of . . . "

Trying to navigate the snag-filled Missouri while fighting off Indian attacks was no picnic for fur traders. This group is trying to get their keelboat past a gathering of unappreciative Sioux (WESTERN HISTORY COLLECTIONS, UNIVERSITY OF OKLAHOMA LIBRARY, NORMAN)

By this time, truth had settled its heavy mantle on the listeners, and snorting in disgust they stomped off to find bedrolls and enough profanity to swear themselves to sleep.

Such stories salted the nightly campfires through that mix of flatlands and steeplands, and in the first four decades of the nineteenth century, helped make legendary the whispered call of the West. By 1820, hundreds of trappers were sprinkled through the northern plains and Rockies. Their birthplaces had been New England, the Original Thirteen, the Ohio Valley, New Orleans, Tennessee. It was this gathering of wanderers that followed Lisa and laid claim to the entire North Dakota-Montana-Idaho region at a time when land ownership depended on who shot first. Enough had been decided, however, so that a boundary between Canada and the United States could be established in 1818. Shortly thereafter, in August of 1820, Manuel Lisa died. With the international boundary fixed, it was as though his work was done. In life he had shown no interest in that boundary or its location, and it's not unfair to add that he gave no apparent allegiance to any nation. Yet more than any other single man it was Manuel Lisa, a Spanish-French-American merchant who placed that boundary where it is today. He provided the thrust that pushed it north to the 49th Parallel.

The other major trader on the northern plains was John Jacob Astor, who was never there himself, but whose men followed Lisa's up the Missouri in search of beaver. Astor showed his financial genius early in life and became the unquestioned king of the American fur trade. He was born in Germany in 1758 and emigrated to New York City in 1783. At first he was a peddler and baker's boy, but by 1787 he had entered the fur trade as a middleman, buying from St. Louis and New Orleans merchants and shipping his furs to Europe and the Orient. He invested much of his income in cheap Manhattan Island farmland, which soon leapfrogged in value. His rise thereafter was meteoric, and by 1806 when Lewis and Clark returned from the Pacific, he was already a millionaire.

As with Lisa, Astor immediately saw that Lewis and Clark had opened the world's most lucrative fur field, and he moved rapidly to capture it. Lisa, on the scene first, got upriver in 1808 while the first Astorians, suffering a burden of complications, didn't make the journey until 1811. Astor's first plan was too complex to be successful. He sent one expedition overland and another by ship from New York to the mouth of the Columbia. The two groups were supposed to meet there on the coast where a fort would be built. The ship would exchange its load of trade goods for a load of furs gathered by the overland expedition. The ship would then head for China, exchange its furs for tea, spices, jade, and other high-value items before returning to New York. Other ships would be sent out and the Columbia River fort, to be called Astoria, would grow into a thriving trade center.

It might have worked. In fact it did to a degree. The little ship *Tonquin* arrived at the mouth of the Columbia in the spring of 1811, and its crew set about building the fort. The overland expedition also made it across the mountains in straggling, battered, small groups after nearly starving during the winter of 1812. That summer, the colony began to prosper, but the War of 1812 scuttled everything. For a time all that northwest country was swamped by British trappers, ambitions, and influence. In response, Astor concentrated his efforts on his American Fur Company and moved it slowly westward from the Great Lakes into the St. Louis and Missouri River trade. Now he was making progress. Year after year, he sent more and more members of his Western Department up the Missouri in well-manned and well-supplied expeditions. By 1828 the Upper Missouri Outfit of Astor's company, under leadership of the veteran Kenneth McKenzie, had built Fort Union at the mouth of the Yellowstone. In the brawling toughness of this trade, McKenzie was so outstanding that he earned grudging recognition as "King of the Missouri," and his Fort Union was soon dominating trade throughout the region. McKenzie even managed a peace conference with the Blackfeet in 1830, and soon after opened trade with them.

So much for the north. There still remained the longed-for trade with Santa Fe. Lisa's hope had been to ascend the Missouri, then drift traders down the east face of the Rockies into Spanish territory. He had been thwarted in that by the assorted hells of the western plains, plus an early death. Official Spanish policy also banned trade with outsiders, and several Americans had long since found the policy was no idle threat. These intruders, when they arrived at Santa Fe, were jailed and their goods confiscated. One large caravan under the St. Louis trader Robert McKnight was captured and all ten of his men were jailed. They remained in that Spanish hoosegow from 1812 to 1822. Word of this was passed about as a warning to other groups. But several nonbelievers, suffering visions of plump Santa Fe ladies, jingling silver, and flowing whiskey, tried their hand and were jailed as well. At St. Louis, therefore, the view was dim for any progress toward the Santa Fe trade, and for years the matter languished.

The wall, oddly enough, was swept away overnight. That series of sporadic uprisings that had started with the little priest in Hidalgo, Mexico, in 1810 finally led the Mexican people to independence from Spain on September 27, 1821. Word reached Santa Fe a few months later. Facundo Melgares, the Spanish governor and former cavalry lieutenant who had chased Pike around the plains, promptly switched allegiances and tossed out all the old Spanish policies. Among these was the opposition to Americans. Melgares also freed McKnight's men and several other traders long held captive, and invited an American trader then at the border to enter the city. The trader was William Becknell of Franklin, Missouri, and by early December 1821, he was trading in the main square of Santa Fe. By the end of December, he and another American trader had sold all their goods and Becknell was headed back to western Missouri laden with bags of silver. On January 29, 1822 he rode into Franklin with one frost-clawed companion and turned his townsmen goggle-eyed with the mounds of silver he poured out. The next day he repaid loans at the rate of $15 for every dollar invested, and with that single stroke the Santa Fe Trail was born.

By May, Becknell launched his second expedition, this time using three heavily loaded wagons and leading a troop of twenty-one men. On his journey to Missouri in January, he had taken a direct route across the fifty-mile Cimarron desert. It had been safe enough on horseback in the dead of winter, and Becknell decided to chance it with his caravan. The decision was almost disastrous. Alkali dust rose in clouds at every step and nearly drove men and mules mad. They ran out of water halfway across, and the last two days were a panic of bone-aching thirst. They cut off the ears of their mules to drink the blood, and killed their dogs for the same purpose. Only the intervention of a newly watered cow buffalo saved them. They killed the animal and drank her stomach juices to survive.

Finally they reached the Cimarron, lowered its level several inches, then eased into Santa Fe for a summer of profitable trading. Becknell had now accomplished two major goals in creation of the Santa Fe Trail. He had found the shortest flatland route, which avoided the steep Raton Pass, and he had shown that wagons could be used in the trade. What he had not shown, however, was how to overcome Comanches and Pawnees. The durable tribesmen were not pleased by white intrusions and blotted up traders and trading parties for the next twenty years. They were tough and courageous, and the horse allowed them lightninglike strikes in force. While armed only with bows and arrows, they were still seen to be extremely dangerous light cavalry. They rode bareback, the horse being equipped only with a bridle and reins, plus a horsehair or leather rope looped around the girth. In battle, what the Santa Fe trader saw over his sights was a galloping, apparently riderless horse. At a distance of fifty to seventy-five yards, the horse would suddenly veer to right or left and a string of four or five arrows, all in the air at once, would whistle toward the trader from beneath the horse's neck. The rider, who made it look simple, had hooked one foot into the girth rope and thrown himself far over on the protected side of the horse. From there, with both hands free, he could pull his short bow, notch another arrow and pull, notch and pull, notch and pull. The trader, and all who used the plains in those days, was restricted to the use of one-shot muzzle loaders, either as smooth-bore muskets or as grooved rifles. The muzzle loader was accurate and deadly at a range of one hundred yards or more, but after that first shot it might take a full minute to reload.

The strength of the Santa Fe venture, therefore, lay primarily in numbers. Becknell engineered a solution to this during the winter of 1823–24. He issued a call throughout the Missouri territory, announcing that a caravan of wagons, a sort of "traveling fortress" would leave Independence in May, and all who would travel the route that year were invited to join for mutual safety. True to his word, in mid-May of 1824 Becknell led a string of twenty-five wagons and eighty-one men out of Independence bound for Santa Fe. The journey was undistinguished by any serious affront against life and limb, and by September, Becknell and company were back in Independence with $180,-000 in gold and silver, plus about $10,000 in furs.

That ratio of much coin and few furs was not an idle coincidence. The opening of Spanish trade three years earlier had also opened the mountain streams of New Mexico to American trappers, and with growing thoroughness the mountain men had been eliminating beaver from the entire region. The pelts could now funnel east to St. Louis along two main routes; down the Missouri River from the north, or up the Santa Fe Trail from the south. In the first few years of trapping the southern mountains, the returns were lush, but they narrowed quickly as stream after stream was trapped out. Because of fierce competition among trappers, no attempt was made to leave a stock of young beaver for ensuing years. Trapping was conducted not only in the fall, but in the spring as well when the young kits, whose pelts were useless, were killed as often as mature beaver.

The development of the Rendezvous System further hurried the demise of the beaver. William H. Ashley, one man who made a fortune in furs, developed the system in 1825. This was a technique of specialization that doubled the number of men in the West, but cut by half the time required to supply trappers and deliver furs to St. Louis. Ashley himself led a band of trappers west in the spring of 1824, and that summer let it be known through the mountains that in July of the following year he would carry large supplies of guns, ammunition, trade goods, and whiskey to Henry's Fork on the Green River. He would wait there and exchange these goods and whiskey for furs. Any free trappers or Indians who might like to join the fun were invited to the party.

Such news rattled up and down the valleys and high meadows of the Rockies like bolts of electricity that winter, and for the parched and lonely, the spring of 1825 passed much too slowly, but was full of dreams. Mostly the dreams were of that trade whiskey, a decoction generally composed about as follows: One gallon 180-proof grain alcohol, one pound black chewing tobacco, one handful red peppers, one bottle ginger (to give it a little snap), one quart black molasses, and some Green River water—more of the last ingredient to be added as the drunks got drunker and the barrel got emptier. Sometimes a little nitric acid replaced the chewing tobacco, which was valuable as a trade item.

That first rendezvous—they called it a "Rendavoze"—nearly

The Trappers' Rendezvous was the occasion for a six-week mid-summer debauch of everyone involved in the plains and mountain fur trade. Here the party is getting started with whiskey, horse racing, card playing, yarn telling and other unmentionable delights. (FRANCIS F. VICTOR, *The River of the West*)

ended in a lynching. Ashley forgot to bring the whiskey. Such an oversight left the high-country dreamers about as humorous as warpath Blackfeet, and they allowed Ashley to keep his hair out of the only hope they had—that next year he would bring a double amount.

True to his word, in the following summer he turned up at the appointed rendezvous—Cache Valley north of Salt Lake— with an ample supply of the grim libation. After that the Rendavoze was everything they all hoped it would be—a six-week carnival of drinking, gambling, lying, swapping, and fornicating with Indian girls. Good times weren't frequent in the mountains. The trappers and Indians reckoned they'd be back next year. Ashley, canny in conquest, sold his company on the spot to Jedediah Smith, David Jackson, and William Sublette, then started for St. Louis with one hundred and twenty-three packs of furs valued at more than $60,000. Lots of hairy bank notes.

All pieces of the jigsaw puzzle were now on the table. The two main lines of supply—the Missouri River and the Santa Fe Trail—had been augmented in 1824 by Jed Smith's discovery of South Pass, that most crucial central opening into the West. Robert Stuart, one of the Astorians, crossed South Pass on his return from the Pacific Coast in 1812, but it remained unknown as a pass until Smith's crossing twelve years later. One reason for the late discovery is that South Pass doesn't look like a pass. It's a high, flat, wind-blown opening that seems more a rolling hillside than a break in the mighty Rockies. In any case, it was soon to become the key to the Oregon Trail. The Rendezvous System, meanwhile, allowed trappers to stay in the mountains and work without interruption while the marketplace, formerly six months to the east, was carried across the Great Plains in Dearborn and Murphy wagons and deposited at the summer gathering. Further, the increasing numbers of trappers and decreasing supplies of beaver forced ever-wider exploration of the Great Basin, the West Coast, and that gnarl of mountains that composes western Montana, Idaho, eastern Oregon, and Washington. It was a forced exploration, aimed at keeping fur companies alive and men employed. The result, however, was something far more important—development of an intimate knowledge of all the remainder of the trans-Mississippi west. In the narrow span of twenty-five horse-backed and hard-walking years, Jed Smith, Joseph Walker, the four Sublette brothers, Tom Fitzpatrick, Moses "Black" Harris, Jim Bridger, and about thirty other leading figures charted the entire West. The information they collected, while not gathered for that purpose, led directly into the next phase of America's westward travel, and the Great Plains, formerly such a formidable obstacle to this traffic, now became the easiest part of a far longer and more grueling journey.

Finally there was Bent's Fort, which opened its massive doors in 1833, and became a harbinger and example of a new and important force on the Great Plains. Bent's Fort was built by Charles and William Bent, those St. Louis youngsters who grew to manhood with the musky smell of beaver fur always in their nostrils. Charles had started working for Manuel Lisa as soon as

Bent's Fort was an adobe structure on the banks of the Arkansas River, built by Charles and William Bent, a pair of St. Louis fur traders. The fort became the most important American strongpoint in the southwest, boasting impregnable walls and huge size. (STATE HISTORICAL SOCIETY OF COLORADO, DENVER)

he was old enough to pole a pirogue, and William had joined him at age sixteen. After Lisa died, the Bent brothers gradually established themselves in the fur trade, and when Becknell opened the Santa Fe Trail, they were soon on their way with wagons of their own. They established a trading company with Ceran St. Veran, a young French trapper, and in this association experienced several profitable years. William married a Cheyenne girl, and his brother Charles successfully protected two other Cheyennes from a Comanche raiding party. In return, the Bents were accorded several years of trouble-free association with this otherwise dangerous Great Plains tribe. When the brothers opened their fort on the banks of the Arkansas, it soon began to prosper. When the fur trade began to decline the Bents merely shifted to other wares. Their position had become an anchor point of American influence on the southern plains.

In 1834 two other important forts opened in the West. Fort Hall, located at the junction of the Portneuf and Snake rivers, provided northern trappers with a center of habitation and trade. The same year, Fort Laramie on the Upper Platte opened its doors. Dozens of other lesser strongholds were scattering through the West in those years, but these three posts became points on a triangle that changed the entire commercial and social development of the West. They anchored the fur trade. They extended the idea of the annual Rendezvous to a seasonal

Rendezvous, and eventually to a year-round trading program. They made clerks out of trappers and businessmen out of mountain men. The two eastern benchmarks, Bent's Fort and Fort Laramie, were located far out on the High Plains. Such locations made best commercial use of that land's unusual geography. They were at the far end of a long, flat, easily traversed wagon trail where the major enemies were dust, thirst, and Indians. But they were easily reached by mountain trappers and high-country Indians seeking trade, thereby providing halfway stations and crucial points on the long journey west. And so the forts prospered.

The face of the West was changed by all this commotion from an unknown wilderness to a well-charted and thoroughly explored continent. In truth, it was the beaver that had brought this change. The fierce search for his hide had transformed the outriders of that generation into their own unique "Corps of Discovery," and the expeditions of Pike and Lewis and Clark now seemed far in the past. Yet barely twenty-five years had passed from the time those explorers returned to St. Louis. And now settlement of the West was getting underway in earnest.

CHAPTER 12

The Ties That Bind
a Nation Together

In the eastern United States by the year 1830, the published and proclaimed views of the Great Plains region were clearly established. Lieutenant Pike had compared the plains to the "sandy desarts of Africa," and reported "tracts of many leagues where the wind had thrown up the sand in all the fanciful forms of the ocean's rolling wave, and on which not a speck of vegetable matter existed." Major Stephen H. Long went west in 1819, leading a group of twenty-one soldiers and seven civilian scientists and his report, published in 1821, strengthened Pike's view. Where Lewis and Clark had surveyed the northern route and Pike the southern route, Long and his party first covered middle ground, going overland from Independence, Missouri, to the Platte River in Nebraska, then west to the Rockies. From there, he essentially followed Pike's footsteps, going south along the Front Range in Colorado. When he arrived at the Arkansas, Long split his party, one group descending the river, while he continued south to the Canadian with the rest of the group. From here they turned east, following the Canadian until they joined the Arkansas River contingent near Fort Smith, Arkansas. Long had thought he was on the Red, not the Canadian, and was sorely disappointed by this Great Plains deception. But he examined a great patch of the plains and so had earned his right to an opinion on the subject. That land was, he said, the Great American Desert.

Back East, such views produced numerous high-collar discussions on the worth of such a barrier. Some thought it would serve as a natural "sand wall" against invasion by any future enemy. Others thought the hated heathen redmen should be sent there. This view was countered by the fear that they were already pretty tough, and sending Indians off to a desert would merely harden them into a new breed of western Tartars. They would doubtless gain strength from the difficulties of that land, then sweep eastward and annihilate all civilized men. By 1830, however, the Tartar thinkers had lost. Congress passed the Indian Removal Act which called for eastern Indian groups to be resettled on the western plains. Both plains and Indians obviously were dangerous and therefore suited to each other. Nation by nation, thereafter, at least forty-two separate Indian peoples either went quietly or were overcome in military round-ups. Those who resisted were driven by troops westward to the so-called Indian Territory. Mostly that was the present state of Oklahoma, although the borders were poorly defined. The first tribes taken west were the "Civilized Nations" of Choctaw, Cherokee, Chickasaw, Creek, and Seminole. Later, lands were set aside for the Osage, Arapaho, Cheyenne, Wichita, Kiowa, and Comanche. The Ottawa, Peoria, Shawnee, Modoc, and Quapaw came a bit later, to be followed in time by twenty-six other tribes. The drives were grueling and often brutal. As they arrived in the new land, the Indians were expected to convert from eastern woodland hunters and farmers to western nomads. That didn't work. But the whites, meantime, had solved their problem; they had gotten rid of the Indian by sending him off to some worthless western lands. Though supposedly a desert, those lands teemed with buffalo and the Indian, it was said, could make his way if he persevered.

This general view of the Great Plains remained essentially unchanged through the 1830s. Seemingly no one voluntarily settled on the plains, and those lands were seen mainly as an unfortunately long, boring, and dangerous place to cross while en route somewhere else.

After 1820, all westering travelers followed one or another of three main routes. One path was up the Missouri and/or the

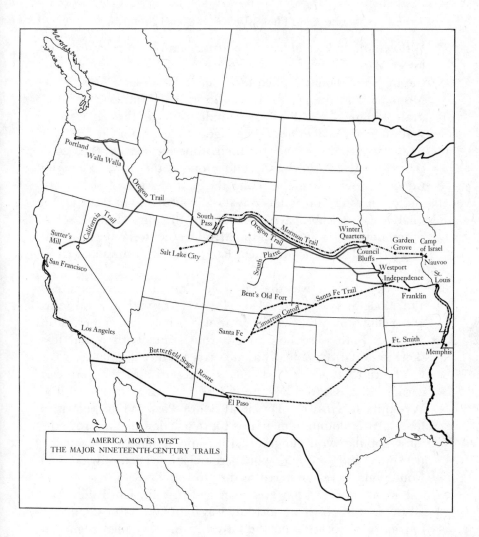

Portland
Walla Walla
Oregon Trail
South Pass
California Trail
Sutter's Mill
San Francisco
Salt Lake City
Oregon Trail
Mormon Trail
South Platte
Winter Quarters
Garden Grove
Camp of Israel
Council Bluffs
Nauvoo
Westport
Independence
St. Louis
Franklin
Los Angeles
Bent's Old Fort
Santa Fe Trail
Cimarron Cutoff
Santa Fe
Butterfield Stage Route
Ft. Smith
Memphis
El Paso

AMERICA MOVES WEST
THE MAJOR NINETEENTH-CENTURY TRAILS

Yellowstone by steamboat. The first steamboat appeared on the lower Missouri in 1819. As years passed, increasing numbers of the big smoky puffers plied the river as far west as Great Falls, Montana, and the falls of the Yellowstone. The boats, shallow draft skimmers, could ease over sandbars where the water was so shallow frogs had to hop. They ignored snags that would tear smaller craft apart and by their superior design they soon claimed both Missouri and Yellowstone as their own. Plenty of wood for fuel was found along the bottomlands of the rivers, and clean water for boilers was usually available in freshets and small clear streams paying tribute to the Big Muddy. Sometimes, however, water from the Missouri had to be used, so that clogged boilers were a frequent hazard of the professional riverman.

A second route was the Santa Fe Trail, being well marked and moderately safe by 1830. However, as with the Missouri and Yellowstone, the Santa Fe run was primarily commercial in purpose. Both were slow freight routes and both would lose their importance gradually as the years advanced.

The third route crossed central Missouri and the northeast corner of Kansas to the Platte River, then passed westward into Wyoming to cross the Divide at South Pass. While known at first only to mountain men, this route was destined to prove the most popular with emigrants. Pike and Long had followed it part way, and it would soon become known nationwide, and would long be remembered, as the Oregon Trail.

For the moment, however, that had to wait. Until the 1840s all traffic west on whatever route was light and seasonal, and the impact of civilization on the Great Plains remained slight. At this time in our history, the force of western expansion seemed stymied by the massive solidity of the plains. If not employed in commerce on the Santa Fe trade or caught by mountain excitement in the beaver pelt industry, easterners had little reason to venture west. Individuals, of course, did make the journey, becoming mountain men and trappers and traders. But large groups came later, and slower, as the promise of the land unfolded gradually.

Still, a vision of that promise was revealed fairly early. In

1833, a well-educated half-Wyandot, half-white named William Walker had visited St. Louis. There he learned that three Flathead Indians had come across the Rockies to ask their friend Red Hair to help them receive the white man's religion. Red Hair—William Clark—still lived in St. Louis, and he had met them and conversed in sign language. When Walker arrived, the Flatheads had disappeared, but Clark told him about them. Walker then wrote a letter to a wealthy Methodist friend in New York City, G. P. Disoway, who had the letter published in a Methodist paper, the *Christian Advocate and Journal.* The Flatheads, the letter said, were good people, but they had no guidance. A Christian had come among them there in the Oregon country, and had pronounced their mode of religion wrong and displeasing to the deity. Shaken by this, they elected a group of three warriors to go to St. Louis, seat of all the white man's activities, to bring back the big medicine. It was contained in a book, they had heard, and they deeply desired both that book and the guidance it offered.

So piteous was Walker's recount of the Flathead's call, and so forceful the resulting desire to save them, that the Methodist laity soon mounted a series of missions to Oregon. The most important was that led by the Rev. Marcus Whitman, who went out to Oregon in 1835 with his bride Narcissa and Henry and Eliza Spalding. Narcissa and Eliza were the first two white women to go west overland, and their arrival in that non-Christian land sent shock waves of disbelief through mountain man and Indian alike. Narcissa was especially beautiful and lively, and all the West was properly impressed thereafter with the virtues of Methodism. The two couples established missions in Oregon and Washington and set about saving Indians. Their letters and descriptions of the Willamette Valley of Oregon were widely circulated in the East and swelled interest in that western settlement. Further, the Reverend Whitman and company had traveled in a *wagon* nearly all the way. That proved the mountains couldn't be so terrible—at least to those who'd never seen them—and besides, if a pair of prayersome eastern ladies could make the journey safely, what could stop a hardknuckled Ohio River farmer? So the missions made a proper dent on eastern concerns about western travel. At least they did until November, 1847, when a group of Cayuse Indians began doubting the wisdom of giving up certain joys of this life for uncertain ones in the next. After measuring these thoughts among themselves, they rebelled at Walla Walla, Washington, and invited the Reverend Whitman and his wife, who kept talking about the hereafter, to try their luck with it first. They also killed about a dozen other mission residents, in a slaughter that induced general discouragement with Indian salvation. That red mayhem soon brought on expected white mayhem, with predictable results. It left a lot of people dead on both sides.

In 1839 another small group seeking western free lands spun its trail across the plains and over the horizon, while in 1841 a rather large group made the journey, proving once and for all that settlement of both Oregon and California was possible even for ordinary people. The latter group was called together by a feverish young man from Missouri named John Bidwell, who enlisted landseekers rather than missionaries. He had lost his Ohio farm in a squabble with a pair of less articulate but better-armed frontiersmen, and being left with nothing went west looking for something. In Missouri, then busily growing, his lack of fortune required diligent attention. Noting that having no property made him an outcast from one society, Bidwell soon reckoned to find another. The result was the Western Emigration Society, which he formed in the fall of 1840. It was a landmark organization, and though not the first to journey west, it was large and early on and it followed a pattern that hundreds of others would use successfully in the next two decades. The method was copied directly from truths gathered by mountain men and merchants who had earlier plied the western trails. The plains, they found, allowed for safe and successful wagon travel when enough whites eased along together to make Indians wary. The tough sod supported heavy wagons and the open country prevented ambush. By following rivers, it was possible to reach the Rockies without ever suffering more than a whiskey thirst. The flats and bottoms bordering the rivers provided timber for wagon repairs plus grazing at night for horses,

Fort Laramie in 1836

Fort Laramie marked the halfway point for travelers headed from St. Louis to the West Coast. This depiction shows the famous bastion toward the end of the fur-trade era and just prior to the big westward migration. (WYOMING HISTORICAL DEPARTMENT, CHEYENNE)

mules, oxen, and other livestock. When sharp inclines were faced, two or three teams could string together to ease each wagon across in turn. When wagons broke down, labor could be divided and resources shared. The plains therefore determined not only the mode of travel, but the form of society as well. Unlike eastern forests where the frontiersman could move alone in fair safety, the Great Plains forced individuals to band together. This sudden shift of social pattern at plains edge brought difficulties that should have been foreseen, but were not. A blue-sky view of the trip across those western lands was easily accepted by men who didn't know them, so that loud pronouncements of good will toward all leaders hazed the air of western Missouri each spring. Three days out of Independence or Westport or Elm Grove, however, and the truth of life's minutiae began to ooze through the seams. Forest-bred loners struggled momentarily with their new social conscience, spat upwind, and started growling about wagon train decisions. The lead wagon went too fast or it went too slow. The column was

too close and raised too much dust—or too spread out to be safe
from Indians. One group split on lines of dog-owning travelers
vs. non-dog travelers. Others split over the route of travel. Leaders who survived both Indian and element in Tennessee and
Kentucky usually reckoned their own decisions wisest. But their
followers seemed always to know better and as hails of abuse
greeted each determination, leaders kept replacing leaders.

Into this melody stepped a number of unemployed mountain
men who had trapped the last beaver and who now sought some
western venture to occupy their time. Such a venture, to be successful, had to allow visits to old haunts and pay enough for
beans and bacon. Beyond that they asked very little. A willing
campfire audience at day's end, perhaps. Some nightly harum-
scarum about Indians and grizzlies, or the mountains ahead.
Unquestioning obedience in times of emergency. That sort of
thing. They spoke with authority and had the scars to back it
up. As often as they stood still long enough to be hired, they
solved the problem of leadership and direction on the western
migrations. Jim Bridger, Tom Fitzpatrick, Moses Harris, Kit
Carson, Milton Sublette, Joe Walker—these were a few of the
trustees who owned the West and ushered newcomers in.

Bidwell's Western Emigration Society of 1841 was clearly a
group that needed such leadership, enjoying at the start all the
grand delusions that pie-eyed land seekers seem to conjure out
of their deeps. But they also plucked a piece of real luck out of
the Missouri air. Tom Fitzpatrick, known throughout the West
as "Broken Hand" after an exploding rifle barrel mutilated his
left hand, joined the group with a patch of freighters. They
were taking supplies out to Fort Hall, southeastern Idaho.
Under his leadership, the little column headed west, reaching
the Platte in good season and South Pass by early July. After
crossing the Green River, however, some members of the party
decided the stubby little man with the gnarled hand was leading
them astray. They sought California to the south. Why was he
going northwest? A great discussion ensued. Some said Fitzpatrick knew the route to Oregon, and that was a valuable bit of
information when all others were ignorant of any route what-

ever. But the California yearners, blinded by the fierce glow of their own convictions, held for a southern route. Fitzpatrick, unaccustomed to making life-and-death decisions for other men, just stood to one side scratching that broken old hand and respecting their ignorance as best he could. When talk was through, half the group headed north with him, thereafter reaching Oregon's Willamette Valley in good season. The other group, headed but not led by Bidwell, angled southwest across the Great Basin to California. They also made it, into the San Joaquin Valley, but it was November when they arrived, and they were dazed, nearly starved, crawling with fear and exhaustion, and damned lucky to be there.

Another small group left Missouri for the Coast the following year, this time without a leader of any sort, though organized by a resolutely ignorant promoter named Lansford W. Hastings. Somehow the sixteen wagons and 112 humans struggled westward across the plains. This was the same quarrelsome band that split into two columns over the dog vs. non-dog issue. But again luck curtsied, and after crossing the plains a discreet dog bark apart, these two trains also found Tom Fitzpatrick, this time at Fort Laramie. Easy master of the trail, he soon guided them through to Fort Vancouver on the Columbia.

Having done it once, Hastings figured the way west was easy. He therefore invented the Hastings Cutoff, a vaguely defined route supposedly angling southwest from Salt Lake to California. Invent is the correct verb. Hastings had never traveled the route, but pieced it together from vagrant bits of conversation, then wrote it into a guidebook for eastern consumption. It's enough to add that the famous and tragic Donner party was among his converts. "We had to kill littel Cash the dog & eat him," wrote thirteen-year-old Elizabeth Reed, one survivor of the Donner ordeal. Her letter to a cousin in Springfield, Illinois, told of her rescue with forty-four other survivors in the snowbound Sierras in 1846. "We ate his entrails & feet & hide & every thing about him. There was 15 in the cabin we was in and half of us had to lay abed all the time. There was 10 starved to death. 3 died and the rest ate them. I have not rote you half of

the trouble we had but I have rote you enough to let you know
that you don't know what trouble is. Never take no cutoff and
hury along as fast as you can."

From such tragedy, ignorance, and modest numbers did the
Great Migration across our land begin. Over the next forty
years, it would slowly increase into a steady stream of westering
peoples. So many passed across the plains that an Indian hope
began to rise that white men came out of the rising sun and
passed away into the setting sun. If that was true, they reasoned,
soon enough all their land would once again be free of the
white blight and they could return unhindered to their homelands.

In any case, now that the sand barrier of the Great American
Desert had been breached, the migration across America pushed
ahead in earnest. The population of states east of the Mississippi
increased an average of about 80 percent from 1840 to 1860;
west of the Mississippi in that same period, the population
increased nearly 700 percent. Three major events brought
about this rapid western growth, created out of our national
policy of Manifest Destiny, that new-nation muscle flexing that
first fixed our attentions so firmly in the 1820s. The events were
annexation of Texas in 1845, settlement with England over
Oregon in 1846, and annexation of California, Nevada, and
parts of Arizona and New Mexico in 1848. In four years, the
fledgling new nation added two-fifths of all the territory it later
would hold in the contiguous forty-eight states. It was a big
gulp of land, and in this time, the attentions of easterners were
riveted on the West. Even the most resolute had to reckon with
the power of that western magnetism.

Whether our western migration caused annexation of those
new lands, or the impending annexation caused the migration is
moot. In any case, the two events occurred together and transformed the Great Plains into a broad highway, busy with traffic.
As noted, most of this traffic followed the Oregon Trail. That
pathway stretched from Independence, Missouri, westward
along the Kansas and Republican rivers, then north a short distance to the Platte. Near the Colorado border, the Platte splits,

the South Branch angling along the Front Range to pass
through Denver, while the North Branch angles into central
Wyoming. It was along this North Branch that literally tens of
thousands of emigrants traveled in wagon trains during the
1840s and 1850s, and they became the backbone of the California and Oregon colonies.

Land was not the only goal that led these hopefuls west; it
was land, gold, and God. Sheer circumstance, of course, brought
these forces together, but few occasions in human history have
seen such a powerful triad of reasons merged in one appealing
geographic region at one intense moment. The land annexa-
tions of 1845, 1846, and 1848 provided impetus for one portion
of the migration, while God and His Promised Land were goals
of West Coast missionaries and the migrant Mormon peoples.
But when California gold was discovered at John Sutter's sawmill in 1848, any easterner who till then hadn't considered a
journey west began to give it ample thought.

Plains travel during that busy season of history was heavy,
and knew many shapes and forms. George Willis Read, a
pioneer headed overland in 1850, noted in his journal on May
19 that his own wagon train was just east of Fort Kearny,
Nebraska, and on that day "170 waggons passed us. Some mules.
Horses, Oxen. Some packing on mules and horses, and some on
their backs. Three men and a boy, 12 years old, passed our camp
this morning, with some provisions on their backs. It looked
hard. 4 men are encamped close to us, going through the same
way. We think it hard going as we do, but oh, how much more
laborious to make the trip on foot and carry all your provisions!"

Another Oregon trailer, Madison Berryman Moorman,
reported on June 29, 1850, that traffic headed toward the California gold mines was so heavy that three hundred wagons per
day were crossing the South Platte ferry in Nebraska and paying
$5 each, "besides multiplied hundreds of oxen, horses, and
mules at from fifty cents to one dollar apiece." Five dollars was
a small fortune in 1850. Besides that, those who crossed were
required to propel the ferry themselves! Miners being mined.

Omaha was an important rail center and stopping point on the eastern margin of the plains. It grew rapidly once the westward migration got under way. (*Frank Leslie's Illustrated Newspaper,* NOVEMBER 6, 1858)

The river, Moorman reported on that date, was 150 yards wide, foaming, and running like a mill race—the spring rise in full flow. Later, he saw a "fat-faced, simple-looking good natured and recently imported German, who started from St. Jo. afoot, driving a cow, packed with his little budget. He was moving on finely and said he used the milk of the cow night and morning."

The inducement of gold seekers to use the central plains route was financial. About 25,000 glassy-eyed easterners raced to California by ship in 1849, going via Cape Horn, or by ship to Panama, then overland to the Pacific, and north to San Francisco on a second ship. But more than twice that number went overland, with an estimated 45,000 using the central route. Overland along the Missouri and the Platte might not be the easiest route, but it was cheapest, by far. A Mississippi or Ohio

River farmer could grease his wagon, load provisions, call his dog, and be on his way. A long ship voyage cost money, a dear and scarce commodity for any average footloose eastern American of the late 1840s.

While the central route was most popular, several other routes were used, including the Santa Fe Trail, plus a swampy and/or sandy pair of ruts that drifted west from Shreveport, Louisiana, across the Llano Estacado of northern Texas. From New Mexico the route split indecisively into several branches before crossing the northern end of the Chihuahuan desert in Mexico and present Arizona. All those branches trailed thirstily into southern California. Any who dared such a route and made it then continued pell-mell up the Central Valley or along the Coast to reach the Sierra's Mother Lode.

And so they went, more than 50,000 strong, "Overland in Forty-Nine," heads full of golden thoughts and pockets full of Great Plains dust. In one year they converted California from a sweetly pastoral Mexican ranch colony into a brawling, violent, scabrous piece of the new America. The place became a state in 1850, having grown from 20,000 to more than 90,000 in one golden season.

The going was always rough, but the large number of travelers clearly lowered the frequency of Indian clashes and grizzly bear encounters. For thirst, starvation, snow-blocked mountain passes and alkali dust, however, there were no easy tonics and the overland trails were marked—and frequently not marked—with graves of those who bit that dust too hard.

By far the most resourceful and successful Great Plains migration, however, was that of the Mormon peoples. In a sense, they were like a large emigration society making the trip west, but they used their numbers to fullest advantage. Mormonism had started at Fayette, New York, in 1830, when Joseph Smith was twenty-five. He said the angel Moroni came to him in a vision and led him to a set of buried golden plates on which the teachings of Mormon were inscribed. Smith's magnetic personality soon captured a strong following, and his church of Latter-Day Saints began to fire the anger of other, more traditional sects.

The anger of religious intolerance always seems the strongest known to mankind, and the rise of Mormonism proved no exception. Smith and his little group were soon hounded from the region of Fayette. From here, they moved to Kirtland in northern Ohio where a converted minister promised sanctuary. The Ohio locals were no more desirous to have their beliefs challenged and once again persecution started. Smith announced that another vision had appeared and that he had been instructed to lead his flock to "Zion, the gathering place, on the borders by the Lamanites." Lamanites was translated loosely to mean the western Indians. In short, he would lead the Mormons to the frontier.

So they started out again in 1838, this time for Far West, Missouri. Another group of Mormons had founded that town, but barely had Smith arrived when a riot broke out and about twenty defenseless Mormons were murdered. Smith was arrested by anxious locals and held prisoner for several months. But the growing flock of Mormons, angered by his imprisonment, were becoming a major problem for local officials. So Smith was allowed to escape jail, after which he led fifteen thousand of his followers upriver to a new townsite on the Mississippi, in Illinois. They called it Nauvoo. Again the Mormons settled down to a busy pastoral life, soon building an imposing temple and two thousand dwellings. Nauvoo quickly became the largest city in Illinois and the Mormons, who were learning to shoot back, were now an imposing strength on the landscape.

Trouble continued through the early 1840s, however, and Smith was jailed once again, this time with his brother Hyrum. On the night of June 27, 1844, a mob attacked their jail at Carthage, Illinois, and after being dragged into the street, both leaders were shot by the rioters.

Brigham Young, one of Smith's closest followers, then assumed command of the church, and as a practical, strong-minded leader he soon had solid control of the Mormon destinies. The church was organized on lines of a cooperative society, a popular approach to frontier survival in those days, and the structural base for most western emigration companies. This made control very direct, and to avoid further persecution, Young now decided the Mormons must move to a land no one else wanted. The most remote location in all the West, he reasoned, was beside the Great Salt Lake. Young knew of the lake from the journals of John C. Frémont, who had gone west with a small military column in 1843. Frémont described the Salt Lake region rather thoroughly, and Brigham Young was canny enough to realize that the land had sufficient fertility, but needed irrigation. Also, the area was a veritable fortress, walled in by mountains on east and north and a salty desert west and south. However, fresh water from mountain streams was available plus plenty of sunshine, and Young expected his farm-bred followers to use these assets in creating their Paradise on the desert. So Young now struck a bargain with local officials. If left in peace, he would remove his entire following to the far west. This agreement was kept, and in the winter of 1845–46 the entire church made extensive preparations for the move.

The backbone of Young's following was what we now call Rural Poor, strengthened by shiploads of immigrants from England's industrial slums. Mormonism held out a hand of practical survival and social unity to these people. In return they gave its leaders a solid internal loyalty. God's will would be done through the leadership of Brigham Young and his disciples, and the flock asked no democracy in that alliance. Young, a stocky, plain-spoken man of little education, also was thunderous in his damnation of any who contested his decisions. They were, by definition, "God's Will." Some of the less enlightened formed splinter groups and broke off or were driven out after Smith's death, but the bulk of the Mormons held together and were willing to follow their new leader to Zion.

To transport his people to the Salt Lake basin, Smith took lessons from the bees and the ants. The Mormons, he told his disciples, must send out advance teams of carefully selected artisans to set up camps along the route. In this way, he explained, the main flock could move west without undue losses. Meantime, all set to work building wagons, preparing and storing food, trading livestock for wagon teams, and creating other necessary equipment. Early in February 1846, the first advance group moved across the icy Mississippi to set up Camp of Israel in Iowa. Log buildings were constructed, crops were planted, and necessary preparation made for arrival of the travelers. The migration continued with trail units leaving Nauvoo during most of 1846. By fall that city, largest in Illinois, was a ghost town and most of the travelers were safely in Camp of Israel. In the meantime, another advance group had forged ahead to establish the next major assembly area. This second stopping point was Garden Grove, located about 150 miles beyond Camp of Israel. Again, buildings were constructed and crops planted. Young men in this advance party sought work in the neighborhood to supplement the Mormon needs, and soon the first small units of travelers began to arrive. Brigham Young himself led the third advance group ahead to the banks of the Missouri, where Winter Quarters was established. Once again construction started and because it was June, extensive planting began. Shortly after, small units of the faithful began to arrive here, too.

Now Young could look back over his shoulder and envision a wagon train of 15,000 of his people, strung out for 300 miles across Iowa in small concise bands. They had divided into units of 100, 50, and 10, and each unit was under command of a leader appointed by Young. By fall, the entire Mormon colony was housed at Winter Quarters, or at one of the rest stops along the way.

In 1847 the same approach was used to cross the Great Plains, except that Young was wise enough to avoid the Oregon Trail. That route, he knew, would cause too many conflicts with others traveling west. So he pioneered his own trail, this time along the *north* shore of the Platte. Grazing for wagon animals was better, game was more abundant, and choice campsites were unused. On April 9, 1847, the Mormon's "Pioneer Band" of one hundred forty-three men, three women, and two children started west from Winter Quarters in seventy-three wagons, led by Brigham Young. Just one hundred five days later, on July 22, nine Mormons in a scouting party led by Orson Pratt came out of the Wasatch Range and passed down Emigration Canyon into the valley of the Great Salt Lake. They camped beside a clear mountain stream they named City Creek. Two days later, Brigham Young arrived with the rest of his party to find the advance group already planting potatoes and laying out the townsite. There is little contemporary evidence to support the popular belief that Young, then sick with mountain fever, rose from his wagon bed, looked across the barren landscape, and said: "This is the place." But whether he did or not is unimportant. The Mormons had found their home, and a look at any contemporary map shows how dominant their city is to the lightly populated western slope. Salt Lake remains today the only city of large size for hundreds of miles in all directions.

One final chapter in the Mormon story bears heavily on the history of the Great Plains. In Temple Square in Salt Lake City stands a life-size bronze sculpture of a pioneer Mormon family pulling and pushing a heavy two-wheel handcart. Handcarts were one of Brigham Young's answers to the difficulty and expense of wagon trains. Handcarts, he reasoned, might be smaller than wagons, but each could carry up to six hundred pounds, and each family could be responsible for its own supplies. They also cost far less and required no food, water, lengthy rest stops, or grazing. Nightly guard work could be cut to a minimum, as Indians would find no horses or mules to tempt their raiding skills. Besides, thousands of new converts were coming from England, and plans for their passage had to be made.

So Young assigned a corps of carpenters and wheelwrights to build hundreds of handcarts in Iowa, and when the first immigrants of the year arrived in Iowa City, the careful Mormon planning again bore fruit. Two companies of the faithful, totaling five hundred persons, left that frontier post shortly after arriving in early June, and after one hundred seven days travel rolled into Salt Lake City, somewhat fatigued but full of spirit. They beat all wagon trains en route, and averaged nearly fifteen miles per day across both plain and mountain. That success, however, was not equaled by two later groups which left Iowa in late July, too late to beat winter into the mountain passes. Of the 1,076 that started, 217 were buried en route, and rescue teams from Salt Lake City had to lead survivors into the valley. Brigham Young was sharply criticized for these losses, and rightly so. He should not have allowed them to start west so late in the season. Nevertheless, handcarts had proved their worth, and for four seasons, 1856 through 1860, nearly three thousand Mormons walked to Salt Lake City. En route, on better days, they chanted trail songs to Zion, among them a cart song called "Some must push and some must pull."

Enough pioneering had now taken place so that standard methods of passage over the plains could be questioned, and experimented with, and in the years prior to the Civil War several innovations appeared. Among these were camels, freighters, the Overland and Butterfield coach systems, and the Pony Express.

The camel idea never really got a good try, arriving on this continent at least one civilization too late. Still, the army did need some form of transport to cross the plains, so in 1857 a herd of bandy-legged, highly nervous, and very vocal dromedaries was imported to Texas. A sweating, bandy-legged, and highly nervous lieutenant named Edward F. Beale was placed in charge of the animals, and he tried to recruit help to handle the critters. The only offers he got came from the guard house. Under threat of court-martial, he finally induced a band of cowed privates and corporals to help him herd the animals across the southwestern desert to Los Angeles. There, to replace deserters from his own force, he tried to find civilian help, but all local teamsters faded as soon as they saw the strange beasts. So Beale started east with his little circus, but unfortunately the experiment ended when the animals, 'tis said, escaped one night across the Arizona desert. Escape was a kindness to both sides. At least the army didn't try to recapture their camels, and the camels seemed content enough with the landscape, some descendants reportedly being seen there as late as 1907.

The freighters were a more successful solution. They followed the westward extension of the army, which followed the

"Divine Handcarts," as the Mormons called them, could move with relative ease through Iowa, as this column is doing. But farther west, the going got tough. (T. B. H. STENHOUSE, *The Rocky Mountain Saints*, NEW YORK, 1873)

westward push of the frontier. During the Mexican War in the late 1840s, the army suffered severely from supply problems, and was only too willing to turn the task over to the contractors —even before the camel experiment. One contractor who bid successfully was James Brown of Independence, Missouri. Brown died of typhus in 1850, but not before aligning himself with the legendary William H. Russell, a gamblin' man if ever the West knew one. Russell teamed with Alexander Majors and William B. Waddell to form the famed passenger, freight, and mail company of Russell, Majors & Waddell. Russell was fiery and imaginative, Majors the rough-hewn plainsman, Waddell the businessman. Together in 1855 at Leavenworth, Kansas, they constructed a freighting empire composed of 1,700 men, 500 wagons, and 7,500 oxen. Majors knew the plains and knew wagons, and he demanded the best—those with slightly curved bottoms, a shiplike prow and a square stern. Each would hold five thousand pounds of provisions and equipment. The com-

pany worked with such efficiency during that and the following
year, that in 1857 they were commissioned to carry five million
pounds of supplies to western forts then operated by the army.
That looked profitable all around. Unfortunately, the Mormon
War, a brief open conflict between Mormons and the rest of the
nation, struck that year, requiring transport of an additional
three million pounds, and on that rock their ship-shaped
wagons foundered. The Mormons caught and burned three
long wagon trains while others, forced to leave home base late
in the season, were marooned by winter snows. Added to that
misfortune, the army ran out of money—having some cost over-
runs even then. The company ended the year with army promises of payment and a lot of unpaid bills.

Russell was undaunted. He now elected to enter the mail and
stagecoach business. Jealous easterners may today claim with
vague foundation that no native Californians exist, but in those
years the allegation clearly was true. California was an island
peopled with self-exiled easterners who yearned steadily for any
news of home. Several local promoters soon found that miners
would willingly pay $16, an ounce of gold dust, for a single
letter and when that itch was revealed it quickly produced various scratchers. These mailmen worked overtime but with
patchy success. After several abortive tries to link East with
West, the United States Post Office finally awarded a mail contract to the Butterfield Overland Mail Company. John Butterfield, also a gambler, was on the scene first. In fact, at the very
moment the wagons of Russell, Majors, & Waddell were being
burned by Mormons, Butterfield was signing his mail contract
with the government. It called for a southern all-seasons route
of twenty-eight hundred miles from St. Louis and Memphis to
Fort Smith, Arkansas, then to El Paso, Texas, west to Los Angeles, and north to San Francisco. He planned to use Celerity and
Concord wagons for these fast runs.

Choice of this southern route in 1857 caused an uproar in the
north, then girding for war, but the contract was signed and the
mails began to run. Butterfield had agreed to provide twenty-
five-day service between St. Louis and San Francisco, and that
called for day and night travel, but his first two wagons, one

starting east from San Francisco and one west from St. Louis, made it with hours to spare.

Russell, meanwhile, fretted over Butterfield's success, and tried every ruse he knew to enter the trade. Majors and Waddell were reluctant to move into this untried territory, but Russell forged ahead anyway. Acting independent of his partners, he started a new company with another freighter named John Jones. Gold had been discovered in Colorado that year, and they gambled that a large rush of easterners would cross the plains the following spring. In the winter of 1858–59, they bought fifty Concord coaches, and on April 18, 1859, the Leavenworth and Pike's Peak Express Company dispatched its first coach west from Leavenworth to Denver. The trip took nineteen days and jolted most of the teeth out of the ten passengers. Russell was hailed as a transportation genius, and for a time hopes were high that success lay ahead. But Butterfield held the mail subsidy, and as costs mounted Russell saw that passenger service alone couldn't pay the bills. He had to find some other way to wrest mail traffic from his rival. His solution was the Pony Express.

The Pony Express was not a new idea. Russell and others had toyed with the thought for some time, but it was risky as a business venture. It could be successful if the mail contract was generous and the setbacks few. Before the government would fund a subsidy, however, the idea had to be set in motion. By February, he had convinced his partners, and the plan was rushed into operation. Riders would make the run in ten days, Russell said, and that meant a phenomenal race of more than two hundred miles per day on horseback. Horses therefore were recruited for their violence, and it was claimed that in shoeing these beasts a blacksmith had to be able to hammer fast and above his head. Riders were selected for the rubber in their bones. Special short-horn saddles were created to cut weight to a minimum. On April 3, 1860, the first rider, Billy Richardson, left St. Joseph, Missouri, with forty-nine letters and some special newspapers. He rode at top speed west across Kansas, changing horses at swing stations located every ten miles. After nearly one hundred miles of this hell-for-leather travel, he tossed his tiny mail pouch to a relief rider who sped away into the night.

The Pony Express was under way, and true to Russell's word, he got the mail through to Sacramento in a whisker under ten days. The route of 153 stations followed the old emigrant trail to the Platte River, through South Pass to Fort Bridger in Wyoming, then south around the lower end of the Great Salt Lake to Carson City, Nevada, and through Donner Pass to Sacramento. When the first rider reached California in nine days, twenty-three hours, the West went wild with joy. The celebrations were out of all proportion to the achievement, but Russell's great victory over time and distance meant the two halves of the continent actually could be tied together. Residents of California and Oregon had worried about that problem, as had loyal easterners, and grumblings at this less than perfect union were frequently laced with talk of founding a separate western nation. But for eighteen months, the Pony Express captured the thoughts of the nation, with eighty riders in the saddle at all

The pony express was an imaginative and romantic success, but a financial failure. It operated from April 3, 1860 to October 24, 1861 and died a quiet death under the tapping keys of the first transcontinental telegraph. (MONTANA HISTORICAL SOCIETY, HELENA)

times, and the mails getting through on schedule. The charge was $5 an ounce at first, later reduced to $1 for half an ounce. Only one bag of mail was lost and the partners continued to hope that Congress would favor them with a mail contract.

But it was all ill fated. War fever was now too high, and in the summer of 1860, southern Congressmen defeated a bill that would have awarded this northern company a sizable subsidy. And when the first coast-to-coast telegraph line was completed on October 24, the doom of this most colorful experiment in the history of the mail service was sealed.

It hardly mattered. East and west were now tied together by wire and trail, and the great division that the plains had created was overcome. For the moment, the nation was united.

CHAPTER 13

Trails North and Trails West

The social history of any land is always destined to ebb and flow between times of hurry and times of repose, and the Great Plains of North America offer no exception to this principle. At present, the plains are probably our most overlooked land. They are not popular as places to visit and residents are not numerous. This is true both in Canada and the United States, and the general public view outsiders express toward the plains lies somewhere between distaste and discouragement.

But generations are faddish and sometimes the history they produce moves ahead in spurts. Such was the case with the people of the Great Plains during the brief period from 1860 to 1890, the span of one generation. So many powerful forces came together on the plains in that period that it has proved one of the richest times in our national history. It produced, for example, the entire folklore of the cowboy western. It included the Pony Express and Custer's Last Stand. There were Civil War battles. The "inexhaustible supplies" of buffalo, which numbered fifty million or more at the start of the period, were slaughtered down to a national total of five hundred fifty-one animals. The great North American Cattle Drive came to life, lived its brief colorful moment, and died. Most of the major Indian-white battles took place, and a final peace of sorts was established. All the best-known town marshals and six-shooter badmen lived in this time, and the list provides a virtual Who's

Who of American folklore. Wyatt Earp, Bat Masterson, Doc Holliday, the Daltons, Wild Bill Hickok, Buffalo Bill, the James boys, Billy the Kid, and a host of others—names burned forever into our hero cult. The transcontinental railways were built. The national diet was changed from acorn-fed pork, pine-fed venison, and grass-fed buffalo to beef ribs raised on hay. The great immigrations of European peoples into the American mainstream occurred, with large numbers settling on the plains. The period produced the Homestead Act, the sod buster, the granger and squatter, the Oklahoma Sooner and Boomer, and finally barbed wire, that love-hate invention that clawed its way across the land, closed the frontier, and brought an end to a way of life. By government announcement, in fact, the frontier was declared officially closed in 1890.

What a time it was, sending such a pageant of colorful figures and claiming events trooping across the stage. All elements of the American character were revealed in their grossness, violence, and youthful purity. It was a period rich and vigorous, tragic and free, brutal and hopeful. It was the American people growing into their new clothes, filling out. And a very large piece of all this burgeoning and greening and becoming took place on our Great Plains.

In several ways, the growth of the railroads provides the clearest picture of what happened. The railroads were central to many of the changes, and provide an excellent jump-off to an understanding of this complex period. The first train west of the Mississippi was a smoky puffer and huffer that traveled five miles on a wriggly collection of ties and rails bearing the grand title "Pacific Railroad of Missouri." The route lay between St. Louis and Cheltenham, Missouri, and was traversed on December 23, 1852. The hoopla occasioned by this event far exceeded its practical significance, capturing public attention and concentrating a growing belief that the nation could someday be spanned by rails. Such expansive thoughts were heard increasingly more often both east and west during the 1850s, and by 1860 they were well planted. It was a time of land boomers and such vibrant self-confidence that growth and wealth seemed assured to anyone who even thought about the subject. Hardly a

CATTLE TRAILS AND RAILROADS
1860s – 1880s

stake was driven west of the Mississippi but the hammer poun-
der expected dangerous amounts of money and fame to flow
forth. Every farmer saw himself commanding thousands of lush
acres, every hamlet saw itself a city, every flash of gold in every
western pan brought visions of such excesses of the good life as
could ever soothe and smooth the imagination. He was a buoyant new freedman, this westerner, and railroads would place life
in his hands like a big red apple.

Such happy thoughts sailed like gospel ships through the
1850s skies, far above certain realities that in ordinary times
would have foundered the strongest. For example, in 1850,
States west of the Mississippi housed only two million persons,
mostly in Missouri, Arkansas, California, and Mississippi.
Mostly, too, these hardy westerners were housed in small cities,
such as St. Louis, San Francisco, Fort Smith, Shreveport. Being
in such smallish camps and isolated unto themselves, thinkers of
beautiful railroad thoughts worked as communities to submerge
whatever stray wisps of reality that might happen past. Minnesota provides a fair example of this craft:

For real assets during the railroad boom, Minnesota was fortunate. Its people were clearly safe from any dangerous offers of
credit, no politician had succeeded in removing the place from
the safety of an unknown territory to the exuberance of statehood, and geographically it was a very far country indeed, an
outrage against normal east-west railroad logic of the day. For
all these reasons, railroad fever could flow like cholera morbus
over the 6,077 immoderately enthusiastic residents of Minnesota
and no hurt could come of it. Railroads were therefore cheerily
projected from the Twin Cities to Duluth, from the Twin
Cities to St. Louis, from the Twin Cities—that hub of the uni-
verse—to Nebraska. Red Wing should be the eastern terminus
of a railroad to the Pacific, and a long east-wester should run
from Winona and La Crosse and Duluth to the West Coast at
least, maybe beyond.

Trouble arose in 1858. Statehood was achieved. And smack in
the depths of a national financial panic. Minnesotans solved the
panic problem by ignoring it. They had, in fact, lived with high
railroad temperatures for so long they would be endangered by

Loading longhorns into freight cars was no task for the timid. This scene in the 1870s might have taken place at Ellsworth, or Abilene, or Dodge City, or any of several other western rail points. (STATE HISTORICAL SOCIETY OF COLORADO, DENVER)

any attacks of normalcy and therefore didn't recognize a panic when they saw it. State-subsidized construction of a railroad began immediately—and ended almost as soon for lack of capital, customers, credit, knowledgeable management, rolling stock, rails, and other minor matters.

Lest the reader consider Minnesotans more vaporous than most, it should be noted that the same difficulty of marrying hope to reason plagued all western railroads throughout the period, though the intensity of the fever was sometimes less extreme in some locales. Minnesota can also claim the only really successful railroad of the period, the Great Northern. This came as a piece of luck for the northern states when James J. Hill, a one-eyed Canadian immigrant, settled in Minneapolis in the 1870s. When the St. Paul and Pacific Railroad went bankrupt in 1878, Hill was there to pick up the pieces. Gaining control, he moved cautiously, building westward and running feeder lines only to those points where sizable quantities of freight and passengers could be assured. Hill was not only canny, he was bold, and when it came time to build to the West Coast, he hired ships and imported Irish laborers, indenturing them to his service to work off their boat fares. They proved able and eager workers, and Hill was once heard to remark that with enough Irish whiskey and asbestos ties, he and they could build a railroad through Hell. The Great Northern, prospering steadily, reached Great Falls in 1887 and Seattle in 1893.

On the other hand, the prestigious banking firm of Jay Cooke & Company, which almost single-handedly kept the Union side afloat during the Civil War, met its match in railroad fever. When the Cooke banks closed their doors in September 1873, the worst financial collapse of the nineteenth century gripped the nation. Cooke, an astute and careful financier, had studied the Northern Pacific Railroad project for nearly four years before taking the plunge. Four years later he was reduced from one of America's wealthiest men to a state of bankruptcy—done in by railroad fever. His case was echoed in dozens of lesser financial organizations both earlier and later.

Despite all this boggy ground, the spirit never flagged. It was in truth an optimistic time, and the widespread indifference to reality that claimed railroaders had an enormous impact on development of the entire West. Where sensible economic reason would have faltered, railroad optimism broke through and the vicious cycle that could have forced a much slower development was overcome. Reasonably, railroads should not have grown where there were no people, because trains need people for riding and bundle-carrying and freight-sending. But before there could be people on such a sweeping land as the great West, transportation was needed. The growth of each depended on existence of the other. In 1860 the plains had neither railroads nor people, and if neither could grow without the other, how could settlement proceed?

The answer was optimism, guided by greed. And that was precisely the remedy that emerged. Within twenty years after the Civil War, the plains and the West acquired extensive oper-

ating railways and millions of new residents. The boomers—
those who lived somewhere between lies and prophecy—believed in railroads. They drove them across the plains and
through the mountains, expecting markets to grow around them
like wet-meadow mushrooms. The speculators fed this fever and
kept a pious face. In the symbiotic process that developed, railroads did get built and once built began to operate, whether in
bankruptcy or not. The process was summed up in the Atchi-
son, Topeka, & Santa Fe Annual Report for 1888. "The history
of western railroad construction for the past quarter of a century," the chastened front office noted, "has demonstrated that
successful results can only be attained by occupying territory
promptly, and often in advance of actual needs."

This rueful look backward raised visions of the past, when
glazed belief in a pair of rails sent state and federal and private
support flowing forth. Building a railroad was so acceptable. It
was an act of public goodwill and faith in America. Many
respected political leaders served both on railroad boards of
directors and in Congress, and unabashedly pushed legislation
favoring their own enterprises. It was, after all, a form of community service, like the Red Cross, or the Salvation Army. Massive grants of public land were given railroads along projected
rights-of-way, lands to be used as railroad officials wished, and
most Americans lauded the practice. Land was seen as worthless
until put to work, and the railroads, it was hoped, would see
that those lands were placed in production. Large blocks of
those lands were sold, sometimes to finance construction work,
sometimes to settle immigrant farmers. Such agricultural communities as might take root were then expected to produce
grains and livestock for shipment—in separate cars—over the
company's lines.

From 1862 to 1872, United States railroads received rights to
180,000,000 acres of public domain lands, an area about the size
of Michigan, Wisconsin, and Minnesota combined. A very large
proportion of this total was on the Great Plains. In 1862 the
Homestead Act also was passed, under which the federal government provided any citizen with 160 acres of land free, provided he worked the land and improved it over a five-year period.

A former Union soldier with the appropriate name of Daniel Freeman was first to accept this bet, settling on his quarter section near Beatrice in southeastern Nebraska on January 1, 1863. His stake was later converted into the 160-acre Homestead National Monument in memory of a law that provided homes and sustenance for half a million families before 1900. Once again, the Great Plains were the key lands settled by homesteaders during this period.

The Civil War also aided settlement of the plains in a very powerful way. Prior to the war, the nation had been divided by the question of the best railway route to the Pacific. Southerners wanted a line from New Orleans or Memphis through Santa Fe or west Texas, then across the Arizona desert to southern California. Northerners wanted to follow the Oregon Trail from Iowa and Missouri through Nebraska and Wyoming, then over South Pass and the Great Basin to northern California. This route would cross the Sierras at Truckee or The Needles. The arguments were bitter and prolonged, and served to delay all decisions. Once war broke out, however, the North was free to answer the question on its own and chose the northern, or Union Pacific route. During war years, construction was slowed in the West, but with the end of hostilities, the pace picked up, both on the main line and on several others as well. The Union Pacific and the Kansas Pacific both stretched westward, crossing the plains immediately after the war.

The growth of these lines soon brought a new quantum into the American scene, one destined to change the face—and posture and growth and health—of the American people. That quantum was beef. Beef was needed in cities of the industrial Northeast. Texas had it and the railroads could carry it. But it was a very different beef than we know today. It was wild, slab sided, and about as chewable as whang leather. Store-bought teeth were tested for their endurance on that beef.

The first bovine cattle to enter North America landed at Vera Cruz, Mexico, in 1521 as part of the settlement program of Cortez. Cortez himself soon founded a large ranch south of Mexico City and named it appropriately Cuernavaca, or Cow's Horn. There the Spanish cattle he imported took root. These

A rare picture of Chinese coolies working on the railroad. This was the Northern Pacific in the 1880s near the Clark Fork River in Montana. (HISTORICAL SOCIETY OF MONTANA, HELENA)

wild-eyed descendants of the Asian ox were smallish but tough, the forerunners of Spanish fighting bulls. In Mexico they began to multiply rapidly and sizable numbers appear to have grown both domestically and in a semiwild state. Coronado, while preparing for his famous expedition to the Great Plains, hunted up five hundred of the beasts and kept a small army of drovers swearing in fluent Spanish as he skittered them north to Arizona, New Mexico, and Kansas. That was in 1541, but it's doubtful if any descendants of these animals survived the expedition. They were much too enraptured with their own ideas of freedom, and were probably all murdered by Coronado's keepers. In Mexico, however, they continued to multiply and spread northward along the West Coast. Once there they appear to have literally mushroomed in numbers from year to year. They entered the northern Mexico colonies in the seventeenth century and so came to Texas, New Mexico, and California. Conditions in those three locations favored cattle raising, and their spread and increase continued unchecked. That is to say, there were few Spaniards and no fences and therefore no check on their growth. Indians, whose teeth had been hardened by eons of chewing at some of the toughest meat land can produce, met their match in the Spanish cow. Though they killed his master, these Indians generally left his animals alone, eating in preference the handy buffalo. However, these leftover cattle had little value in commerce. Through Indian depredations and strained relations between Spain and France, these cattle could not be driven to markets such as New Orleans or Shreveport. They supplied their scattered Spanish owners with hides, tallow, and meat, but their numbers increased far beyond this limited use.

After about 1770, however, the Apaches, Lipans, and Comanches found some comfort in the shortage of Spaniards by slaughtering their cattle. Scores of thousands of such cattle were killed before Americans began to enter the southern plains, yet sizable numbers still ran wild all over the region as American settlement progressed. By 1860 farmers had sparsely settled most of eastern and northern Texas, and were raising cotton and chasing cattle as steady occupations. The Civil War cut into this pastoral development and loosened whatever restraints Texans had clamped on those semiwild Spanish beasts. Once again cattle increased freely, this time with little interference from either Indians or whites.

At the close of the Civil War, Texans drifted home to find large numbers of these free-roaming animals scattered across much of the state, most of them unbranded, and all resolutely convinced that Mr. Lincoln had freed them, too. The battle of wills that now began between cow and man forged the American cowboy—that word cowboy then being used with a smile, for he was neither boy nor worker of cows. More accurately, he was a cattle-thumper, attempting to place a sort of vague domination over those four-legged collections of bone, gristle, and horn, a domination always subject to dispute and likely to disappear momentarily in sudden fits of free thought. The longhorn had been born, and now came stampeding into American history about twenty yards ahead of a storm of profanity, whistling lariats, and galloping semi-insane cow ponies. Astride the latter was America-on-the-move, personified. The longhorn came to this contest with his textured Spanish past, but he was America's own, at least as tough and colorful and free as his two-legged opposition.

The longhorn, however, was born as much from railroad fever as Spanish introduction. "Occupy territory promptly, often in advance of actual need"—that was the railroader's thought that gave the cowboy and longhorn their chance for glory in the American kaleidoscope. As the rails pushed west, cattle were driven north. The two came together in a shower of howls, bellows, gunfire, and other air pollution at such locations as Abilene, Ellsworth, Dodge City, and Wichita. The first major trail drive of longhorns was carried north in 1866, and while only moderately successful economically, it was a big hit back home. Mainly it offered new occupations for men and their horses, plus purposeful use of a lot of aimless cattle. An estimated six to fifteen million of these animals roamed over the plains of Texas after the Civil War, with ownership depending almost solely on who controlled the land they grazed. There were few fences, and barbed wire had not come into use. As a matter of practice, most men figured they had enough trouble handling their own cattle without trying to claim those found on lands of another, and this tradition of recognizing the "accustomed range" of semiwild cattle now gave rise to a new social activity called the "cow hunt." Not yet a roundup, or cattle drive, but just a cow hunt.

Cow hunts started in the spring when the sage was new and the grass a pale blue-green and the plains air perfumed by the annual carpet of flowers, and the whole countryside fresh and alive. In those weeks of new warmth and singing meadowlarks, the male members of a farm community—not ranches yet, either—would turn out on horseback and head off across the landscape in search of the cows. They carried their own flour and beans and branding irons, and they camped each night in a different location as a sociable group of friends and neighbors.

Cattle were the stakes for the nightly poker game, with a valuable—that is, catchable—animal bringing upward of $5, while yearlings were fifty cents and calves "was throwed in free" with their mommies. There were so many cattle available that sometimes the poker games got downright large. Since there was little actual money, however, bits of paper were used for betting, each marked one cow, two cows, five cows, etc. The story is told of one such legendary game in which two gambling cowboys named Chicken Breast Bartlett and Smelly Johnson bumped each other night after night while the competition between them gradually grew more and more intense. One night Bartlett would win, the next night Smelly. As more and more cattle were collected, the stakes got higher and higher. One night Bartlett got on a winning streak and nearly cleaned Smelly out. Finally, however, Smelly's luck turned and for once he got a good hand.

"I'll bet a cow," said Bartlett routinely, glancing at his hand.

"I'll see your bet, and raise you two cows," said Johnson. Bartlett, surprised, guessed Smelly was making a desperate bluff, and so came right back. "I'll see that and raise you five head of the best darned cattle in Texas."

These triple-decker freight cars were bunkhouses for railroad gangs during construction days. They were all right for the plains, but they later had to be sawed off to get through tunnels in the mountains. (HISTORICAL SOCIETY OF MONTANA, HELENA)

Johnson barely hesitated. "All right, I'll see your bet and raise you ten head."

Bartlett saw Johnson had now used up the last of his cattle notes and could no longer keep up the pace. "I'll see that and raise you twenty head," he said triumphantly.

Smelly, desperate, looked at his hand, looked around wildly, finally anchored on another cowpoke. "Here Willy," he said, "hold my hand while I go out and round up enough cows to call that bet."

A successful cow hunt, however, had to end in the marketplace. As word spread through Texas in the late '60s that the railroad was pushing west, some individuals arranged to take gatherings of these animals north. There being little money in the country but lots of honor, such business was normally handled on verbal credit. The drover would head north out of Texas with gatherings of cattle from a dozen of his neighbors. When he returned in the fall, he divided proceeds accordingly. In years of loss, all suffered, and the drover wasn't penalized. But one hedge against such losses was invented by an enterprising cattle pusher whose idea lingers in the English lexicon in the phrase "watered stock." His plan was simple. Feed the cattle plenty of salt in their hay the day before being sold. The thirst this caused forced the cattle to take on great quantities of water before weigh in, thereby raising their price by eight pounds per gallon.

In 1866, the first big year of the cattle drive, an estimated 260,000 head were driven north, not only to the Kansas Pacific in eastern Kansas, but also north to new pastures in Missouri and Iowa. The several routes first taken all lay across Indian lands in Oklahoma. Most Indians had by this date seen enough of white men to know they spelled trouble, so any man traveling through their territory with several thousand longhorns could expect a lively trip. Their pathways north out of Texas endured as legendary highways under the names of Chisholm Trail, Goodnight-Loving Trail, Texas Road and Osage Trace, Western Trail, and several others. Of them all, the Chisholm Trail remains the best known, though the facts about it are generally freighted with myth and misunderstanding.

Jesse Chisholm's father was a Scot and his mother a Tennessee Cherokee. He was born in Tennessee in 1805 and emigrated across the Mississippi as a young man, beginning his life's work as a merchant and cattle supplier to Great Plains military posts such as Forts Riley and Harker, and to Forts Zarah and Scott farther east. He had a natural facility with Indian languages, once answering modestly when asked about this that he knew "only six." Because of this knowledge, and because he was a mixed blood, he found it easy to move among the Plains Indians. Soon he was trading with the Wichitas and Caddos in west central Oklahoma. In the early 1840s that was dangerous country, both for Indians and whites, but Chisholm survived rambles by the nomadic Comanches and Kiowas as well as other more settled tribes. He was later adopted into the Wichita tribe, and suffered with them in their losses of life and property during the Civil War. After the war, he established a ranch between the Kansas and Little Kansas rivers, northeast of present Wichita, and was soon actively trading cattle and frontier merchandise once again. Though the country was still largely unorganized, Chisholm seemed to move through it casually, and in the spring of 1865 blazed a wagon trail due south 220 miles across central Kansas and into southwestern Oklahoma to the new Wichita Indian agency on the Washita River. This original wagon trail later became the spine of the Chisholm Trail over which several million longhorns were driven. The trail had many offshoots north and south, and those who followed it north might start anywhere in central Texas and complete their journey in Kansas, Missouri, Iowa, or Nebraska. There was, in short, a great divergence of understanding about the true location of the Chisholm Trail, and the many recollections of the many men who cursed their cattle northward must be respected when they say they "followed the Chisholm Trail." For all of that, however, the only trail Jesse Chisholm blazed was his wagon road to the Wichita Indian agency, across central Kansas and Oklahoma, in 1865. Chisholm died in 1868, and is buried near Greenfield, Oklahoma. His tombstone says simply: "Jesse Chisholm. Born 1805, died March 4, 1868. No one left his home cold and hungry."

Meantime, the Kansas Pacific was building its way southwest, and in 1867 had arrived at Abilene, Kansas. There an Illinois cattleman and promoter named Joseph G. McCoy was arranging for eastern cattle buyers to meet western drovers. There being no trail across the plains, the first of these herds was led about aimlessly for days while its herders looked for the market. To solve that, the following spring McCoy—from whom the phrase "the real McCoy" derives—sent out a surveyor and work parties to throw up a line of dirt mounds. Each of these was topped with a flag bearing a crudely drawn Lone Star to guide the herds in.

With Texas cattle now plugged into the railroad market, the annual cattle drives increased in size and frequency. No one knows how many longhorns traveled those trails to the north, but estimates range from four to six million between 1866 and 1886 when the practice came to an abrupt end. Cattle were driven north to the Kansas and Missouri railroads, and also to northern ranges in Colorado, Nebraska, Wyoming, Montana, and the Dakotas.

During these drives, cattlemen were subjected to constant and usually justified harassment from Indians, whose lands they crossed, and from grangers and sod busters, whose crops they trampled. Sometimes pitched battles left men dead on both sides. At other times, lone farmers lay in wait along the trail and exacted tribute by shooting a stray steer or two—known locally as "slow elk." Such trouble caused a national convention of stockmen to urge, in 1884, that a "National Cattle Trail" be established from the northern boundary of Texas—the Red River—all the way to Canada. The trail was to be six miles wide, and was to be open land, free to the use of any cattleman. Settlers and Indians were to be excluded. The idea was squelched by railroad interests and disgruntled settlers who, by that date, had enough trouble from cattlemen to last a lifetime.

Meantime, the northern plains during this period produced other stories. In 1860 the entire region was largely unsettled, being still the province of the Indian and the buffalo. Nebraska did not convert from a territory to a state until 1867, and Colorado followed eleven years later. Montana and North and South Dakota did not attain statehood until 1889, and Wyoming in

1890. Nevertheless, settlement was underway much earlier throughout the region and a nucleus population had taken hold by 1860. Between 1860 and 1890, however, the entire ownership and character of the northern plains was converted to the white man's ways. What had grown as a balanced relationship between land and man over thousands of years was wiped away in an instant, and an entire new way of life was planted in its place.

These were the years in which the great buffalo herds were destroyed. It was a wanton destruction, almost malicious in nature. That revered hero of American folklore, Buffalo Bill Cody, reputedly killed forty-three hundred of the big woollies in eight months, from October 1867 to May 1868, while working as a railroad supplier. Buffalo hides brought a high enough price to make it worth a man's time to hunt them, and professional teams went onto the plains with wagons to more efficiently manage the slaughter. Hunters used the Sharps Buffalo Rifle that fired a piece of lead half an inch in diameter and weighing one and one-half ounces. The rifle had a very long barrel, and hunters generally used it in the kneeling position. To steady this sixteen-pound weapon, they carried a pair of "buffalo sticks." These were straight wooden canes, about three feet long, tied together near one end, so they could be spread out like a pair of scissors to form a bipod. The rifle barrel was placed in the notch and the buffalo were shot from a distance, often a quarter of a mile or more. Having poor eyesight, buffalo could not see the hunter. They could smell the blood, and they milled about in confusion, but they usually failed to stampede, so a hunter in a good location often was able to kill an entire herd without moving from one spot. To cool the barrel of his rifle, and to remove carbon buildup from black powder, he would simply pour water down the tube, then load again and continue to fire. Such rifles were unbelievably accurate. One Billy Dixon at the battle of Adobe Walls reputedly killed an Indian from a distance of 1,538 yards, shooting a fifty-calibre Sharps Buffalo Rifle.

An English hunter named Sir George Gore—from whom we get the words gore and gory—carried the practice of buffalo killing to a high art. He came to America in 1854 with an arsenal

of weapons and a retinue of beaters. For three years he killed
the great herds of Wyoming, Colorado, and New Mexico. It
could hardly be called hunting. Sir George had himself placed
in a blind in a likely looking location. Then a small army of
beaters would drive local game past. Seated on a camp chair,
Gore would fire at anything that approached. He would hand
each emptied gun to one of his helpers who would, like a surgeon's aide, hand back a loaded weapon. Gore didn't even stop
to eat; food was brought and he continued to fire between bites.
Several thousand buffalo, elk, deer, and other animals were
killed during this three-year tour of the plains.

Other similar expeditions were fairly common during the
period, but the major portion of the slaughter was carried out
by the hide hunters. Traveling in teams, killing was the easiest
work. One hunter could keep three or four other men busy
skinning and scraping the hides, and buffalo were so numerous
and the plains so easy for wagon travel that scores of these teams
were at work each season. Between 1860 and 1889, when the
slaughter was ended for lack of targets, the original herd of 50,-
000,000 Great Plains buffalo were reduced to a miserly 551 animals. Today, about 10,000 survive in scattered colonies throughout North America, most of them protected on state or federal
ranges.

Following destruction of the great herds, a new industry arose
—bone collection. Buffalo bones were useful in making potash,
and after the wolves, vultures, and ants had finished their work,
the whitened bones were gathered and stacked like cordwood
beside railroads for shipment east.

With this destruction came an end to the Indian's traditional
way of life, and having lost his source of food, he was reduced to
a state of hunger, anger, and resentment. Badgered by the white
man's army, scattered in fragmentary bands, and pushed beyond
the pale of advancing civilization, the Indian sought in desperation for some road back. A moment of vengeance showed itself
in 1876, when the arrogant cavalry general, George Custer,
decided to attack several thousand Sioux with a force of 650
men. Custer—34th in his West Point class of 34—had been
assigned to find an Indian village known to be located in southeastern Montana and to bring the inhabitants to a reservation.

This depiction of Custer's Last Stand, one of many, shows Custer and his 7th Cavalry being attacked by mounted Sioux under Crazy Horse and Sitting Bull. Custer's two brothers and a nephew died with him at the "Battle of the Little Bighorn" on June 25, 1876. (WESTERN HISTORY COLLECTIONS, UNIVERSITY OF OKLAHOMA LIBRARY, NORMAN)

He located the village in late June. Believing he faced about 1,000 poorly-armed Sioux, he divided his force into three units and prepared to attack. Taking leadership of the right flank, Custer ordered the center of his line to charge. Major Marcus A. Reno commanded the center, and soon found himself embroiled in more trouble than anyone had expected. He retreated with his force into a range of hills, where he was joined by members of the left flank. Custer meanwhile was surrounded on the right flank, and his entire force was wiped out. One of the Sioux leaders, Crazy Horse, was soon captured, but Sitting Bull escaped to Canada where he remained until 1881

After returning to the Sioux reservation he was killed in 1890.

Repercussions of this Battle of the Little Bighorn were wide-spread, and did much to sharpen tempers between whites and Indians for decades afterward. One tragic consequence was the killing of about two hundred Sioux men, women, and children at Wounded Knee Creek, South Dakota, in 1890. The Indians had been captured by federal troops and were being disarmed when a rifle discharged, setting off the slaughter.

The removal of buffalo and Indians from the northern plains region progressively opened those lands to settlement by whites, and among the most obvious uses for the now-uninhabited plains was cattle raising. Accordingly, Texas cattle were soon trailed north to these vacant ranges, where they found sufficient water and plenty of nutritious buffalo grass during summer months. Here the trail-weary animals could be fattened and readied for market close beside the westering railroads. Both the Union Pacific and the Northern Pacific offered freighting service to eastern markets, and the combination of cattle, land, transportation, and markets all suggested a sudden boom time for the northern plains.

It was not long in coming. The only scarcity throughout the region was an active supply of capital, and this was soon remedied. Eastern investors who watched western developments as a habit soon poured sizable funds into the northern plains cattle industry. Also, in one of the more unusual turns of American finance, large amounts of English money were invested in the Wyoming, Colorado, Nebraska, Dakota, Montana region. Nearly all of it centered in the cattle industry. How much was invested will never be known, but eleven typical English and Scotch cattle companies operating in the plains states from 1883 to 1885 owned and leased a total of nearly 3,500,000 acres of rangelands. The West had the cattle, the grass, and the experience; the East poured in the capital, and the railroads held the two together.

This introduction of the polished eastern dude and the English gentleman into the crusty society of experienced western cattlemen has provided stereotypes for countless films, dime novels, and magazine fiction. But in the early '80s, the scenes were true life and frequent. Cattlemen parked their mucky

boots beneath mahogany bank conference tables and waxed elo-
quent. Eastern investors—their audience—listened wide-eyed
and invested wide open. Cattlemen could name their price, and
in that day before securities controls, plenty of bogus companies
were mixed with legitimate enterprises. As a result, the entire
northern plains stock-raising industry was steadily overcapital-
ized by speculators. If owning one ranch could make a man
wealthy, owning two could make him rich beyond dreams. Competition for the purchase of land and cattle thus hoisted prices
far beyond their real worth. Prices continued to spiral upward,
and cattle continued to pour into the northern plains as the
late 1870s advanced into the early '80s. The crash had to come
and unfortunately for the cattle it came on the winds of the
worst blizzard in western history. The winter of 1885–86 was
bad enough, and should have warned owners on the crowded
northern ranges that trouble lay ahead. That winter some
ranches lost up to 85 percent of their cattle. Mostly, however,
these losses occurred in Oklahoma, Colorado, and Kansas where
the herds were generally smaller.

The summer of 1886 saw business as usual once again, and
almost no one set aside any winter feed. Hay storage was not the
habit, and cattle normally rustled enough grass to see themselves through with losses of only 5 to 10 percent. That summer
was dry, however, and both range and cattle headed into the fall
in poor condition. A heavy snowfall in late November blotted
out what range there was, and almost immediately many
crowded herds were in trouble. The snow continued to burden
the range as cattlemen prayed for a chinook. It came finally in
early January, a strong warm wind from the south that evaporated the snow and revealed the range to the starving cattle. But
barely had this relief appeared when the blizzard of January 28
hit. It howled in out of the north as the most ferocious storm of
wind and snow ever seen. Vision was reduced to zero. Men got
lost going a few yards from house to barn and were found days
later, frozen, having wandered in circles before falling. Cattle,
for a moment, were forgotten in the fierce human struggle for
survival. The storm continued for days, battering the entire
plains region from Canada south to Texas. When the worst was
over, there were still weeks of swirling snow. Temperatures

dipped to forty below, and stayed there for days, while stockmen dared not think what was happening on their ranges. At night they tried to close their ears to the plaintive bawling of dying cattle outside their cabins. The only hope men had was for another chinook to warm the ranges and free the grass, poor as it was. But the chinook never came, and the weeks dragged into March, with snow and bitter cold singing a message that would never be forgotten.

When the weather finally broke, deeply humbled cattlemen drifted out to survey the loss. They found horrible sights. Dead cattle were piled atop each other where they'd been stopped by fences. Battered, dazed animals with frozen feet, ears, and tails had to be dispatched with rifles to end their suffering. Men were revolted by the sight, and speculating stockmen who had failed to provide winter feed were heaped with abuse by press and public. Overnight, the bubble had burst, and dozens of companies with heavy investments in cattle and land were swept into bankruptcy courts. An estimated ten million head of livestock were lost in the Great Plains region that winter, all the way from Alberta to Texas. The disaster had been complete, and brought a virtual revolution to the cattle industry. Many men, sickened by the sights they saw that spring, left the business entirely. Those who survived bankruptcy vowed never again to overstock their ranges, and to lay up sufficient winter foods to see them through future blizzards. Wyoming had had about three million cattle in 1880, at the start of the boom period, and nine million at the peak in 1886. After the disaster of the blizzard, the herd was shattered, and ten years later had climbed back only to the three million level. Other states throughout the plains region were similarly jolted back to earlier, lower levels.

The Great Plains had now been shocked into a new way of life. What had been a monolith of cattle and open ranges had survived by political power, great wealth, and range wars. But a growing tide of impoverished, tough new immigrants were now filling up the plains states with other visions in mind. These were members of the "New Migration" that were beginning to flow west and they would inevitably claim the plains as their own. The story of this peopling of the plains now became the center of the greatest mass migration in the history of mankind.

CHAPTER 14

Peopling the Plains

The American frontier was officially closed in 1890. "Up to and including 1880 the country had a frontier of settlement," a census official wrote, "but at present the unsettled area has been so broken into by isolated bodies of settlement that there can hardly be said to be a frontier line."

That wasn't really a very accurate pronouncement. Certain words do sing little songs in the human brain, and "frontier" rang like crystal on this continent for nearly three hundred years. Throughout most of the nineteenth century, however, and until very recently, the frontier was reduced more to a state of mind than a geographical condition. The entire West had been broken into "by isolated bodies of settlement" as early as 1840. By 1850, strong lines of travel threaded westward over the plains, through the mountains, into the Great Basin, and up and down the West Coast. The greatest migration of humans since the Crusades was getting under way, and it would continue throughout the century. The migrants came from the eastern United States and from Europe, and from the late 1840s onward to the days of the railroads, those ribbons of white-topped wagons rippled across the plains in every month they were green. Most followed the "Nebraska Seacoast"—the Platte River—going west to plant stakes and make states out of California and Oregon. Others, who figured they'd need a bit more sunshine, angled off across Kansas and some other vaguely known

lands toward a place called Santa Fe. Nobody would know it as
New Mexico for half a century; it was merely a land of opportunity, some said, where there was a town and people who liked to
trade, and anyway it was *West*. That was the important part.
The whole West was a new land to be tried for a home, and it
had a furry carpet of buffalo, and there was a funny, stiff sort of
short mat underneath called buffalo grass that tickled the bellies
of the prairie dogs—but fed the oxen and mules and milch cows
of the pioneers year after year. And the way west was so well-
known by the 1850s that "prairie navigation is simple"—or so
an emigrant's guide book said. "Merely follow the wheel ruts of
the wagons which have preceded you. . . . If you travel at the
normal rate for oxen of eight miles a day, there are enough natural beacons so that you will never need a compass."

In those fanciful years all the West, and the plains in particular, were seen as a sweet and open land, beckoning anyone seeking a new and wonderful home. The land was flat and bare and
easy to plant. If crops failed, there was always a gold rush under
way or about to start. Seven took place between 1848 and 1900.
Slower rushes called more people west to discoveries of silver,
copper, lead, and other metals. "When I wash my face in the
Yellowstone," one jackass miner wrote home from Montana, "I
comb $10 nuggets out of my beard." An Iowa newspaper noted:
"A Colorado miner is reported to be sitting on a nugget of solid
gold weighing 839 pounds, which he can't move and doesn't
dare leave. When last seen, he was offering $27,000 for a plate of
pork and beans." After the Homestake lode was found in South
Dakota in 1876, miners were warned not to hang their laundry
outside during dust storms. "The pockets fill with gold and,
becoming heavy, break the clothesline." The Homestake proved
out as the largest gold mine in the Western Hemisphere and visitors were advised: "If you stub your toe on a rock, don't cuss it,
cash it."

The myth and hoopla surrounding Great Plains gold might
be doubted in some quarters, but not the more sober view of
that land as a frontier. Having been bypassed by migrants
sweeping to the Coast twenty years earlier, the plains now
focused the attentions of land-hungry settlers. California had

Crossing the plains during our great westward migration had all the markings of a Conestoga traffic jam. This was a scene taken along the Oregon Trail in 1862. (STATE HISTORICAL SOCIETY OF COLORADO LIBRARY, DENVER)

been accepted to statehood in 1850, Oregon in 1857. Now East and West, separated by the plains, needed tying together. As a step in this direction, Kansas was given statehood on January 29, 1861—and seventy-four days later the Civil War broke out.

Statehood for Kansas was, in fact, as much a cause of the Civil War as any single factor. The region was long a hotbed of pro-slavery and antislavery forces, and Congress bickered for months over whether it should be a slave or free state. Finally a compromise was reached. Those who lived in the state would decide for themselves which side Kansas would join. When that was announced, sympathizers from northern and southern states both formed committees to send strong-willed and short-fused adherents into the Kansas Territory. A large number of restless settlers took up residence there as a result. Among other fire-brands, John Brown moved into the state in 1855 to start his desperate little march into history. With five of his sons he served as a leader of the antislavery forces and began raids on the opposition. In one encounter, he brutally murdered five

defenseless slaveholders at Potawatomie Creek, thereby earning
the name "Old Osawatomie Brown," along with an outlaw's
brand. Four years later, with the flames in Kansas burning
brightly, Brown attacked the government arsenal at Harper's
Ferry, Virginia, and, after failing to escape, was hanged for treason on December 2, 1859. But he had done his work well.
"Bleeding Kansas," as it came to be known, entered the Union
within a year after his execution, its people voting to join the
Northern cause. With feelings against slavery so strong, Kansas
sent more troops into Union service in proportion to its population than any other northern state.

But those Kansans who stayed home also saw some bloody
fighting. Among other lesser encounters, William Clarke Quan-
trill and his guerrilla raiders attacked the city of Lawrence on
August 21, 1863, burned the city, and left one hundred and fifty
Northern sympathizers dead. Then he disappeared into the surrounding plains.

After the war, great changes faced the plains states. All the
industrial power that had grown to feed northern military
forces suddenly needed new markets. Railroad construction
across the plains provided one immediate outlet, supported by
government land grants and a work-hungry populace. The
Union army, left with a bulky framework, added its thrust to
Great Plains settlement. Having fought Indians before and
during the Civil War, it now turned full attention to the western front, bringing on at one stroke the saddest era in the history of the plains.

Much has been written about our Indian wars, and much
made of the brutality invading whites visited on our resident
Indians. Unfortunately much of this writing grows from a deep
sense of white guilt and red outrage, neither emotion helping to
clarify what actually happened. About two hundred minor and
major conflicts involving bloodshed took place on the Great
Plains in the last half of the nineteenth century. They were the
last collection of Indian-white battles in America, and they grew
because a veritable tide of settlers swept onto the plains in general disregard of prior Indian occupation. From 1850 to 1900,
white populations increased elevenfold, from about 700,000 to

more than 8,000,000. Plains Indian populations, though not known with accuracy, declined from a high of about 135,000 in 1830 to 30,000 or 40,000 in 1900. Smallpox, battles, massacres, and severe disruptions of family and social patterns battered tribal numbers and brought them steadily downward.

Some of these encounters between white men and red men are classics in the annals of racial hatred. The so-called Battle of Sand Creek is a case in point, standing as one of the whites' worst outrages against humanity. In the fall of 1864, a small group of disruptive Indians kidnapped several white women and children from a settlement in eastern Colorado. Local Union forces, garrisoned far west of most Civil War action, had been itching for some contest to prove their merit. Soon after the kidnapping, a mixed force of volunteer and regular militia under Colonel J. M. Chivington set out from Denver with the express purpose of "killing Indians." Chivington had, in fact, ordered his officers to kill Indians "wherever and whenever they are found." William Bent, founder of Bent's Fort, tried to reason with the colonel, but to no avail. Bent's wife, a full-blooded Cheyenne, had been so angered by other white excesses in those troubled times that she took their two sons and returned to tribal life. As husband and father and long-time friend of the Cheyennes, Bent was sickened by the lengthening list of skirmishes leaving both whites and Indians dead. His discussion with Chivington brought only a terse response. "I am on the warpath," Chivington told him. "I am not authorized to make peace."

Meantime, about 400 Cheyennes under the aging Chief Black Kettle had approached Major Scott J. Anthony, commandant at Fort Lyon in southeastern Colorado, asking for peace. The major, frightened and fearing a trick, advised them to camp on Sand Creek, hunt nearby, and wait for a forthcoming peace conference. As soon as the Cheyennes departed, Anthony sent for Chivington. When the colonel arrived, he and Anthony drove their combined force of about 950 men on an all-night march toward the Indian encampment. They were located on a bend in what is now Big Sandy Creek about ten miles southeast of present Kit Carson, Colorado. A fair amount of drinking was

This grim mass burial of Indians followed the slaughter at Wounded Knee Creek in South Dakota. The soldiers had been disarming the Indians one winter day in 1890 when a rifle discharged, precipitating the bloody encounter. About 200 Sioux were killed. (WESTERN HISTORY COLLECTIONS, UNIVERSITY OF OKLAHOMA LIBRARY, NORMAN)

under way during the march, and the local militia was soon unruly. When morning came on November 29, the attack started. The drunkenness probably helped about two-thirds of the Cheyennes escape up and down the river and into surrounding foothills. But 130 to 150 others were not so lucky. Congressional inquiry revealed that infants were shot and scalped, genitalia hacked from both men and women, and the wounded were indiscriminately shot. No prisoners were taken. Chief Black

Kettle raised both a white flag and an American flag as soon as the shooting broke out, holding to a blind faith that some tragic mistake had been made. He was promptly shot and the slaughter continued sporadically most of the day.

This atrocity so inflamed the Plains Indians that old tribal hatreds were forgotten and a general coalition of Cheyennes, Arapahos, and Comanches gathered for all-out war. Their raids and destruction continued off and on for nearly thirty years.

Farther north, the Sioux nation also lashed at the white man, as settlers moved into the Dakotas and Montana. In 1876 the brilliant Sioux strategist Crazy Horse lured General George Crook's cavalry forces into the Battle of the Rosebud in south-eastern Montana and gave them a thorough thumping. The Custer massacre occurred the following week only a short distance away. Sitting Bull and Crazy Horse correctly expected an early white attempt at vengeance for these twin encounters, and therefore split their forces into small bands and scattered. Sitting Bull escaped to Canada where he remained until 1881. Crazy Horse was captured, then soon after was killed "while trying to escape." No authentic photograph or drawing of him has ever surfaced.

The year following Custer's defeat, Chief Joseph refused to take his Nez Perce people to a reservation and began a brilliant 1,000-mile escape trek across Montana, first moving south, then back to the north. But when he paused to rest at Bear Paw Mountain, only thirty miles from the relative safety of Canada, the whites caught up and after a five-day battle he surrendered. The Nez Perce were forced back onto the reservation to suffer and dwindle.

In the south, the Apaches fought stubbornly and longer under such sage leaders as Cochise, Victorio, and Geronimo. But the white invaders kept coming and gradually claimed more and more territory. These bitter and cruel Apache-white wars continued for nearly forty years with no quarter given on either side, and they kept west Texas and New Mexico in a constant turmoil. The last great leader of the Apaches, Geronimo, surrendered and was imprisoned in 1886, but he had by then so inspired his people that they continued the struggle until 1906.

Cold, exhausted, and surrounded, Chief Joseph finally surrendered the remnants of his Nez Perce tribe to General Miles only a short distance from the sanctuary of Canada. (CYRUS TOWNSEND BRADY, *Northwestern Fights and Fighters*, NEW YORK, 1909)

But then it was over. "I am tired of fighting," Chief Joseph said in his surrender speech. "Our chiefs are killed. The old men are all dead. The little children are freezing to death. My people have run away to the hills, and have no food. No one knows where they are. I want to have time to look for my children. Maybe I shall find them among the dead. Hear me, my chiefs, I am tired. My heart is sad and sick. From where the sun now stands I will fight no more . . . forever."

Some have thought that Indian wars and rampaging buffalo herds prevented settlers from occupying the plains and with those menaces removed, settlement under the Homestead Act of 1862 should proceed smoothly. In fact, however, the lands of the plains were consumed by railroads and speculators at the same moment that hide hunters were decimating buffalo and the army was destroying Indians. Settlers, being outmaneuvered and threatened on all sides, threaded their impoverished path between these powerful forces, built their sod houses, and dug in. They lost scalps both to Indians and speculators. Railroads, their only link to a market and survival, calculated the settler's money more accurately than the settler, then charged all the traffic would bear. Blizzards, droughts, and floods hammered entire communities into the ground. Grasshoppers "ate everything but the mortgage." A three-foot drift of the insects stopped Union Pacific trains in Nebraska in 1874. "In God we trusted; on the plains we busted."

But there's no hope like the land hope, and whether outraged by speculators, embezzled by railroads, or crippled by acts of nature, more and more settlers took root on the plains. After Kansas entered the Union in 1861, Nebraska followed in 1867 and Colorado in 1876. Being central on the route West, those three states gathered enough settlers, inn keepers, ferry boaters, and provision suppliers to achieve statehood as a by-product of West Coast settlement.

The northern plains remained open territories for a longer time. Montana had 20,000 people as early as 1870, but was not accorded statehood until 1889 at which date it had 140,000. North and South Dakota suffered similar fates, being settled early but not being allowed to enter the Union until 1889.

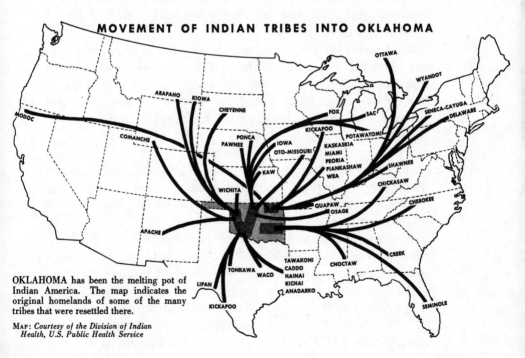

MOVEMENT OF INDIAN TRIBES INTO OKLAHOMA

OKLAHOMA has been the melting pot of Indian America. The map indicates the original homelands of some of the many tribes that were resettled there.

MAP: *Courtesy of the Division of Indian Health, U.S. Public Health Service*

Wyoming had to wait until 1890, though the state had 10,000 residents as early as 1870.

The southern plains, though settled earliest, became in public thinking the last of our plains frontiers. Oklahoma long suffered stigma as "The Indian Nation," and though settled in the 1840s did not receive statehood until 1907. Even the 50,000 Sooners and Boomers who poured into the Cherokee Strip on— and before—September 16, 1893 saw themselves as frontiersmen. Being free land located next door to a whole nation of Indians qualified the Strip as frontier, and these frontiersmen showed their mettle by gobbling up the 6,500,000 acres of free land in a matter of hours.

New Mexico also found it difficult to achieve statehood. Despite being the second oldest white settlement in North America, New Mexico long suffered from the Apache wars, but was finally settled enough to enter the Union in 1912. Yet as early as 1850 it had 62,000 residents and was hardly a frontier. Of the ten Great Plains states, only Texas lost its frontier label before 1850, having entered the Union with a population of 200,000 in 1845.

Recognition of early settlements in Alberta, Saskatchewan, and Manitoba was likewise delayed, but for different reasons. The main block was ownership and governmental control. From about the 1850s, public pressure began to mount for creation of Canada as a separate nation within the British Empire. Parliament had long heard scattered demands for this action, and in 1867 finally passed "The British North America Act" establishing the Dominion of Canada. That Act compares approximately to the United States Constitution in delegating powers to legislative, judiciary, and executive branches of government.

Soon after, the Dominion opened negotiations with the Hudson's Bay Company for control of Rupert's Land. That was a massive tract of western and northern Canada given in 1670 under its original charter to the HBC ("Here Before Christ," as rival fur buyers dubbed it). Rupert's Land, named for Prince Rupert, included the land drained by all rivers entering Hudson Bay, which in effect meant all of southern Canada west to the Rockies. Negotiations for the Canadian take-over lagged, but in 1869 all of Rupert's Land finally became part of the Dominion.

The change of ownership did not sit well in the Canadian west, however, where a group of tough-minded Indians and mixed bloods known as Métis feared their lands would soon be swamped by a flood of settlers. To present their cause, they chose the son of a former leader, an educated twenty-five-year-old Méti named Louis Riel. Riel pleaded for protection of Méti rights, but the government turned a deaf ear to the lightly respected half-breeds. With that the die was cast, and by fall of 1869 the Red River Rebellion was under way in southern Manitoba. Riel's followers were poorly equipped and badly outnumbered, and after sporadic fighting a rumored promise of amnesty swept their ranks. The uprising fell apart, and Dominion militia rounded up the rebels. Riel, however, soon realized amnesty would not be forthcoming and fled to the United States. Although back home his popularity remained intact, and his followers elected him to the Canadian House of Commons in 1873 and 1874, he was denied his seat and declared an outlaw. He took up residence in Montana and stayed there several years while events directly to the north in Alberta were once more coming to a head. In the spring of 1885, the whole region of southeastern Alberta was seething with unrest. Indians everywhere were angered by white intrusions and white indifference. On the morning of April 2, a band of Cree Indians led by Chief Big Bear attacked the settlement of Frog Lake, Alberta, caught most of the townspeople in the church, and massacred nine of them. With that act, Riel's second rebellion was under way.

This time the Métis set up a provisional government with Riel as president. Once again the Dominion sent out several troops of militia and after scattered fighting Riel was captured and the rebellion crushed. A sensational and racially bitter trial followed, in which Riel was found guilty of high treason. Despite pleas of moderates on both sides, he was hanged on November 16, 1885. As those moderates had expected, however, his gallows cast long shadows, and racial and religious unrest continued for years afterward.

The hanging of Louis Riel aroused lasting angers, and a lengthy period of troubled relations came between Métis and white settlers. Even Queen Victoria pleaded for clemency, but to no avail. (ROYAL ONTARIO MUSEUM, TORONTO)

At the time of his hanging, the Canadian Pacific Railroad was pushing west across Canada, and the lands of southern Saskatchewan and Alberta were being steadily settled by immigrants and easterners. Among those who moved into the territory were thousands of Americans who filtered across the border to become new Canadians, though most settlers came at first from the British Isles and eastern Canada. The pattern of settlement on the plains provinces was, therefore, very similar to that of the plains' states, again following the railroad and again dispossessing the Indians and mixed bloods.

One interesting group that came to the Canadian plains were the Doukhobors. *Doukhobor* is a Russian word signifying "Spirit Fighter" and was applied in derision to a sect of nonconformist peasants that broke from the Orthodox church in the mid-eighteenth century. They were scattered across Russia and adopted the belief that God resides within each man and directs each from within. Therefore, no church or hierarchy is necessary. Their outlook may best be described as sublime, and they were models of industry and dedication. But denying the church was cause for persecution, and they were soon hounded off their lands and sent to a rocky, marginal hill country near the Turkish frontier. Through perseverance and community dedication, they turned those lands into a garden and became the envy of the region.

In 1887, however, universal military conscription was proclaimed in Russia and, being nonviolent pacifists, they were soon suffering new persecution, Cossack brutality, and dispersal. Then Tolstoy heard of their plight and through Quaker acquaintances in England arranged for aid and transportation of about 7,500 to Canada. All arrived in 1889 in several contingents. The government welcomed them warmly and assigned them farm lands in southern Alberta and Saskatchewan. Here once again they prospered and grew and by 1910 their numbers had increased to 13,000. They built a highly successful cooperative based on farming, brick and tile manufacture, and sawmill operations.

But relations with other religious groups were sometimes troublesome, and in 1924 the Doukhobor leader, Peter Verigin, was killed when a bomb exploded in his railway car. His son, Peter II, took over, but the cooperative went bankrupt in the Great Depression and the sect gradually began to lose its strength.

Then in the 1930s, a highly militant splinter group calling themselves "Sons of Freedom" broke away and began active demonstration against what they believed was heretical behavior by other Doukhobors. They burned schools because they did not believe in compulsory education. They burned the homes of those they believed were living in sin. They bombed the Canadian Pacific Railway, and they paraded in the nude. In World War II, they refused even to work as conscientious objectors. The Canadian government finally disenfranchised the Doukhobors and imprisoned about 500 Sons of Freedom.

However, most plains settlers differed little from those found elsewhere. Mostly they were farmers. To 1900, we were 80 percent a nation of farmers. In Europe and our eastern states, small farms and plenty of rain provided a wide range of crops, both in the ground and on the hoof. A family could live on what it grew, and be independent of money, cities, or commerce. Financial panics and a lack of markets were a nuisance, not a calamity. Naturally this spawned individual views of personal inde-

pendence and self-sufficiency. Such attitudes led the immigrant
farmer and the American hopeful westward across the Mississippi in the last half of the nineteenth century where, at first, all
went well. Newcomers on the plains blotted up the waterholes,
planted their edibles, raised pigs, cows, and chickens. They even
had enough timber for houses, all found along the river bottoms
and down in the coulees. For them the land could provide as it
had in the East.

Their numbers of course were small, though large enough to
deceive others into believing similar good fortune lay out there
on the open plains. The vagrant fact of a thin rainfall was slow
to strike home. Anybody could plant corn, but it took waiting
through a long dry season to learn that it wouldn't grow. Millet,
sorghum, oats, and rye were planted with a similar lack of success. An almost total lack of wood required a new form of hous-
ing and fuel. The settler's eastern plow failed in attempts to
break the heavy sod. Against these obstacles he developed the
sod house, twisted lumps of dried grass for fuel, and a new type
of steel-bladed plow, curved and sharpened to chisel its way into
the tough, centuries-old mat of grasses. Against the lack of
water, he converted windmills to new needs of this dry land.
Against marauding buffalo, wandering Indians, and trail-driven
herds, he developed barbed wire—the Devil's Hatband—a key
element in subduing the plains. Invented in the early 1870s,
manufacturers were producing large quantities of this fencing
in a short time. Dozens of ingenious designs were tried, gradually narrowing to the few types known today. More than eight
million pounds were sold, mainly on the plains, in the single
year of 1880. From then on its success was never questioned,
and the Great Plains today is the world's largest outdoor example of strong fencing. Fences there offer studies in both design
and type unrivaled anywhere on the globe, being maintained
with great care and diligence.

Some of the resourcefulness of those early settlers is contained
in the memories of Mary Starr Frost, who went out to the
Nebraska plains as a ten-year-old with her family in 1871:

"We traveled in our covered wagon, drawn by an ox-team,
with our plow tied securely on, while at the back of the wagon

was a few chickens in a coop. Our cows were driven along as well. We started from Buffalo County, Wisconsin, crossed the Mississippi at Wabasha on a ferry boat, and were on the trail six weeks.

"Near Blue Earth, Minnesota, we fell in with three other families and traveled on together. When in camp, the mothers baked their bread over a bed of hot coals in a 'Dutch oven.' I can still hear in memory the swishing and groaning of the tall grass as the wagons rolled across southern Minnesota.

"When we arrived near what is now Plainview, Nebraska, we decided to stop. About the first thing to do was to dig a well. Next to build a house. This called for turning over the sod, cutting it into 2 or 2½ foot lengths after which it was laid up into walls, very much as the mason lays brick, breaking joints and making a solid wall. Such walls were warm in winter and cool in summer and of surprising durability due to the thick grass roots which had grown unmolested for countless years without being cut by the plow-shares of the pioneer. We had the ground for the floor, which was swept daily with a broom made of willows. Our house was plastered with alkali mud and whitewashed. Mother tacked old sheets to the rafters up over our beds. The rafters were poles from the woods. These were covered with strips of bark (smooth side down) cut from the larger trees. Hay was next placed on top of the bark, then sod laid like shingles. Father had the credit of finishing the first house in the settlement.

"Life in those sodhouse days was full of experiences. The first winter the snow drifted over our house so that many a morning the door would be banked and father had to dig his way out. Every prudent settler saw that his shovel was parked inside at night, for we had many blizzards lasting three days at a time. Some of the settlers used to tie a rope to the door when they went out to feed their stock, so as to have a guide back to the house as one could easily get lost in that trackless waste of white, lose all bearings and perish of cold within a few rods of home. It must be remembered that practically no trees or landmarks existed at this early period, and nothing in the shape of a wind-break broke the cruel fury of those northwesters.

Great Plains Gothic. All worldly goods were carried outside or marched into position for picture-taking ceremonies. This sodhouse is in western Nebraska, circa 1880s. (DENVER PUBLIC LIBRARY WESTERN COLLECTION, PHOTO BY S. D. BUTCHER)

"The fall of 1871, prairie fires swept the landscape until every foot of ground was black as far as the eye could reach. This did not happen once, but nearly every fall until the country was settled up. We had our fire breaks made by plowing strips of ground around our homes and burning out between. Then we would start a backfire when the flames came too near.

"Our door was fastened with a wooden latch to which was tied a leather string passing through a tiny hole to the outside. To lock our door, we drew in the string. But the latch string was always out to welcome any neighbors or weary travelers passing through.

"Our bread was made of corn meal, and as coffee was almost unknown for the first two years, mother browned corn and corn meal for a substitute.

"One night mother left her washing on the line. A big wind came up and scattered the clothes over the prairie so that some were not found until the snow melted in the spring. But the thaw came so fast that several inches of water came into the house. We had to live on a platform. Those were stirring times for all. The coyotes and wolves howled at night making music for our lonely little band of settlers.

"The grasshoppers visited us three years in succession. They usually stayed with us three days, eating every green thing excepting the grass and sorghum cane—they drew a line at that. When that happened, father left us and found work near Norfolk where the crops were not destroyed by grasshoppers, working through the harvest, then returning in the fall. That way he could earn $50 or $60 in cash, plus a supply of meat, flour, and potatoes to tide us over until the next crop could be raised. All our supplies were purchased at Norfolk thirty miles away. It took three days to make the trip with the ox teams."

At about the same moment young Mary Starr Frost was beginning her years near Plainview, a group of traders in central Montana began trekking northward into Alberta to find new markets. The border between Canada and the United States was not a carefully dotted line in those days after the Civil War, and passage between the two countries was free and easy. The traders, faced with Cree and Blackfoot Indians, set up a series of forts to protect their operations. In itself that wasn't illegal, but sales of whiskey and firearms to Indians, plus non-payment of duties on merchandise, soon aroused Dominion authorities. They became particularly disturbed about an American post named Fort Whoop-Up, where whiskey was used to pry horses, cattle, furs, and other valuables away from the Indians.

To end this threat, the Canadian government formed the North West Mounted Police in 1873—now the Royal Canadian Mounted Police—and sent them west on a one-thousand-mile tramp across the plains. The Mounties, about three hundred strong, reached the region in October 1874, promptly smashed the whiskey trade, and built a post named Fort Macleod, near present Lethbridge. They were guided into the region by a bow-legged little plainsman named Jerry Potts, son of Irish and Blood Indian parents, who remained as guide and aide for the Mounties until his death in 1896. Francis Dickens, son of the English author Charles Dickens, was an inspector in the early Mountie troops and served in Alberta in those troubled territorial years. Through the work of all these men, the region became safe for settlers and Alberta and Saskatchewan became provinces of the Dominion in 1905.

Settlement of the plains—now that legal action was bolstering lever action—progressed in waves, depending mostly on political and economic conditions in Europe and the eastern United States. People came to find a new life or get away from an old one. The German revolution of 1848–49 drove nearly a million people to America in the 1850s, with half arriving in 1852–54. Probably a fourth of these Reichs-Deutsch settled in Texas and formed the first large bloc of immigrants to enter a Great Plains state.

Following the Civil War, however, this settlement pattern developed rapidly. One of the largest and most important groups of farmer-settlers was the Germans from Russia. In 1762, Catherine the Great, the Prussian princess who became Empress of Russia, invited farmers from Germany to settle in the Caucasus Black Sea region. She knew they were sturdy people and excellent farmers and she wanted to stabilize a politically tormented region. A large number of settlers made the move. For about a century they prospered, maintaining their native German identity. In 1871, however, their special privileges were abolished, persecution began, and with it came immigration to the United States and Canada.

The Canadian Northwest Mounted Police were formed in 1873 and a first column was sent west to the plains to break up the whiskey trade in 1874. Here they search traders' carts for the illicit hooch. Their name later was changed to the present Royal Canadian Mounted Police. (SASKATCHEWAN ARCHIVES, REGINA)

The first major wave of these peoples came in 1873, first to
Nebraska and Kansas, then to Oklahoma and Texas. Most, however, came in the late 1880s and early 1890s, and were bundled
onto through trains from the East Coast to the Dakotas. The
Chicago, Milwaukee, and St. Paul Railroad had pushed into the
heart of the Dakotas by this date and now literally tens of
thousands of these German-Russians were dumped onto the
barren plains at the end of the line.

All these immigrant families came to the plains equipped for
survival, and the main piece of baggage each carried was a
bushel or two of hard Red Turkey winter wheat. This grain was
new to America, but soon came to dominate all crop production
in the entire central and northern plains regions. It is today the
basic grain stock of that bread-basket region, and Russia's growing call for supplies to feed her people must come as ironic tribute to many Great Plains families driven here a century ago by
Russian persecution.

They were a clannish determined people, admirably equipped
for Great Plains settlement. The land was their life. They
had struggled for centuries as peasants, serfs, and farmers.
They were frugal and could withstand harsh conditions. In
Russia they had fashioned their cattle manure into squares
called "mistholz" and used them dried as fuel. Thus, what the
French had called "wood of the cow"—bois de vache—and
what we call buffalo chips became a natural fuel for these immigrant peoples. The harsh winds of the plains were akin to those
of the Steppes in Russia, and arid climate and brutal winters
were not unknown to these people. Their communities spread
and increased and by 1910 they had sizable centers in every one
of the ten Great Plains states. Most were Protestant, with large
numbers being Lutheran, while smaller centers of Catholics and
Mennonites also flourished. Alberta, Saskatchewan, and Manitoba also gathered large numbers of German-Russians, and like
their counterparts in the United States they maintained close
and strong community ties.

Mixed into the bushels of wheat they carried was another
immigrant seed, however, this one known as the Russian thistle.
We call it the tumbleweed. Unfortunately, it proved just as

hardy and tough as the farmers who sowed it into those first fields of winter wheat. It is today of course a great, bounding, lively pest of a weed that infests many regions of the Great Plains, exulting in those flatlands and sweeping winds that bounce it along and spread its seeds so fruitfully.

The German-Russian experience was bolstered by Germans, Scandinavians, and Ukranians who came after the Civil War in successive waves of settlers, particularly to the northern and central plains—the southern plains states having by then been settled by Indians, Mexicans, and earlier white settlers. So strong were these waves of European and Scandinavian immigrants that the census of North Dakota in 1890 showed that 43 percent of the white people were foreign born and 33 percent more were of foreign or mixed parentage. The Scandinavians were mainly Norwegians and at one time their numbers exceeded the total population of their homeland. Other plains states showed similar immigrant strength.

Gradually these settlements began to drift almost unconsciously into a new life style, one that grew steadily more dependent on railroads and distant markets. The plains were, in fact, becoming one end of the assembly line in a new factory-farm production system unseen before in world history. Though the plains would not grow a great diversity of crops, they would grow large amounts of certain commodities that the rest of the world needed. Partly this became possible through mechanization. Cyrus Hall McCormick had developed a crude mower and reaper system in the 1830s, and by the end of the Civil War had a thriving factory operating in Chicago. His reaper used horses for power, but on the flatland of the Great Plains that was enough to allow vast acreages to be planted with wheat. Such an implement helped farmers move toward the single-crop approach to survival, trading their surplus wheat, beef, cotton, wool, or mutton for barbed wire, windmills, steel plows, lumber, and other imports. In the exchange they became mortgaged to those very cities that manufactured such necessities. The city now became dependent on the farmer, the farmer on the city, and the railroad on both.

By 1915 the basic settlement pattern of the plains was largely

As the buffalo slaughter of the 1860s and 1870s advanced, their sun-bleached bones lay strewn mile after mile across the plains. Thrifty and dead-broke settlers gathered them in wagon loads for shipment to eastern potash, fertilizer, and carbon factories. (SASKATCHEWAN ARCHIVES, REGINA)

completed. A few large cattle companies remained, mostly those that had enough capital and resilience to survive the disastrous winter of 1886–87, later picking up land and cattle at cheap prices from other ranches bankrupted by that winter. But such large companies now controlled far less land and cattle than they had earlier. Many small ranches also grew in the region, mainly as a response to the dangers of maintaining larger herds. Small self-contained family operations could store enough hay and work enough cattle to survive with modest capital. These family operations herded their cattle closely on smallish plots, often less than one thousand acres, and continued to use some of the free government grazing lands then available. A third group was the new breed of farmer that developed irrigation for both forage and grain crops. These were often older residents, the earlier immigrants, who occupied favorable waterholes, or newcomers with enough money to buy their way in. Next came the "grangers," or farmers with small landholdings who had come as immigrants to lands lacking good water, or to settlement on broken and rough landscapes where the farming would be uncertain. These were still homestead lands, but firstcomers had preempted the watered sites and in the plains, water determined settlement.

Finally in this broadening farm community came the sheep herders. Large and small, sheep ranching was becoming big business on the Great Plains by the turn of the century and especially on the more northerly plains. In Wyoming, for example, barely 250,000 sheep were pastured before the blizzard of 1886–87. By 1902, nearly 3.5 million were owned in the state. Beef cattle by comparison slumped to about half a million in Wyoming by 1890 and remained near that level well into the twentieth century.

By 1930 the settlement and agricultural patterns had become so entrenched it appeared they might remain intact indefinitely. What happened next was capped nicely by a weathered old-timer in eastern Montana who lived through it. "Land is patient stuff," he said ruefully, "but God help the man that provokes it." In the 1930s we found there were still some things to learn about this vast landscape called the Great Plains. We had, in fact, "provoked it." The question we face today is whether we learned a lesson from those dust bowl years, and if so what that lesson means for the future.

CHAPTER 15

Present Tense,
Future Tenser

By the strength of their character, the Great Plains claim the attentions of their residents with uncommon force. The sky is larger, the land more demanding, the weather always roaring off on one tangent or another, and the history marked with violence and the movement of great events. It is a land that will not be ignored very successfully and it has a way of pushing with great frequency into thoughts and conversations of those who live and travel there.

This is demonstrated to some degree by place names. The naming time of course goes back well before the arrival of white men, when Indians translated their thoughts into names for settlements, rivers, mountains, and plains. Few of these survive in original form, though many are seen as Spanish or French or English corruptions. Nebraska is such a name, deriving from *Nebrathka*, an Oto word meaning "flat water," after the principal river system of that region, the Platte. And Platte is of course the French translation with the same meaning. *Kansas* means "People of the South Wind," and is a Kansa, or Kaw, Indian word. Texas comes from the Caddo word, *Tejas*, and means "allies" or "friends"; the Caddos applied it to the region, then the Spanish cemented it into place in the sixteenth century. *Oklahoma* is the white man's version of two Choctaw words that in their spoken language sounded like "Okla," and "Homa," and when used together meant "Red People."

Wyoming is also an Indian word, though in this case it happens to be from the Delaware Indians, and was first applied to that western region by a white congressman from Ohio. He suggested it be used to designate the area when Wyoming became a territory in 1868. The Delaware word is *m'cheuwomink*, meaning "upon the great plain," and the white congressman heard it from easterners who settled the Wyoming Valley of Pennsylvania.

Colorado is another word chosen because the land seemed to demand it, though in this case it derives directly from the Spanish and means "colored red." It turned up as a place name after early explorers saw the Colorado River flowing over a series of red rock ledges. *Montana* is also directly from Spanish, meaning simply mountain.

Manitoba and *Saskatchewan* are Indian words. *Manito bau* is Ojibway meaning "spirit strait," and derives from the sound of waves dashing against limestone cliffs in a narrows of present Lake Manitoba. *Saskatchewan* is from the Assiniboin *kis-is-ska-tche-wan* meaning "river-that-turns-around-when-it-runs," or fast flowing.

Other place-names paying deference to the land and its products and peoples tell us much about how early residents viewed or responded to these vast open plains. Buffalo left their mark as community or place-names in twelve of the thirteen Great Plains states and provinces. And interestingly enough, the animal we all call buffalo is really a bison, not related to true buffalo of the world that are found only in Africa and Asia. In a minority supporting biological accuracy are towns named Bison in Kansas, North Dakota, and Oklahoma.

The flatness of the land provides another rich source for names. There are towns named Plains, Stony Plain, Porcupine Plain, Plainview, Plainville, and Plano. There's a Prairie City, a Prairie County, two Prairie Views, a Prairie Village, a Prairie Hill, a High Prairie, a Grande Prairie, and a Golden Prairie. If that isn't enough, Texas has Levelland, Pampa, Grass Plains, and Earth.

With the plains being so wide and open, one might expect the sun to play an important role in namings. And so it does:

Sunburst, Sun Prairie, Sun River, Sunnyside, Sunnyvale, Sunray, Sunset, Sun City, Sundance, Sunrise, Sunnybrook, Sunnynook, and Sunnyslope.

Some unusual names are also found in the region, as might be expected, from its rich tapestry of people and events. There is, for example, a Bairoil and a Chugwater in Wyoming, an Okay, a Bowlegs, and a Stringtown in Oklahoma. There's a Broken Bow and a Weeping Water in Nebraska, while Colorado has Climax, Cripple Creek, Leadville, Silt, Steamboat Springs, and Yellow Jacket. Texas has towns named Comfort, Muleshoe, Grapevine, Happy, Idalou, Lovelady, Panhandle, Rising Star, Wink, Sourlake, and Sweetwater. Wyoming has a Ten Sleep and Alberta a Seven Persons. There's a Protection in Kansas, a Truth or Consequences in New Mexico, a Livelong in Saskatchewan, and a Fairplay in Colorado. There's a Goodland in Kansas, an Eden in South Dakota, an Elysian Fields in Texas, and a Choiceland in Saskatchewan.

Truth or Consequences gained its name in 1950 from a radio show of the same name on the promise that an annual fiesta would be held in the town if highlighted on the program. All the other names, however, go back half a century or more, telling us forcefully about the plains of yesterday. Happily, most such names still comfortably fit their surroundings and their people. Hopefully, that will remain the case for a long time. However, it might be wise to travel there soon—if you hope to see this land at its historic best, for some rather significant changes are coming to the plains—and not all are to the liking of the residents, nor in keeping with its historic past.

The basic reason for these impending changes arises from the fact that the plains are becoming, and must remain, the major food and fuel-producing region of North America. The significance of this truth is steadily making itself felt as the world becomes more and more dependent on Great Plains products.

Looking back to the beginnings of life in this region, we found the plains as a grassland that proved attractive to large numbers of wild animals. They grazed and browsed across this mixture of grassy opens and tree-dotted "park lands," and were hunted by various animal predators. The region was a rather well-balanced ecological community that existed for thousands of years.

Sometime within the last 30,000 years, however, man arrived on the plains and rather rapidly began to exterminate many of the larger, more vulnerable species. By extensive use of fire, he also removed trees that had encroached in many places, so that the plains now became an open, prime grazing ground. The buffalo, being the largest mammal in North America, soon came to dominate this grazing land, steadily increasing its numbers until many millions roamed the region in enormous herds.

In the sixteenth century, the white man arrived and by the end of the eighteenth century, descendants of the horses he brought had spread over the entire region, thereby allowing Indians to take buffalo at any time of year, and in large numbers. These tribesmen, who formerly had to spend most of their time hunting, were now largely freed for other interests. They were converted from a people constantly haunted by starvation into a food-rich culture. The new leisure they obtained with the horse was soon turned into social activities including war, arts, dance, decorative dress, ceremonies, and many other cultural pursuits.

In the nineteenth century, however, the white man wiped all of that away and came into dominance over the entire region. The Indian peoples were sharply reduced in numbers and removed to enclaves. The buffalo were destroyed. In their place, the white man brought settlers, cattle, sheep and, most of all, the plow. With that implement the eastern farmer soon introduced eastern agriculture to the plains—adapted, however, to produce monoculture crops over vast stretches of the region. Hundreds of thousands of acres in continuous fields stretching to the horizon were planted with wheat, or cotton, or sorghum. When tractors began to be used in that country, they were equipped with compasses. Farmers then literally set a course in order to plow across miles of open field.

This change from grassland to tilled fields was dramatic and far-reaching and was without question the most profound and rapid—and dangerous—shift in the use of a large piece of land ever to occur in North America. The plains had been converted in the bare span of fifty years from a stabilized grassland complex into a plowed cropland. The thick mat of grasses that had for eons tied down the soil and protected it from wind erosion was now gone. Wind erosion followed as night the day, and in the 1930s, everyone east of the Rockies knew when dust storms were under way on the plains. Fine filtered traces of Texas and Oklahoma and Kansas drifted eastward with every wind to settle on window panes and tabletops in Georgia and Alabama. The same grayish-yellow traces of Colorado, Nebraska, and the Dakotas turned up in New York, Pennsylvania, and Ohio.

World War II pulled us out of the Great Depression and made us forget the Dust Bowl years. And we have since been so busy with other affairs that we scarcely remember the severe drought and dust blows that hit the plains in the 1950s. Yet far more land blew away in the 1950s than in the 1930s. United States Soil Conservation Service (SCS) records show that the worst year of the Dust Bowl was 1938 when about 9 million acres were severely damaged. In 1954, however, 16 million acres were "blown away." Just under 10 million additional acres were similarly damaged the following year, while over 10 million more were carried off in 1956. The Great Plains region is about 550 million acres in total size, including sizable regions in Canada. In the thirty-two years from 1934 through 1966, the SCS shows a total of more than 100 million acres sustaining severe wind damage in the United States portion alone.

Dr. Carle C. Zimmerman, an agriculture and land-use specialist in North Dakota, believes this problem may have staggering world implications before the end of this century. "Plains erosion is on such a vast scale now," he said recently, "that its potential for endangering future use of the soil as a source of food and support of life is very alarming."

Our rising use of fertilizers and irrigation, and generally rising per-acre productivity has, for the moment, tempered or masked the effects of this lost acreage. Soil loss to wind erosion is cumulative, however, and once a field is blown out, it may require centuries to rebuild even a thin topsoil. We must therefore face the certainty of very severe food shortages worldwide when the next lengthy drought hits the plains. Famines in some

The Great Plains traveler these days will see frequent dead-level fields being irrigated, with water pumped from wells or nearby rivers. This field is in western Kansas. (PHOTO BY THE AUTHOR)

regions of Africa, Asia, and Latin America may be expected. Fully two-thirds of all the world's wheat exports are shipped from the Great Plains of Canada and the United States, an amount not expected to decline. Dr. I. Arnon, a specialist on crop production in dry regions, says: "Although rice probably constitutes the staple diet of more people, wheat is the first in importance on a world scale of all the grain cereals, as regards both the total area sown and the annual production." Zimmerman backs this statement, calling wheat "the most outstanding source of human food, even surpassing rice." He adds that, unfortunately, it is also the only food we can increase materially, and immediately, for the world. Such increases must be drawn from the Great Plains in particular, of all the world's wheat-growing regions.

This conversion of the plains to agriculture was of course necessary for national policy in the nineteenth century and remains necessary today for world survival. It will certainly be carried forward in the decades ahead. Georg Borgstrom, a renowned authority on food supplies, notes that the world is adding the population equivalent of one United States every three years. The grain surpluses we had in the late 1950s and early 1960s built a false sense of national optimism—and left farmers with a wary outlook toward overproduction and low prices. Those surpluses are now gone, and the price of wheat continues to set record highs. The world's population increased from 1.5 billion in 1900 to 3 billion in 1970. It will double from 3 billion to 6 billion by the year 2000. That's the distance of one generation ahead, barely a moment away.

Great Plains cattle also represent a drain on lands and grain, a matter that must come under increasing scrutiny in the years ahead. It requires six to ten pounds of forage foods to produce one pound of beef on the table. In the political and economic decisions that lie just ahead, the value of Great Plains wheat on the world market may become so high that beef will simply be priced out of reach. Lands now used to raise forage crops may have to be converted to wheat production, and cattle may well be relegated to use of only the most marginal lands.

A further deep concern about food production that seemingly never will be eliminated from Great Plains life is the general scarcity of water. Water has always been in short supply. Nature has dictated a rainfall of fifteen to twenty inches per year over most of the Great Plains region. If the average came every year, that would be sufficient for a comfortable if restricted agricultural program. But what happens when a farmer receives twenty-five inches one year and five inches the next? Or five inches per year for ten years at a stretch, then several years of drenching rains? While the world's population was down around two billion people, such an up-and-down pattern destroyed farms and caused ripples of difficulty along the entire length of our food production chain. But it wasn't calamitous to the world at large. Now the world has three billion people, and the Great Plains have been cast as the main gladiator to fight famine on a dozen world fronts. In such a battle, "average annual rainfall" is a concept providing only a dangerous hope.

Dry-land farming has been the Great Plains answer to even out some of these highs and lows of rainfall. Under dry farming, the landowner plants alternate patches of ground, growing wheat on one strip several hundred feet wide and a mile or more in length, then leaving unplanted an adjacent strip of the same size. The following year the farmer switches his planting program onto the fallow lands and gives last year's wheatlands a

These combination steam harvesters and threshing machines worked well on the Great Plains wheatlands, but they were a constant fire hazard in the dry stubble. (DENVER PUBLIC LIBRARY)

rest. The alternation back and forth from year to year provides time for the fallow lands to regenerate nitrogen and other nutrients, but primarily the purpose is one of water conservation. In a way, it is a system of irrigation where the water can't be seen. That which does not evaporate settles down into the soil and becomes a reserve for the following year. The farmer meantime keeps the fallow lands tilled and harrowed, both to keep weeds out and to provide an open, spongelike surface into which water can trickle.

Dry-land farming has proved most successful on the northern plains—roughly all lands north of the Kansas-Nebraska border. One reason is the cooler northern climate, allowing the average of fifteen to twenty inches rainfall to evaporate more slowly and therefore to stretch farther. More moisture is retained in soils of the fallow lands, so the practice in general is more fruitful. The same amount of precipitation falls on the southern plains, but higher daily temperatures cause much more rapid evaporation. Dry-land farming without supplements from irrigation is therefore less successful as a practice. This accounts for the generally more widespread use of that other major weapon now being used against southern plains drought—deep-well irrigation.

Deep wells first came into play in the Texas Panhandle in the 1940s, then soon spread to Oklahoma and western Kansas. They suck away at ancient water supplies that for centuries have percolated drop by drop down through the sands and gravels of the southern plains and now rest in great pools on the bedrock. Some of this water has also sloped off the Rockies to trickle eastward along underground routes. For a time, in fact, it was widely believed that most water lying beneath the plains had drained off the Rockies, but later discovery of various fault lines and other underground obstacles now belies that thought. Whatever their origin, sizable quantities of water do lie beneath the plains, puddled into the sands and gravels at depths varying from 100 to 1,200 feet. In western Kansas, wells with pipes six to eight inches in diameter pull water from depths of 400 to 600 feet. Such large wells can extract enormous quantities of water from underground resources—far more than can be regenerated by natural percolation from year to year. Irrigation as a general practice provides water to crops, of course. And some portion of that well water does filter back down into deep reservoirs, to be sure. But on the southern plains in particular, most well water used for irrigation simply evaporates and is carried away on dry, fast-moving winds.

The bounty from this relatively new source of southern plains water is sizable. It has turned former low-quality grazing lands into valuable croplands producing cotton, sorghum, and wheat in vast quantities. Even water-heavy vegetables such as cucumbers, tomatoes, and watermelons, plus popcorn, sugar beets, and dry beans are being produced in small but valuable quantities. The Dust Bowl has become a fruit bowl, and in many places the plains are blooming like a garden.

But the real cost of these crops is not being paid today. That bill will have to be met by those generations now coming up, starting ten to thirty years hence. Southern plains irrigation, both from ponded sources at the surface and from deep wells, is as noted steadily using more water from year to year than nature provides. This is causing a rapid decline in those deep formations, and as that water begins to play out, the practice of irrigation will gradually end. One study of a seventeen-county area in the Texas Panhandle, dead center on the most intensively irrigated region in North America, showed production in 1970 to be 38 percent cotton, 41 percent grain sorghum, and 15 percent wheat—nearly all irrigated. By the year 2015, with the water nearly gone, cotton production will have declined 65 percent and grain sorghum by 90 percent, while wheat production will rise only about one-fifth under dry-land farming. Most lands formerly used for cotton and sorghum will have to be used to produce that extra wheat. Total income from those lands will drop more than 60 percent, with the decline probably beginning around 1980. The same time frame, perhaps a bit later, has been projected for western Kansas. Irrigators in eastern portions of New Mexico and Colorado, on the other hand, have long been more dependent on surface runoff from the Rockies than from deep wells. Those water supplies are more dependable and less inclined to create a boom-to-bust economy.

The northern plains are in a generally better position. Water for irrigation there is drawn from reservoirs of surface water. Mainly this water comes from the Missouri River system, including its tributaries. In addition large areas are under irrigation along the Yellowstone, the South Platte, the main stream of the Platte in eastern Nebraska, and the Republican River along the Nebraska-Kansas border. At present, about two million acres are under irrigation, while the Missouri River Project, begun in 1944, is reaching for a goal of five to six million irrigated acres by the year 2000. The major effort now in the works is the so-called Garrison Diversion Unit, designed to carry about five percent of the Missouri's stream flow eastward across the ridge of the Coteau into central and eastern North Dakota. About a million acres will be irrigated. Reservoirs will be constructed and flowages of the Souris, Sheyenne, James, and Red rivers will be increased enough to allow the additional irrigation. All those rivers, except the James, flow north to Hudson Bay, so the project will divert some of the Big Muddy's waters away from the Gulf of Mexico. That means those waters will be forced northward into the drainage they knew historical-

An Oklahoma dust storm in 1937 at the height of the Dust Bowl years. When plowing removed the native grasses, the landscape was left wide open for this sort of disaster. (WESTERN HISTORY COLLECTIONS, UNIVERSITY OF OKLAHOMA LIBRARY, NORMAN)

ly—before glacial action constructed the barrier of the Coteau and forced their flow southward.

These trends and countertrends, however, provide only a scattering of clues to the future of the Great Plains as a food-producing region. Some areas now under irrigation will be lost to crops when the water runs out. Others will replace them when irrigation projects now in the works crank up. Irrigation in any case is planned or under way on only a modest portion of the total region. Wind erosion looms as a more widespread and disabling problem, yet from year to year, total grain yield from the Great Plains have continued to rise. Hybrid grains, fertilizers, irrigation, and more effective harvest practices have to date offset those soil losses. How long this can continue is moot, but certainly not indefinitely. Conversion of many lands from cattle pasturage to cereal grain production now seems a certainty, though this shift will arise in a highly uncertain time frame, out of very complex and unforeseeable market forces. It could take decades.

But if the Great Plains must become the most important single contributor to the world's breadbasket, it must also continue to serve as the nation's center of energy resources. For decades, most of our domestic petroleum has come from Great Plains states, and though national reserves are dwindling rapidly, the region will remain supreme for the foreseeable future. Only Alaska's North Slope can possibly challenge Texas and Oklahoma as the oil and gas center of the United States. To date, we have used about half our domestic petroleum resources —over the span of about a century. However, the second half will disappear far faster. The most generous estimates indicate domestic reserves will, for all practical purposes, be gone by the end of this century. Other estimates, based on reasonable assumptions, place the end point only fifteen to twenty years down the road. Imports of foreign oil may increase enough to offset some of this drain, but the plain truth of American fuel reserves is that petroleum is over the hill and on the way out. The whole industry is now crisis oriented. The federal government is pushing distributors to prorate supplies of propane and fuel oil. Within a short time we must expect rationing of all petroleum products. We may expect crisis after crisis from now on—in the auto industry, in home heating, in tooling up for mass transit to replace automobiles, and not least of all, in social and economic conditions of people living in the Great Plains states, where more than two-thirds of our petroleum is now produced.

Two major changes will be seen, and both are already well under way. The impact of declining petroleum supplies, as noted, must inevitably affect the economic well-being of the oil-producing states. All the plains states and provinces produce oil and gas, but most is produced in Texas, Oklahoma, and Kansas. When the crunch comes, it will come there with the greatest impact. Fortunately, those states have steadily diversified their economies so that conversion from oil production to other pursuits may succeed without calamitous dislocations. But severe unemployment problems must be expected, retraining programs

will have to be instituted, and the base of capital investment
will undergo grinding shifts.

The other change is in strip mining for coal. Eighty percent
of America's fossil fuel reserves are in coal, and coal is the only
ready resource of fuel we have to replace petroleum. Nuclear
fission is years behind in schedule, and today after three decades
of existence, still provides only 5 percent of America's electrical
needs. On the other hand, industrial conversion from oil and
gas to coal can be managed rather swiftly because all necessary
equipment is known or available, and the technology is well
understood. Industry, which uses about half of all American
energy, will therefore be called upon to convert back to coal
within a few years.

Two very serious difficulties arise in this context. First, North
American coal reserves lie in enormous deposits in the Canadian plains provinces, in eastern Montana and Wyoming, and
in western portions of Nebraska and the two Dakotas. Lesser
deposits are found in eastern Colorado. Most of these lands are
owned by farmers and ranchers, and by the federal government.
But ownership as we usually think of it does not normally
include "mineral rights," and that is very largely the case with
the coal lands of the northern Great Plains. Resident owners
there own for the most part only the surface rights. They can
plow and plant and pasture and live on the land, but if the
owner of the mineral rights decides to mine, he can move in his
equipment, tear up the surface, and extract the minerals. Often,
depending on state law, the surface owner does not even have to
be consulted. Sixty percent of the mineral rights to the coal
lands of the northern Great Plains belong to the federal government, 20 percent are held by railroads and coal companies, and
the other 20 percent are held by landowners. The federal government will, of course, auction off its mineral rights to coal
companies when the time is ripe and the coal is needed.

This coal lies in vast sprawling seams, usually thirty to fifty
feet beneath the surface of the plains. That means strip mining
will be used to extract it, a practice that has virtually ruined the
surface of large areas of Appalachia and southern Illinois. In
strip mining, huge scoop shovels lift aside the overburden, pile

it in long steep-sided rows, then dig out the coal beneath. Normally the overburden is left where it's piled—topsoil buried, steep slopes exposed to erosion, the surface rock and stone worthless for any plant-growing purposes. Entire mountains have been flattened in West Virginia and Kentucky. Parts of Illinois have been left like craters of the moon, with barren, eroding rock piles fifty to one hundred feet high lying in long rows, centuries removed from usefulness. Strip mining has rightfully gained a bad name, and there is as yet little reason to believe amends will be made out there on our northern Great Plains.

However, with American petroleum reserves dwindling rapidly, there is virtually no question that northern Great Plains coal will have to be stripped for use. Stubborn and lingering attempts will be made to prevent this, or slow it down, but these will be defeated. The raw political and economic power that will be used in making the decision does not lie on the side of the thinly populated northern plains states; it is held in the industrial centers of the Northeast, the central South, and the West Coast. Some strip mining is already under way, in a flurry of controversy, in eastern Montana, Colorado, and the western Dakotas. Pious pronouncements by the coal companies that the land will be "reclaimed"—that is, put back more or less as it was found—have not persuaded residents.

The second difficulty arises from the fact that those coal fields are a thousand miles or more removed from the nearest major industrial centers. That means either industry must move to the fuel source, or the fuel must be transported to industry. In advance of that decision, a massive power-generating complex is already being built in southeastern Montana and northeastern Wyoming. No less than twenty electric utility companies have banded together to build steam generators that will use local coal and water to produce 53,000 megawatts of power by the year 2000. That single plant will increase present United States electrical energy by 15 percent. Industry must then make a choice, at least for that particular energy. It can move to the plains and gain low local energy prices, or it can stay put and pay the high costs of electrical transmission. Probably both decisions will be made, depending on costs of moving versus staying. That electrical complex is, of course, merely the first fragment of a vast enterprise that will grow up around those coal resources. They are without question the most important energy reserves in North America today, and tied up in their future is the future of this continent. Some, in fact, see the northern plains becoming a second Ruhr Valley, or a multiple Gary, Indiana, or a cluster of Pittsburghs.

Whatever happens, the northern plains will be deeply affected—socially, economically, scenically, and environmentally. Some residents will see the change as a boost and a boom, others are already gloomily predicting the end to a unique, quiet, and pleasant way of life.

Finally, there is the big question of the future of human populations on the Great Plains. There are no large cities on the Great Plains, and in general the population is quite thin. Omaha-Council Bluffs, Kansas City, and Dallas-Fort Worth are all on the eastern edge of the plains. Kansas City and Dallas-Fort Worth each have populations of a million-plus, while Omaha and Council Bluffs combined total less than half a million. On the western border, Denver has about 500,000 people while El Paso has 350,000. Edmonton and Calgary combined, on the northern extremity, are growing steadily but still total less than a million, while San Antonio on the southern boundary is reaching toward the million mark. But out there on the plains proper, the biggest cities are still rather modest in size. Oklahoma City, largest of all, is about 400,000. Wichita has 300,000 while Amarillo and Lubbock are each under 200,000. There are no other Great Plains cities over 100,000 population, and the entire region averages less than ten persons per square mile. In 1961 a congressman from Oklahoma named Tom Steed stood up in his home state and told an assembly of university staff members that it was at that time the intentional policy of the federal government to rapidly resettle fifty million people onto the Great Plains. The purpose of this policy, Steed said, was to decentralize some of our population away from the industrial Northeast, both for better land use and as a national defense measure. That has not happened thus far, though some activities now underway suggest a national effort is being made to at least stabilize Great Plains populations. Federal irrigation and power programs, federal land reclamation, farm price supports and soil conservation efforts, water impoundment and government-backed loan programs—all are aimed at keeping people on the plains and keeping the plains productive.

In truth, however, while many urban areas continue to increase in size, rural areas of the plains are losing residents. Young people in search of education and stimulation are leaving the land to make a life for themselves in the cities. This is of course not true everywhere, but as a general rule, bigger and bigger tractors are being sold to those plains farmers so fewer and fewer hands will be needed to do the work. Getting and keeping good farm and ranch hands, after all available sons and daughters troop off to college, is a major problem. And there's just not much money available for wages anyway. Capital investment in those ranch and farmlands is enormous, but the annual return of an average big wheat or cattle operation is only 3 to 5 percent. That's in a good year. The dollar value is there in land and equipment, but the young people have sensed that the land is an anchor they don't need, and that their futures lie elsewhere.

Perhaps this is the most serious problem facing the plains—if a paucity of people can be considered a problem. Some of course see low populations as a benefit, a mark of hope that the land may be allowed to keep its native charm. Sublette, Kansas, named for that famous family of western mountain men, may have clods of tractor-packed mud in its streets, and may be only a small collection of wind-toughened buildings and people. But maybe it's big enough for the plains and all the work it has to do. When the sun sets on any given summer evening, the golden wheat outside that town glimmers with a magnificence bearing a hundred centuries of man's deepest hopes. Each kernel of grain is the nucleus of the best man has ever accomplished for himself; each stalk holds enough promise of life for generations yet unborn.

Somehow the over-riding insistence of our industrial society is always headed toward growth and a profusion of products; not a bad goal, merely an uncontrollable one. The Great Plains, in their homely cloak, shunned for so long by so many, have somehow retained a flavor of a different America, outside this framework of growing and multiplying. If they lose population, if they sustain injury from strip mining, if the oil wells play out and the deep wells run dry, it may not in the end matter very much. The plains can still remain a unique and vital experience for all who live and travel there. Hopefully they can sustain man's worst attacks and yet keep their subtle beauty. Hopefully, too, they will still be largely intact when all of us and all of our progeny are long gone. They are, in the end, a very great piece of country and truly well named—the Great Plains of North America!

APPENDIX

A Great Plains Journey

The Great Plains are an insurmountable obstacle to anyone attempting land travel across our continent. There is no escaping that awesome flatness, except of course in air travel. Even there, the width of the plains adds an hour to otherwise brief flights. Any journey straight across the plains might be a four-hundred-mile passage. Angles thrown in could easily raise this to six hundred miles, and in a few places the trip is that long on an east-west beeline.

The federal interstate highway system is a pretty good statement of American feeling for the plains. If you look at a highway map of the United States, you will find seven major east-west concrete ribbons crossing through the plains, but only one partial north-south ribbon. The highways are Interstate US-94, US-90, US-80, US-70, US-40, US-20, and US-10. The one partial north-south route is US-35. Here in concrete terms may be seen our national attempt to hurry in as straight a line as possible, across the strange and unknown Great Plains. We are today not much different in our outlook toward this flatland than our pioneering forefathers of a century ago. On those seven east-west routes an Easterner of today can travel west on the shortest route from the Twin Cities, Milwaukee, Chicago, St. Louis, Memphis, Jackson, or New Orleans. But if you want to dally your way across or if you want to go from North Dakota down to the Texas Panhandle, it's big detours or back roads all the way.

Since the Great Plains are a durable geographical fact that highly mobile North Americans must learn to deal with, probably with

This road sign's appropriate to the Texas Panhandle countryside, dead center on one of the most heavily irrigated agricultural regions of our continent. (PHOTO BY THE AUTHOR)

more and more frequency, it seems obvious that anyone sentenced to a crossing may as well try to enjoy it. In that spirit of adventure and necessity, an unprejudiced journey into the Great Plains is hereby suggested.

Two basic approaches suggest themselves, depending on time available. For the retired and traveling, or younger people on the loose, or anyone with a month or more of unstructured time available, an unplanned trip from south to north, or north to south—following the seasons—and zigzagging back and forth through the countryside on back roads provides a truly fascinating venture. Here you'll find the face of a different America, close up, no cosmetics, warmhearted, friendly. And by going unplanned, you also happen on many wonderful surprises. Small town rodeos, for instance, are one patch of great fun; not the big organized gatherings where thousands view the professional cast of traveling bull ropers and bronc busters, but a Sunday afternoon gathering of real-live local ranchers trying their hand at cattle roping, usually in a casually fenced ring near some small Great Plains town. That's real stuff. Also, the horses throughout that country are singularly magnificent and always an attraction. Whether kept for show, or work, or just to look at, it may be claimed without prejudice that Great Plains horses as a totality are the most handsome, well-kept, healthy group of domestic animals in the world. They fit the land and the land fits them.

Those who would wonder what life is like on the back lands of the Great Plains can find out by traveling there—without plan. If in plumbing those back roads you can arrange to become lost three or four times a day, it is possible to engage in conversation those unusual people who could choose to live so far from civilization. Keep in the car some gifts of good table wine, get lost just about dinner time, and when asked your business, demur in modest tones that you are writing a book about their country. That tickles them pink, and is sure to produce another plate at table, for you. Then you can get down to some real talk. Being a transient passing through, they will be more inclined to level with you about concerns they feel for their land and their families, about their knowledge and experiences with weather, soil, and water, and the plant and animal life that surrounds them. On balance, very direct views and more often than not you come away with the feeling that these people do not see themselves as residing on the land so much as they believe themselves a part of it. It is, perhaps, a vaporous distinction. Still, a tone of directness is conveyed therein, and you observe a sense of reality and easy acceptance of all the powerful natural forces surrounding them.

Unplanning your sleeping accommodations also produces adventures. You can park your pickup or smallish trailer along most any side road in that country and not be disturbed. Tenting is all right, too, though the winds tend to be tough at times. If you have a sturdy little vehicle with enough room for sleeping inside, that would be the best of all. Beware of camping on open ground in cattle country; those beefers will bawl you awake at four in the morning, or sniff around with snorts in your ear that sound like little tornadoes. Very disconcerting before breakfast.

Cattle should always be approached cautiously. When standing around quietly they are putting on pounds of nice tender prime beef; when rattled and running away—as from your car—their meat goes down in value and quantity. Also, you should not drive across dry grasses in range country, as one such maneuver is sometimes sufficient to kill the vegetation and open the car's tracks to wind erosion.

The other approach to plains travel, a planned venture, also has its rewards, the most important of which may be to view a great deal of country in a limited amount of time. Included in this appendix are major sources of information to enable such planning, arranged by state and province, including major public lands and interest points, Indian lands and activities as available, and a selection of museums dealing with plains history. These are not definitive lists, but are meant more as suggestions. In particular, the museums are a mixed bag—some truly top drawer and highly unusual, others simply local collections of pioneering relics and antiques gathered in the neighborhood. The federal and state museums are of almost uniformly high quality, while certain of the private museums are also excellent. A few that should not be missed include the Museum of the Plains Indian at Browning, Montana; the Buffalo Bill Historical Center and Whitney Gallery of Western Art at Cody, Wyoming; the Museum of the Great Plains at Lawton, Oklahoma; and the Cowboy Hall of Fame at Oklahoma City.

Also, you will find that the plains states still retain a sort of ambient indifference to tourists that is both refreshing and economical. So while you may wish to plan your plains trip thoroughly, large dollops of uncertainty may of necessity fall into the mix. Off main tracks of travel, motels are infrequent and some small hotels in some small towns may prove more of a lost rest than a last west venture. But then, nobody ever claimed the Great Plains to be a tourist mecca, and if it's a tourist mecca you seek, seek elsewhere. The Great Plains call only the more venturesome. So have at it friend, go with a light heart and don't plan more than one hundred fifty to two hundred miles per day, less if possible. That forces lots of stopping and looking and allows for fine rhythm against the beat.

Note that the following lists include points of interest and facilities only in the plains portions of the states and provinces mentioned. Other attractions in those states, but outside the plains region, are not included.

ALBERTA

For general information, write the Alberta Travel Bureau, Edmonton. *Major Attractions*—Elk Island National Park east of Edmonton; Fort de L'Isle; Fort Vermilion Historic Site; Fort

Macleod near Lethbridge; the Cypress Hills; many provincial parks; Porcupine Hills Forest; and Calgary and Edmonton, two of the largest cities in the plains region. *Museums*—Barrhead Centennial Museum; Calgary Brewery Horseman's Hall of Fame; Glenbow-Alberta Institute in Calgary; Camrose and District Museum; Drumheller and District Museum; Provincial Museum and Archives of Alberta in Edmonton; Fort Saskatchewan Historical Society; Hanna Pioneer Museum; Rainy Hills Pioneer Exhibits at Iddesleigh; Sir Alexander Galt Museum in Lethbridge; Medicine Hat Historical and Museum Foundation; Pas-Ka-Poo Historical Park in Rimbey; St. Albert Parish; Viking Historical Society; Reynolds Museum in Wetaskiwin; Historical Village and Pioneer Museum at Willingdon.

SASKATCHEWAN

For general information, write the Saskatchewan Travel Bureau, Saskatchewan Power Building, Regina. *Major Attractions*—Prince Albert National Park; Batoche Rectory National Historic Site; Fish Creek Memorial Park; Fort Battleford National Historic Park; Old Wives Lake National Wildlife Refuge; the Great Sand Hills; Cypress Hills Provincial Forest; Porcupine Hills; Fort Qu'Appelle; and many provincial parks. *Museums*—Prairie Pioneer Museum at Carik; Duck Lake Historical Museum; Raymore Pioneer Museum; Royal Canadian Mounted Police Museum at Regina; F. T. Hill Museum at Riverhurst; Saskatoon Museum of Ukrainian Culture; Vigfusson Museum at Saskatoon; Western Development Museum at Saskatoon; Grand Coteau Museum at Shaunavon; Swift Current Museum; Doukhobor Society Museum at Verigin; Soo Line Historical Museum in Weyburn.

MANITOBA

For general information, write the Manitoba Travel Branch, Legislative Building, Winnipeg. *Major Attractions*—Riding Mountain National Park; Lower Fort Garry National Historic Park; Duck Mountain Provincial Park; Spruce Woods Forest Reserve; Porcupine Hills; many parks. *Museums*—B. J. Hales Museum of Natural

History in Brandon; Minnedosa and District Pioneer Co-op Museum; Fort LaReine Museum in Portage La Prairie; the Sam Waller Little Northern Museum at The Pas; Manitoba Museum of Man and Nature at Winnipeg; Manitoba Historical Society at Winnipeg.

COLORADO

For general information, write the Colorado Travel Department, State Capitol, Denver 80203. *Major Attractions*—Bent's Old Fort National Historic Site near La Junta; Pawnee Buttes; Bonny Reservoir; Garden of the Gods; Cheyenne Wells. *Museums*—Carriage House Museum at Colorado Springs; Colorado State Museum at Denver; Denver Museum of Natural History; State Historical Society of Colorado at Denver; Kit Carson Memorial Chapel at Fort Lyon; Greeley Municipal Museum; Julesburg Historical Museum; Kit Carson Historical Society at Kit Carson; Koshare Indian Museum at Las Animas; Fort Francisco Museum at LaVeta; Littleton Area Historical Museum; Loveland Museum; Fort Vásquez Visitor Center at Platteville; Rocky Ford Historical Museum; Overland Trail Museum at Sterling; Baca House at Trinidad; Bloom House at Trinidad; Wray Museum.

KANSAS

For general information, write the Kansas Department of Economic Development, State Office Building, Topeka 66612. *Major Attractions*—Fort Larned National Historic Site; Kirwin National Wildlife Refuge at Kirwin; Quivira National Wildlife Refuge west of Hutchinson; the Buffalo Preserve; Castle Rock, Great Spirit Springs, Monument Rocks; the Red Hills; the Pony Express Station, many state parks. *Museums*—Dickinson County Historical Society at Abilene; Western Museum at Abilene; Cherokee Strip Living Museum at Arkansas City; Pioneer Museum at Ashland; Santa Fe Museum at Ashland; Rawlins County Historical Society at Atwood; Old Castle Museum at Baldwin City; Dalton Museum at Coffeyville; Sod Town Prairie Pioneer Museum at Colby; Comanche

County Historical Society Museum at Coldwater; Douglass Museum; Lanesfield Historical Society in Edgerton; Fort Leavenworth Museum; The Garden of Eden in Lucas; U.S. Cavalry Museum at Fort Riley; Original Pony Express Home Station at Marysville; Last Indian Raid Museum at Oberlin; John Brown Cabin at Osawatomie; Butterfield Trail Historical Museum at Russell Springs; Kansas State Historical Society Museum at Topeka; Wichita Historical Museum Association; Davis Memorial at Hiawatha; Charley Crosson grave at Minneapolis.

MONTANA

For general information, write the Montana Advertising Department, Trail Country Information, Helena 59601. *Major Attractions* —Big Hole National Battlefield at Wisdom; Custer National Forest at Billings; Custer Battlefield National Monument at Crow Agency; Lewis & Clark National Forest at Great Falls, the Charles M. Russell National Wildlife Range and the Benton Lake, Black Coulee, Bowdoin, Hewitt Lake, Lake Mason, Medicine Lake, Pishkun and Willow Creek National Wildlife Refuges. Also, Bears Paw Battlefield near Havre, Little Belt Mountains, Big Snowy Mountains, Bighorn Canyon, Pompey's Pillar, many state parks. *Indian Lands and Activities*—Blackfeet Reservation, Browning; North American Indian Days in July with dances, ceremonials, rodeo. Crow Reservation at Crow Agency: Tribal Sun Dances in early June; Custer Battle Re-enactment in late June; Crow Fair and Rodeo, third week in August. Fort Belknap Reservation at Harlem: Natural Bridge in Mission Canyon, St. Paul's Mission at Hays. Fort Peck Reservation at Poplar (the old capital of the Assiniboin and Sioux tribes) : Oil Discovery Celebration with Indian ceremonial dances in August; Wolf Point Wild Horse Stampede at Wolf Point each July. Northern Cheyenne Reservation at Lame Deer: Head Chief Battlefield; Custer's Last Camp; Two Moons Monument at Busby; Indian Parade and Saddle Club Rodeo with dancing in late May; Sun Dance first week in July; tribal fair in late August. Rocky Boy's Reservation at Box Elder: Tribal ceremonials and Indian dances, no fixed dates; camping at Beaver Creek State Park adjacent to the reservation. *Museums*—Museum of the Plains Indian and Crafts Center at Browning; Northeastern Montana Threshers and Antique Association at Culbertson; Carter County Museum at Ekalaka; Fort

Benton Museum; Frontier Gateway Museum at Glendive; C. M. Russell Museum at Great Falls; H. Earl Clack Museum at Havre; Montana Historical Society at Helena; Chief Plenty Coups State Monument at Pryor.

NEBRASKA

For general information, write the Information and Tourism Division, Nebraska Game & Parks Commission, State Capitol, Lincoln 68509. *Major Attractions*—Chimney Rock National Historic Site near McGrew; Homestead National Monument of America at Beatrice; Nebraska National Forest at Lincoln; Scotts Bluff National Monument at Gering; Agate Fossil Beds National Monument near Agate; Fort Niobrara National Wildlife Refuge at Valentine; Massacre Canyon Monument; Pioneer Village; the Sand Hills region; many state parks. *Museums*—Dundy County Historical Society at Benkelman; Museum of the Fur Trade at Chadron; Fort Robinson Museum at Crawford; Oregon Trail Museum at Gering; Pony Express Station at Gothenburg; Stuhr Museum of the Prairie Pioneer at Grand Island; Hastings Museum; Fort Kearny State Historical Park at Kearney; Plains Historical Society at Kimball; Ash Hollow State Historical Park at Lewellen; Nebraska State Historical Society at Lincoln; High Plains Museum at McCook; Pioneer Village at Minden; Buffalo Bill's Ranch at North Platte; Trails Museum at Ogallala; Willa Cather Pioneer Memorial and Educational Foundation at Red Cloud; Heritage House Museum at Weeping Water.

NEW MEXICO

For general information, write the New Mexico Department of Development, State Capitol, Santa Fe 87501. *Major Attractions*—Capulin Mountain National Monument at Capulin; Carlsbad Caverns National Park at Carlsbad; Fort Union National Monument at Watrous; Gran Quivira National Monument at Mountainair; White Sands National Monument at Alamagordo; and the Bitter

Lake, Bosque del Apache, and San Andres National Wildlife refuges. Also, Philmont, Fort Sumner, and graves of Billy the Kid, and Kit Carson. *Indian Lands and Activities*—mainly located in the western mountains, but including the Mescalero Apache Reservation at Mescalero; with its St. Joseph's Catholic Mission; ruins of Blazer's Mill (site of a famous battle during the Lincoln County War), and a year-round scenic gondola lift at Sierra Blanca ski area. *Museums*—Artesia Historical Museum and Art Center; Ernest Thompson Seton Memorial Library and Museum at Cimarron; Old Mill Museum at Cimarron; Rough Riders Memorial and City Museum at Las Vegas; Picuris Pueblo Museum at Penasco; Blackwater Draw Museum at Portales; Paleo-Indian Institute and Museum at Portales; Institute of American Indian Arts Museum at Santa Fe; Museum of Navajo Ceremonial Art at Santa Fe; Museum of New Mexico at Santa Fe; "Old Cienaga Village" Museum at Santa Fe; Governor Bent Museum at Taos; Kit Carson Memorial Foundation at Taos; Tucumcari Historical Research Institute.

NORTH DAKOTA

For general information, write the North Dakota Travel Division, Highway Building, Bismarck 58501. *Major Attractions*—Theodore Roosevelt National Memorial Park at Medora; Sully's Hill National Game Preserve; the Elkhorn Ranch; many state parks. Also, the following National Wildlife refuges: Ardoch, Arrowwood, Chase Lake, Des Lacs, Florence Lake, Hobart Lake, Kelly's Slough, Lake Ilo, Lake Zahl, Long Lake, Lostwood, Lower Souris, McLean, Shell Lake, Slade, Snake Creek, Stump Lake, Tewaukon, Upper Souris, White Lake. *Indian Lands and Activities*—Fort Berthold Reservation at New Town has the Four Bears Park and Indian Museum; Fort Totten Reservation at Fort Totten; Standing Rock Reservation at Fort Yates; Turtle Mountain Reservation at Belcourt has an International Peace Garden of twenty-three hundred acres, partly in Manitoba, with lakes and camp grounds. *Museums*—Divide County Museum-Historical Society at Crosby; Buffalo Trails Museum at Epping; Fort Abraham Lincoln State Historical Park at Mandan; De Mores Historic Site at Medora; Richland County Historical Museum at Wahpeton; Cass County Historical Society at West Fargo; Frontier Museum Society at Williston.

OKLAHOMA

For general information, write Oklahoma Tourist Information, 500 Will Rogers Building, Oklahoma City 73105. *Major Attractions* —Arbuckle Recreation Area at Sulphur; Platt National Park at Sulphur; Wichita Mountains Wildlife Refuge (bison and longhorn cattle) north of Lawton; also the Salt Plains, Tishomingo, and Washita National Wildlife refuges, Fort Sill, Jesse Chisholm's grave near Greenfield, plus many state parks. *Indian Lands and Activities* —Listed here by town or city center: Anadarko Agency, Anadarko— Indian City, traditional Indian village. Ardmore Agency at Ardmore. Concho Agency at Concho. Five Civilized Tribes Agency at Muskogee. Okmulgee Agency at Okmulgee (the old Creek capital and meeting place of the present Creek Indian Council). Osage Agency at Pawhuska. Pawnee Agency at Pawnee. Miami Agency at Miami. Shawnee Agency at Shawnee. Talihina Agency at Talihina. Wewoka Agency at Wewoka. *Museums*—Homesteader's Sod Home at Aline; Museum of the Western Prairie at Altus; Cherokee Strip Museum at Alva; Anadarko Museum; National Hall of Fame for Famous American Indians at Anadarko; Southern Plains Indian Museum and Crafts Center at Anadarko; Tucker Tower Museum at Ardmore; Black Kettle Museum at Cheyenne; Will Rogers Memorial at Claremore; Western Trails Museum at Clinton; Fort Washita at Durant; Canadian County Historical Society Museum at El Reno; Cherokee Strip Museum at Enid; Fort Gibson Stockade; Fort Sill Museum at Fort Sill; No Man's Land Historical Museum at Goodwell; Chisholm Trail Museum at Kingfisher; Museum of the Great Plains at Lawton; Five Civilized Tribes Museum at Muskogee; National Cowboy Hall of Fame and Western Heritage Center at Oklahoma City; Creek Indian Museum at Okmulgee; Osage County Historical Museum at Pawhuska; Pawnee Bill Museum at Pawnee; Cherokee Strip Historical Society at Perry; Pioneer Woman Statue with Museum and State Park at Ponca City; Ponca City Cultural Center and Indian Museum; Kerr Museum at Poteau; Sequoyah's Log Cabin at Salisaw; Shawnee Indian Mission at Shawnee; Cherokee National Historical Society at Tahlequah; Chickasaw Council House Museum at Tishomingo; Thomas Gilcrease Institute of American History and Art at Tulsa; Chisholm Trail Historical Museum Association at Waurika; Pioneer Museum and Art Center at Woodward.

SOUTH DAKOTA

For general information, write the South Dakota Department of Highways at Pierre 57501. *Major Attractions*—Badlands National Monument at Interior; Black Hills National Forest (addressed at Custer, Wyoming;) Jewel Cave National Monument at Hot Springs; Mount Rushmore National Memorial at Keystone; and Wind Cave National Park at Hot Springs. Also, parts of the Custer National Forest, headquartered at Billings, Montana, and the Lacreek, Lake Andes, Sand Lake, and Waubay National Wildlife refuges; Slim Buttes, Oahe Dam and Reservoir, the geographical center of the fifty states, Dells of the Sioux, and many state parks. *Indian Lands and Activities*—Rosebud Reservation at Rosebud has Ghost Hawk Canyon and camping grounds off Highway 18 near the approach to the reservation, and the annual Rosebud Fair and Powwow, usually at the end of August. Lower Brule Reservation at Lower Brule. Crow Creek Reservation at Fort Thompson; Standing Rock Reservation at McIntosh—has a monument to Sacajawea (the other third of the Lewis and Clark expedition) ; and the grave of Sitting Bull. Pine Ridge Reservation at Pine Ridge has an annual Sun Dance and Powwow in the first week of August, also the Wounded Knee Monument. Cheyenne River Reservation at Eagle Butte, and the Yankton Agency at Wagner. *Museums*—Dacotah Prairie Museum at Aberdeen; Western Woodcarvings Museum at Custer; Wiehe's Frontier Museum at Custer City; Soper's Sod Museum at Gregory; Custer State Park Museum at Hermosa; South Dakota State Fair Pioneer Museum at Huron; Petrified Wood Park Museum at Lemmon; Prairie Village of Prairie Historical Society at Madison; Friends of the Middle Border Pioneer Museum at Mitchell; Land of the Sioux Museum at Mobridge; Timber of Ages Petrified Forest at Piedmont; South Dakota State Historical Society Museum at Pierre; Minnilusa Pioneer Museum at Rapid City; Sioux Indian Museum and Crafts Center at Rapid City; Great Plains Zoo at Sioux Falls; Buechel Memorial Sioux Indian Museum at St. Francis; W. H. Over Dakota Museum at Vermillion.

TEXAS

For general information, write Travel and Information Division, Texas Highway Department, Austin 78763. *Major Attractions*— Amistad Recreation Area at Del Rio; Chamizal National Memorial at El Paso; Big Bend National Park at Big Bend; Fort Davis National Historic Site; Alibates Flint Quarries at the Texas Panhandle Culture National Monument north of Amarillo; the Paint Rock Pictographs; Caverns of Sonora; Chisos Mountains; Frio Canyon; Guadalupe Peak; Odessa Meteor Crater. Also, the Buffalo Lake, Hagerman, and Muleshoe National Wildlife refuges and the Sanford Recreation Area. *Museums*—Museum of the Big Bend at Alpine; Texas Memorial Museum at Austin; Frontier Times Museum at Bandera; Hemphill Museum at Canyon; Crosby County Pioneer Memorial Museum at Crosbyton; Dallas Historical Society; Whitehead Memorial Museum at Del Rio; the Texas Ranger Museum at Falfurrias; Fort Bliss Replica Museum at Fort Bliss; Annie Riggs Memorial Museum at Fort Stockton; Amon Carter Museum of Western Art at Fort Worth; Pioneer Museum and Country Store at Fredericksburg; Presidio La Bahia at Goliad; Deaf Smith County Museum at Hereford; Iraan Archeological Museum; Comanche Trails Museum and Zoo at Kermit; Judge Roy Bean Visitor Center at Langtry; South Plains Museum Association at Levelland; Llano County Historical Museum at Llano; Permian Basin Petroleum Museum and Hall of Fame at Midland; T & P Section House Museum at Monahans; Odessa Meteorite Museum; White Deer Land Museum at Pampa; Carson County Square House Museum at Panhandle; West of the Pecos Museum at Pecos; TSA-MO-GA Memorial Museum at Plains; Fort Concho Restoration and Museum at San Angelo; the Alamo at San Antonio; Hall of Texas History Wax Museum at San Antonio; Spanish Governor's Palace at San Antonio; Pioneer Town at Wimberley.

WYOMING

For general information, write the Wyoming Travel Commission, Cheyenne 82001. *Major Attractions*—Bighorn National Forest at Sheridan; Bridger National Forest at Kemmerer; Devils Tower

National Monument at Devils Tower; Fort Laramie National Historic Site at Fort Laramie; Medicine Bow National Forest at Laramie; the Shoshone National Forest at Cody; Independence Rock; Teapot Dome; Dinosaur Graveyard; Hell's Half Acre; South Pass. Also, the Bamforth, Hutton Lake, and Pathfinder National Wildlife refuges. *Indian Lands and Activities*—The Wind River Indian Reservation, near Thermopolis, has the Wind River Mountains, Boysen Dam and Reservoir, and the Indian Petroglyphs at Dinwoody Lake; annual Sun Dances. *Museums*—Bradford Brinton Memorial Museum at Big Horn; Johnson County and Jim Gatchell Memorial Museum at Buffalo; Homestead Museum at Carpenter; Fort Casper Museum and Historic Site at Casper; Fort Bridger State Museum at Cheyenne; Fort Fetterman State Museum at Cheyenne; Wyoming State Archives and Historical Department at Cheyenne; Wyoming State Museum at Cheyenne; Buffalo Bill Historical Center and Whitney Gallery of Western Art at Cody; Guernsey State Museum at Guernsey; Laramie Plains Museum at Laramie; Trail End Museum at Sheridan; Wyoming Pioneer Home at Thermopolis.

BIBLIOGRAPHY

ADAMS, J. T., editor. *Album of American History*. Charles Scribner's Sons, New York, 1967.

ALDRICH, LORENZO D. *A Journal of the Overland Route to California and the Gold Mines*. Dawson's Book Shop, Los Angeles, 1950.

ARCHER, SELLERS G., and BUNCH, CLARENCE E. *The American Grassbook*. University of Oklahoma Press, Norman, 1953.

ARNON, DAVID ISAAC. *Crop Production in Dry Regions*, in two volumes. Leonard Hill, London, 1972.

ATHEARN, ROBERT G. *High Country Empire, The High Plains and the Rockies*. McGRAW-HILL Book Company, Inc., New York, 1960.

ATHERTON, LEWIS E. *The Cattle Kings*. University of Nebraska Press, Lincoln, 1961.

ATWOOD, WALLACE W. *The Physiographic Provinces of North America*. Ginn and Company, New York, 1940.

BANNON, JOHN FRANCIS, editor. *Bolton and the Spanish Borderlands*. University of Oklahoma Press, Norman, 1964.

BELL, JOHN R. *Journal of the Stephen H. Long Expedition*. The Arthur H. Clark Company, Glendale, California, 1957.

BENNETT, J. D. "Oasis Civilization in The Great Plains," in the *Great Plains Journal*, pp. 26–32, fall, 1967.

BILLINGTON, RAY ALLEN. *The Far Western Frontier, 1830–1860*. Harper & Row, New York, 1956.

——. *The Frontier Thesis, A Valid Interpretation of American History?* Holt, Rinehart and Winston, New York, 1966.

——. *Westward Expansion, A History of The American Frontier*. Second edition. The Macmillan Company, New York, 1960.

BLACKER, IRWIN R. *The Golden Conquistadores*. Bobbs-Merrill, Indianapolis, 1960.

BOATWRIGHT, MODY COGGIN. *Folk Laughter on the American Frontier*. Collier Books, New York, 1961.

BOLTON, HERBERT E. *Texas in the Middle Eighteenth Century*. University of California Press, Berkeley, 1915.

BOLTON, HERBERT E. and MARSHALL, THOMAS M. *Spanish Exploration in the Southwest—1542–1706*. Charles Scribner's Sons, New York, 1908.

——. *The Colonization of North America, 1492–1783*. The Macmillan Company, New York, 1936.

BORGSTROM, GEORG. *The Hungry Planet*. Collier, Macmillan, Ltd., London, 1965.

BREBNER, JOHN BARTLET. *The Explorers of North America, 1492–1806*. The World Publishing Company, Cleveland, 1964.

BREIHAN, CARL W. *Great Lawmen of the West*. Bonanza Books, New York, 1963.

——. *Outlaws of the Old West*. Bonanza Books, New York, 1957.

BROWN, EVERETT SOMERVILLE. *Constitutional History of the Louisiana Purchase*. University of California Press, Berkeley, 1920.

BUCHANAN, JAMES SHANNON, editor. "French Interests and Activities In Oklahoma," *Chronicles of Oklahoma*, Vol. 2, No. 3, Oklahoma City, September, 1924.

BURPEE, LAWRENCE J. *Journals and Letters of Pierre Gaultier de Varennes de la Vérendrye and His Sons*. Publications of the Champlain Society, Toronto, 1927.

——. *Pathfinders of the Great Plains*. Volume 19, Part VI in "Pioneers of the North and West." Glasgow, Brook, and Company, Toronto, 1920.

——. *The Journal of Anthony Hendry, 1754–55*. Transactions of the Royal Society of Canada, Ottawa, 1907.

——. *The Search for the Western Sea, The Story of The Exploration of North-Western America*. The Macmillan Company of Canada, Ltd., Toronto, 1935.

BURROUGHS, R. D. *The Natural History of the Lewis and Clark Expedition*. Michigan State University Press, East Lansing, Michigan, 1961.

BUSCH, F. E. and HUDSON, J. D. *Ground Water Levels in New Mexico, 1965, and Changes in Water Levels, 1961–1965*. Technical Report No. 34, New Mexico State Engineer, Santa Fe, 1967.

CATLIN, GEORGE. *Letters and Notes on the Manners, Customs, and Conditions of the North American Indians*. Ross & Haines, Inc., Minneapolis, 1965.

Century Magazine. "Dry Farming—The Hope of The West." Volume LXXII, July, 1906.

CHIDSEY, DONALD BARR. *Lewis and Clark, the Great Adventure*. Crown Publishers, New York, 1970.

CHITTENDEN, HIRAM MARTIN. *A History of the Fur Trade of the Far West*. In two volumes. Academic Reprints, Stanford, 1954.

CLARK, IRA G. *Then Came the Railroads. The Century from Steam to Diesel in the Southwest*. University of Oklahoma Press, Norman, 1958.

CLEMENTS, F. E. "Climatic Cycles and Human Populations in the Great Plains." *Scientific Monthly*, Vol. 47, No. 3, pp. 193–210, New York, September, 1938.

COLTON, RAY C. *The Civil War in the Western Territories*. University of Oklahoma Press, Norman, 1959.

COX, ISAAC JOSLIN. "The Louisiana-Texas Frontier," a series of three articles in the *Southwestern Historical Quarterly*: Volume 10, pp. 1–75 for 1906–07; Volume 17, No. 1, pp. 1–42 for 1913–14; and Volume 17, No. 2, pp. 140–187 for 1913–14. The Texas State Historical Association, Austin.

DAVIDSON, GORDON CHARLES. *The North West Company*. University of California Press, Berkeley, 1918.

DEMPSEY, HUGH A. *Historic Sites of Alberta*. Alberta Government Travel Bureau, Edmonton, undated.

DEVOTO, BERNARD. *Across the Wide Missouri, A Considered Tribute to the Mountain Man, Rapacious, Tough, and Anti-Social*. Houghton Mifflin Company, Boston, 1947.

——. *The Course of Empire, A History of Three Centuries in Which a New Race Engulfed a Continent*. Houghton Mifflin Company, Boston, 1952.

——. *The Journals of Lewis and Clark*, edited, with comments. Houghton, Mifflin Company, Boston, 1953.

DICK, EVERETT. *Vanguards of the Frontier, A Social History of the Northern Plains and Rocky Mountains from the Fur Traders to the Sod Busters.* University of Nebraska Press, Lincoln, 1941.

DOBIE, J. FRANK. *The Longhorns.* Grosset & Dunlap, New York, 1941.

DOUGHTY, A. G. and MARTIN, CHESTER. *The Kelsey Papers.* The Public Archives of Canada, Ottawa, 1929.

DRAGO, HARRY SINCLAIR. *Great American Cattle Trails, The Story of the Cow Paths of the East and the Longhorn Highways of the Plains.* Dodd, Mead & Company, New York, 1965.

——. *The Great Range Wars, Violence on the Grasslands.* Dodd, Mead & Company, New York, 1970.

——. *Wild, Woolly, and Wicked, The History of the Kansas Cow Towns and the Texas Cattle Trade.* Brownhall House, New York, 1960.

DRUMM, STELLA M., editor. *Down the Santa Fe Trail and into Mexico, Diary of Susan Shelby Magoffin, 1846–47.* Yale University Press, New Haven, 1926.

DVORACEK, MARVIN J., and PETERSON, SAM H. *Development of Systems for Ground Water Recharge into the Ogallala Formation.* Texas Tech University, Lubbock, 1971.

ECCLES, W. J. *The Canadian Frontier, 1534–1760.* Holt, Rinehart & Winston, New York, 1969.

EISELEY, L. C. "The Fire Drive and the Extinction of the Terminal Pleistocene Fauna," *American Anthropologist,* Volume 48, Menasha, Wisconsin, 1946.

FARB, PETER. *Man's Rise to Civilization, As Shown by the Indians of North America from Primeval Times to the Coming of the Industrial State.* E. P. Dutton & Company, New York, 1968.

FARNHAM, THOMAS J. *Travels in the Great Western Prairies, the Anahuac, the Rocky Mountains, and the Oregon Country, 1804–1848.* Poughkeepsie, Killey and Lossing, Printers, London, 1841.

FENNEMAN, NEVIN M. *Physiography of Western United States.* McGraw-Hill Book Company, Inc., New York & London, 1931.

FOLMER, HENRI. "Etienne Veniard de Bourgmond in the Missouri Country," *Missouri Historical Review,* Volume 36, October 1941–July 1942, pp. 279–298. Missouri State Historical Society, St. Louis.

——. *Franco-Spanish Rivalry in North America, 1542–1763.* Arthur H. Clark Company, Glendale, California, 1953.

——. "French Expansion Toward New Mexico in the 18th Century," Volume 36 of the *Missouri Historical Review,* April, 1942, pp. 279–298. Missouri State Historical Society, St. Louis.

——. "The Mallet Expedition of 1739 Through Nebraska, Kansas, and Colorado to Santa Fe," *The Colorado Magazine,* Volume XVI, September 1939, pp. 161–73. Denver.

FOWLER, HARLAN D. *Camels to California,* Stanford University Press, Stanford, California, 1950.

FRAZER, ROBERT W. *Forts of the West.* University of Oklahoma Press, Norman, 1965.

FREMONT, JOHN CHARLES. *Memoirs of My Life.* Belford Clarke & Co., Chicago and New York, 1887.

——. *Narratives of Exploration and Adventure.* Edited by Allan Nevins. Longmans, Green, & Company, New York, 1956.

FROST, MARY STARR. "A True Story of Pioneer Days," personal correspondence, Chicago, 1935.

GABRIEL, RALPH HENRY. *The Lure of the Frontier.* Yale University Press, New Haven, 1929.

GARDINER, DOROTHY. *West of the River.* Thomas Y. Crowell Company, New York, 1941.

GERLACH, ARCH C., editor. *The National Atlas of the United States of America*. U.S. Department of the Interior, Washington, D.C., 1970.

GILBERT, E. W. *The Exploration of Western America, 1800–1850*. Cooper Square Publishers, Inc., New York, 1966.

GLADWIN, HAROLD STERLING. *Men Out of Asia*. Whittlesey-House, McGraw-Hill Book Company, Inc.

GREAT PLAINS COMMITTEE REPORT. *The Future of the Great Plains*. U.S. Government Printing Office, Washington, D.C., 1936.

GREGG, ANDREW K. *New Mexico in the 19th Century*. University of New Mexico Press, Albuquerque, 1968.

GREGG, JOSIAH. *The Commerce of the Prairies*. Edited by Milo M. Quaife. University of Nebraska Press, Lincoln, 1926.

GRINNELL, GEORGE BIRD. *The Last of the Buffalo*. Reprinted from *Scribner's Magazine*, Volume XII, July–Dec., 1892, by Arno Press, Inc., New York, 1970.

HAFEN, LEROY R. and HAFEN, ANN W. *Handcarts to Zion*. The Arthur H. Clark Company, Glendale, California, 1960.

HAINES, FRANCES. *Horses in America*. Thomas Y. Crowell Company, New York, 1971.

HAWGOOD, JOHN A. *America's Western Frontiers*. Alfred A. Knopf, New York, 1967.

HAWORTH, PAUL L. *Trailmakers of the Northwest*. Harcourt, Brace & Company, New York, 1921.

HEWITT, RANDALL H. *Across the Plains and Over the Divide*. Argosy-Antiquarian, Ltd., New York, 1964.

HIBBEN, FRANK C. *The Lost Americans*. Thomas Y. Crowell Company, New York, 1968.

HILL, DOUGLAS. *The Opening of the Canadian West*. The John Day Company, New York, 1967.

HITCHCOCK, A. S. *Manual of the Grasses of the United States*. U.S. Government Printing Office, Washington, D.C., 1951.

HITCHCOCK, RIPLEY. *The Louisiana Purchase and the Exploration, Early History, and Building of the West*. Ginn & Company, Boston, 1903.

HOLLON, W. EUGENE. *The Great American Desert, Then and Now*. Oxford University Press, New York, 1966.

———. *The Southwest, Old and New*. Alfred A. Knopf, New York, 1967.

HOSMER, JAMES K. *The History of the Louisiana Purchase*. D. Appleton & Company, New York, 1902.

HUMPHREY, R. R. "The Desert Grassland, Past and Present," in the *Journal of Range Management*, Vol. VI, pp. 159–64.

INMAN, COL. HENRY. *The Old Santa Fe Trail*. Manuscript of 1897 published by Ross and Haines, Minneapolis, 1966.

ISE, JOHN. *Sod and Stubble*. University of Nebraska Press, Lincoln, 1936.

JACKSON, DONALD. *The Journals of Zebulon Montgomery Pike, with Letters and Related Documents*. Two Volumes, edited and annotated. University of Oklahoma Press, Norman, 1966.

JOHNSON, VANCE. *Heaven's Tableland, the Dust Bowl Story*. Farrar-Straus, New York, 1947.

JOHNSON, W. D. "Report on The Conditions of the Great Plains," in the 21st Annual Report of the U.S. Geological Survey for 1899–1900, pp. 601–741, and in the 22nd Annual Report for 1900–1901, pp. 631–669. Washington, 1901 and 1902.

KAVANAGH, MARTIN. *La Vérendrye, His Life and Times*. Published by Martin Kavanagh, Brandon, Manitoba, 1967.

KELLOGG, LOUISE PHELPS. *Early Narratives of the Northwest, 1634–1699*. Madison, Wisconsin, 1917.

KENNEDY, MICHAEL, editor. *A Great Plains Issue, Montana, Magazine of Western History*, Helena, Winter, 1958.

KRAENZEL, CARL FREDERICK. *The Great Plains in Transition.* University of Oklahoma Press, Norman, 1955.

LANGMAN, R. C. *The Great Plains, The Anatomy of a Region.* McGraw-Hill of Canada, Ltd., Toronto, 1971.

LAVENDER, DAVID. *Bent's Fort.* Doubleday & Company, Inc. Garden City, New York, 1954.

LEE, JOHN D. *Mormonism Unveiled.* Pease-Taylor Publishing Company, St. Louis, 1891.

LEONARD, JONATHAN NORTON. *Ancient America.* Time, Inc., New York, 1967.

LEWIS, ANNA. "DuTisne's Expedition into Oklahoma, 1719," *Chronicles of Oklahoma*, Volume III, pp. 319–323. Oklahoma City, 1925.

———. "French Interests and Activities in Oklahoma." *Chronicles of Oklahoma*, Volume II, pp. 254–268. Oklahoma City, 1924.

———. "LaHarpe's First Expedition in Oklahoma, 1718–1719," *Chronicles of Oklahoma*, Volume II, No. 4., pp. 331–349. Oklahoma City, 1924.

———. "Oklahoma as a Part of the Spanish Dominion, 1763–1803," *Chronicles of Oklahoma*, Volume III, pp. 45–58. Oklahoma City, 1925.

LEWIS, G. MALCOLM. "William Gilpin and the Concept of the Great Plains," *Annals of the Association of American Geographers*, Volume 56, No. 1, pp. 33–51, March, 1966.

LEWIS, LLOYD, and PARGELLIS, STANLEY. *Granger Country.* Little, Brown and Company, Boston, 1949.

LONGSTREET, STEPHEN. *War Cries on Horseback.* Doubleday & Company, Garden City, New York, 1970.

LOOMIS, LEANDER V. *A Journal of the Birmingham Emigrating Company, 1850.* The Arthur H. Clark Company, Glendale, California, 1928.

LOOMIS, NOEL M., and NASATIR, ABRAHAM P. *Pedro Vial and the Roads to Santa Fe.* University of Oklahoma Press, Norman, 1967.

LORCH, FRED W. "Iowa and the Gold Rush of 1849," *Iowa Journal of History*, Volume XXX, pp. 307–376. Iowa City, 1932.

LOWIE, ROBERT H. *Indians of the Plains.* American Museum of Natural History, New York, 1954.

MCCALEB, W. *The Aaron Burr Conspiracy.* Argosy-Antiquarian, New York, 1966.

MCCALLUM, HENRY D. and MCCALLUM, FRANCES T. *The Wire that Fenced the West.* University of Oklahoma Press, Norman, 1965.

MCDERMOTT, JOHN FRANCIS. *The Frontier Re-Examined.* University of Illinois Press, Urbana, 1967.

MACEWAN, J. W. GRANT, and FORAN, MAXWELL. *West to the Sea.* McGraw-Hill of Canada Ltd., Toronto, 1968.

MACGOWAN, KENNETH. *Early Man in the New World.* The Macmillan Company, New York, 1950.

MACKENZIE, ALEXANDER. *Alexander MacKenzie's Voyage to the Pacific Ocean in 1793.* The Lakeside Press, Chicago, 1931.

MARSHALL, THOMAS MAITLAND. *A History of the Western Boundary of the Louisiana Purchase, 1819–1841.* University of California Press, Berkeley, 1914.

MATTICE, W. A. "Precipitation in the Great Plains," *Monthly Weather Review*, Volume 66, No. 5, May, 1938.

MOODY, RALPH. *The Old Trails West.* Thomas Y. Crowell Company, New York, 1963.

MOORMAN, MADISON BERRYMAN. *The Journal of Madison Berryman Moorman, 1850–1851.* Edited, with notes, by Irene D. Paden. California Historical Society, San Francisco, 1948.

MORRISON, LORRIN L. and MORRISON, CARROLL SPEAR. *Great Plains Number*, in *Journal of the West*, Volume VI, No. 1, Los Angeles, January, 1967.

MORTON, ARTHUR S. *A History of the Canadian West to 1870–71*. Thomas Nelson & Sons, Ltd., Toronto (undated).

NASATIR, A. P. *Before Lewis and Clark*. In two volumes. St. Louis Historical Documents Foundation, 1952.

NATIONAL PARK SERVICE. *Prospector, Cowhand, and Sodbuster*. U.S. Department of the Interior, Washington, D.C., 1967.

NORMAN, CHARLES. *Discoverers of America*. Thomas Y. Crowell Company, New York, 1968.

OGLESBY, RICHARD EDWARD. *Manuel Lisa and the Opening of the Missouri Fur Trade*. University of Oklahoma Press, Norman, 1963.

OSBORN, JAMES E.; HOLLOWAY, MILTON; and WALKER, NEAL. *Importance of Irrigated Crop Production to a 17-County Area in the Texas High Plains*. Texas Tech University, Lubbock, 1972.

OSGOOD, ERNEST STAPLES. *The Day of the Cattleman*. The University of Minnesota Press, Minneapolis, 1929.

PETERS, J. A. "Extinction, Its Causes and Results," in *Biologist*, Volume 32, pp. 4–8. Columbus, Ohio.

PREUSS, CHARLES. *Exploring with Frémont*. University of Oklahoma Press, 1958.

RASKY, FRANK. *The Taming of the Canadian West*. McClelland and Stewart, Ltd. Toronto, 1967.

READ, GEORGE WILLIS. *A Pioneer of 1850*. Little, Brown and Company, Boston, 1927.

RICH, E. E. *The History of the Hudson's Bay Company, 1670–1870*. In two volumes. The Hudson's Bay Record Society, London, 1958.

RICHARDSON, RUPERT N. *The Frontier of Northwest Texas, 1846–1876*. Arthur H. Clark Company, Glendale, California, 1963.

RICHMOND, ROBERT W. and MARDOCK, ROBERT W. *A Nation Moving West*. University of Nebraska Press, Lincoln, 1966.

RIEGEL, ROBERT EDGAR. *True Story of the Western Railroads*. The Macmillan Company, New York, 1926.

RIEGEL, ROBERT EDGAR., and ATHEARN, ROBERT G. *America Moves West*. Holt, Rinehart and Winston, New York, 1964.

ROE, FRANK GILBERT. *The Indian and the Horse*. University of Oklahoma Press, Norman, 1955.

———. *The North American Buffalo*. University of Toronto Press, 1951.

RORABACHER, J. ALBERT. *The American Buffalo in Transition*. North Star Press, St. Cloud, Minnesota, 1970.

SANDOZ, MARI. *The Beaver Men, Spearheads of Empire*. Hastings House Publishers, New York, 1964.

SAUER, CARL O. "A Geographic Sketch of Early Man in America." *The Geographical Review*, Volume 34, No. 4, pp. 529–573. October, 1944.

———. "Grassland Climax, Fire, and Man," *Journal of Range Management*, Volume III, pp. 16–22. 1950.

SCHANTZ, H. L. "The Natural Vegetation of the Great Plains Region," *Annals of the Association of American Geographers* (AAAS), June, 1923.

SELWYN, ALFRED R. C., and DAWSON, G. M. *Descriptive Sketch of the Physical Geography and Geology of the Dominion of Canada*. Dawson Brothers, Montreal, 1884.

SHELDON, A. E. "The Battle at the Forks of the Loup and the Platte, August 11, 1720. Extermination of the Spanish Army by Otoe Tribe of Indians. A New Chapter In Nebraska History," *Nebraska History and Record of Pioneer Days*, Volume VI, pp. 1–32. Lincoln, 1923.

SOCOLOFSKY, HOMER E., editor. *Great Plains Number, Journal of the West*, Volume 6, No. 1, Los Angeles, January, 1967.

STECKMASTER, KENT LADD. *The Westward Movement.* McGraw-Hill Book Company, New York, 1969.

STEPHENS, F. F. "Missouri and the Santa Fe Trade," two articles in the *Missouri Historical Review.* Volume X, No. 4, pp. 233–262, July, 1916, and Volume XI, No. 3, pp. 289–312, April, 1917.

STEWART, EDGAR I., editor. *Penny-an-Acre Empire in the West.* University of Oklahoma Press, Norman, 1968.

STEWART, OMER C., "Why the Great Plains Are Treeless," *Colorado Quarterly,* Vol. 2, No. 1, pp. 40–50, Denver, Summer, 1953.

———. "Burning and Natural Vegetation in the U.S.," *Geographical Review,* Volume 41, pp. 317–320. Quarterly publication of the American Geographical Society, New York, 1951.

STOVER, JOHN F. *American Railroads.* University of Chicago Press, Chicago, 1961.

TERRELL, JOHN UPTON. *Zebulon Pike, the Life and Times of an Adventurer.* Weybright and Talley, New York, 1968.

THOMAS, ALFRED BARNABY. *After Coronado.* University of Oklahoma Press, Norman, 1935.

———. "The Massacre of the Villasur Expedition at the Forks of the Platte River, August 11, 1720," *Nebraska History.* Nebraska State Historical Society, Volume VII, No. 3, pp. 68–81, Lincoln, 1924.

———. "Spanish Exploration of Oklahoma, 1599–1792," *Chronicles of Oklahoma,* Volume VI, pp. 186–213, Oklahoma City, 1928.

THORBURN, J. B. "Notes on Pierre and Paul Mallet," *Chronicles of Oklahoma,* Volume VI, No. 2, pp. 181–185, Oklahoma City, June, 1922.

THWAITES, REUBEN GOLD. *Early Western Travels.* Cleveland, The Arthur H. Clark Company, 1905.

TROTTER, REGINALD GEORGE. *Canadian History; A Syllabus and Guide to Reading.* Macmillan Company, New York, 1926.

TURNER, FREDERICK J. *The Frontier in American History.* Holt, Rinehart & Winston, 1962.

TWITCHELL, RALPH EMERSON. *The Leading Facts of New Mexican History.* Horn & Wallace, Albuquerque, 1963.

U.S. SOIL CONSERVATION SERVICE. "Facts About Wind Erosion and Dust Storms on the Great Plains." Leaflet No. 394, United States Department of Agriculture, Washington, 1955.

VANDIVEER, CLARENCE A. *The Fur Trade and Early Western Exploration.* The Arthur H. Clark Company, Cleveland, 1929.

VAN ROYEN, WILLIAM. "Prehistoric Droughts in the Central Great Plains." *Geographical Review,* Volume 27, No. 4, pp. 637–650.

VESTAL, STANLEY. *Jim Bridger, Mountain Man.* University of Nebraska Press, Lincoln, 1946.

———. *The Missouri.* University of Nebraska Press, Lincoln, 1945.

WAGNER, HENRY. *The Plains and the Rockies, A Bibliography of Original Narratives of Travel and Adventure, 1800–1865,* third edition. Longs College Book Company, Columbus, Ohio, 1953.

WARKENTIN, JOHN, editor. *The Western Interior of Canada, A Record of Geographical Discovery, 1612–1917.* McClelland & Stewart, Toronto, 1964.

WEAVER, J. E. and ALBERTSON, F. W. *Grasslands of the Great Plains, Their Nature and Use.* Johnson Publishing Company, Lincoln, Nebraska, 1956.

WEBB, WALTER PRESCOTT. *The Great Plains.* Blaisdell Publishing Company, Waltham, Mass., 1931.

WEDEL, WALDO R. *Prehistoric Man on the Great Plains.* University of Oklahoma Press, Norman, 1961.

———. "The Central North American Grassland; Manmade or Natural?" Social

Science Monograph No. 3, pp. 39–69. Studies in Human Ecology, Social Science Section, Pan-American Union Department of Cultural Affairs. Washington, D.C., 1957.

WINSHIP, G. P. *The Coronado Expedition, 1540–1542.* 14th Annual Report of the Bureau of Ethnology, 1892–1893, Washington, 1896.

WISSLER, CLARK. *The American Indian.* Oxford University Press, New York, 1922.

WYCKOFF, JEROME. *Rock, Time, and Landforms.* Harper & Row, New York, 1966.

WYMAN, WALKER D., and KROEBER, CLIFTON B., editors. *The Frontier in Perspective.* University of Wisconsin Press, Madison, 1965.

WYMAN, WALKER D. *The Wild Horse of the West.* University of Nebraska Press, Lincoln, 1945.

ZIMMERMAN, CARLE C., and RUSSELL, SETH. *Symposium on the Great Plains of North America.* The North Dakota Institute for Regional Studies, Fargo, 1967.

INDEX

Index